Diploma in
Home-based Childcare
For childminders and nannies

Sheila Riddall-Leech

www.heinemann.co.uk
✓ Free online support
✓ Useful weblinks
✓ 24 hour online ordering

01865 888058

Heinemann is an imprint of Pearson Education Limited, a company incorporated in England and Wales, having its registered office at Edinburgh Gate, Harlow, Essex, CM20 2JE. Registered company number: 872828

Heinemann is a registered trademark of Pearson Education Limited

© Sheila Riddall-Leech, 2006

First published 2006

10 09 08
10 9 8 7 6 5 4

British Library Cataloguing in Publication Data is available from the British Library on request.

ISBN: 978 0 435 402 11 2

Edited by Gavin Fidler
Designed by GD Associates
Typeset by Tek Art
Original illustrations © Pearson Education Limited, 2006
Cover design by Wooden Ark
Printed in China by South China Printing Co.
Cover photo: © Alamy Images
Picture research by Chrissie Martin

Every effort has been made to contact copyright holders of material reproduced in this book. Any omissions will be rectified in subsequent printings if notice is given to the publishers.

Websites
Please note that the examples of websites featured in this book were up to date at the time of writing. It is essential for tutors to preview each site before using it to ensure that the URL is still accurate and the content is appropriate. We suggest that tutors bookmark useful sites and consider enabling students to access them through the school or college intranet.

Contents

Foreword

Welcome to this book, which has been specially written to back up our updated qualification – the Diploma in Home-based Childcare (DHC). In January 2006, together with the Council for Awards in Children's Care and Education (CACHE), we launched the DHC. This new award takes the place of the Certificate in Childminding Practice, and it takes account of developments in the childcare sector, including the new National Occupational Standards.

Inside this book you will find information, case studies based on real situations, and pointers to think about when working with children in a home-based setting. A wide range of topics is covered, from play theory to child protection, and from observing children to safety in the kitchen.

Whether you are a childminder or a nanny, reading this book will help you to gain a further understanding of your job. Enjoy taking your professionalism to a new level!

Liz Bayram
Chief Executive
National Childminding Association

Acknowledgements

Author acknowledgements

I would like to thank the editorial team at Heinemann and everyone at NCMA for all the support and helpful suggestions made during the writing of this book. Sincere thanks must go to all of the registered childminders and nannies who have provided anecdotes and material for the case studies. Special thanks to Peter for his continued love and support, and not forgetting my late father who inspired me so much and to whom the first Childminding book (which this replaces) was dedicated.

Picture acknowledgements

Sally & Richard Greenhill – page 7
Pearson Education Ltd / Gareth Boden – pages 21, 34, 37, 41, 42, 44, 47, 68, 107, 139, 159, 162, 217, 220, 228, 234, 245, 257, 262
Alamy Images – page 54, 150
Getty Images / PhotoDisc – page 57, 233
Pearson Education Ltd / Tudor Photography – page 76, 153
Pearson Education Ltd / Haddon Davies – page 89, 103, 120
Photolibrary – page 109, 193
Corbis – page 114, 175, 264
Pearson Education Ltd / Jules Selmes – page 129(a), 129 (b), 130, 131, 145
Digital Vision – page 136
NCMA – page 188
Illustrated London News – page 206
Getty Images – page 213
Getty Images / Photodisc – page 250 (a,b,c & d)
Pearson Education Ltd / Gerald Sunderland – page 271

The author and publishers would also like the thank the National Childminding Association (NCMA) for their kind permission to reproduce material on pages 4 and 5.

About the author

Sheila Riddall-Leech began her professional career as a primary school teacher and has worked in many settings within various parts of the UK and abroad, eventually becoming a deputy head of a large primary school with a thriving nursery unit. She moved into further education in the mid-1990s, teaching on a wide range of early years courses and awards. Sheila became an Ofsted Inspector in 1998 and is an assessor for the NCMA Children Come First childminding networks.

For a number of years the author worked closely with the assessment team at CACHE on several awards. Sheila now runs her own training company, as well as writing for numerous professional journals and Heinemann. She continues to deliver CACHE awards and teach Foundation Degree modules. This is her fifth book for Heinemann.

Sheila is married to Peter and lives in rural Shropshire. She has two grown-up daughters. In her spare time she enjoys gardening and walking her two dogs. There are also numerous ducks, hens and geese that require attention, not to mention a large greenhouse and maintenance of the 300-year-old cottage where she lives.

Introduction

The Diploma in Home-based Childcare is a joint initiative qualification between CACHE and the National Childminding Association, replacing the Certificate in Childminding Practice. This Level 3 qualification is an inclusive course for all individuals who care for other people's children in their own homes, the child's home or another person's home. These people are often referred to as nannies or childminders.

People who provide home-based childcare offer a very valuable service to a great many children and their parents. It requires not only a love of children, but also a good understanding of them and a professional approach to the work. Gaining this qualification will raise the professional profile of home-based childcarers and will hopefully improve the quality of service to families.

How to use this book

This book is designed to support the Diploma in Home-based Childcare, providing both the information that you will need to complete the course and practical help in completing the assignments that form the assessment requirements of the qualification. It is divided into six sections, five of which follow the syllabus of the Diploma:

• Unit 1 Introduction to childcare practice (home-based).

• Unit 2 Childcare and child development (0–16) in the home-based setting.

• Unit 3 The childcare practitioner in the home-based setting.

• Unit 4 Working in partnership with parents in the home-based setting.

• Unit 5 Planning to meet the children's individual learning needs in the home-based setting.

The final section of the book covers study skills and other information to help home-based childcarers complete the assessment requirements of each unit.

Throughout the book there are *Case study* feature boxes with questions that link theory to practice. These case studies are based on real situations and people, some will reflect good practice whilst others are designed to make the reader question and reflect on possible situations. The less than ideal case studies are not intended to portray either nannies or childminders in a negative light, merely to encourage reflective practice in the reader. The quotes from home-based childcarers have been gathered through actual interviews and discussions. In all case studies and quotes, names have been changed to maintain confidentiality of all concerned.

In addition to the case studies there are *Find out!* feature boxes which provide opportunities for the reader to find out more, developing and extending their knowledge. There are also *Think about it* features, which are informative and raise issues that you are asked to think about and which give you the opportunity to test how much you have learned and know about home-based childcare. The *Keys to good practice* features reinforce the professional standards required in caring for children in a home setting. The *Key terms* feature boxes include definitions of important terms explained as they occur in the text; there is also a glossary of definitions at the end of the book.

The *Link to assessment* feature boxes in each unit link directly to the assessment requirements for that unit and will provide hints and opportunities for individuals to attempt the higher pass grade criteria, particularly for Units 2–5. Multiple-choice questions are included at the end of each section in Unit 1. At the end of the book there are suggestions for further reading and information sources.

Introduction to Childcare Practice (home-based)

This unit is designed for people beginning their career in home-based childcare and will help you to prepare for your new profession as a nanny or registered childminder. It is also an appropriate unit to study for people beginning formal training in home-based childcare.

This is a stand-alone unit and is individually assessed. You must successfully complete one assessment in order to be accredited with this unit. An assessment which consists of 25 multiple-choice questions will be provided by CACHE.

Several of the topics introduced in this unit are covered in greater detail within Units 2 to 5.

This unit will help you understand how to:

- establish a safe and healthy childcare environment in a home-based setting
- establish routines for home-based childcare
- provide play and other activities for children in a home-based setting
- introduce children and their families to your childcare service
- manage children's behaviour in the home-based setting
- consider inclusion and anti-bias practice
- protect children in the home-based setting
- start a home-based childcare service.

Establishing a safe and healthy environment in a home-based setting

Anyone who looks after other people's children under the age of eight, in their own home, for reward and for over two hours a day, must be registered with the Early Years Directorate of Ofsted in England or the Care Standards Inspectorate in Wales (CSIW). They must also meet minimum standards of care. This is a legal requirement under the Children Act 1989. Any environment where children are cared for must be safe and secure, and the people caring for the children should have taken every possible action to prevent accidents and reduce risks.

If you are to take your responsibilities seriously and be professional, it is essential that you understand how to keep children safe at all times and how to prevent accidents. Accidents can, and do, happen; however, there are important things that you can do to reduce the chances of an accident happening to you, or to the children that you are caring for.

Think about it

Research from the Royal Society for the Prevention of Accidents (RoSPA) suggests that most serious accidents in the home happen in the kitchen and on the stairs, and that most accidents occur in the living room or dining room areas.

RoSPA research shows that children at 0–4 years of age are most at risk from accidents in the home. Most accidents happen between late afternoon and early evening in the summer and during school holidays. Boys are more likely to have accidents than girls.

Every year almost 70,000 children are involved in accidents in the kitchen, and 66% of these accidents involve children under the age of four years.

Risk assessment

It is good practice to undertake a risk assessment for each of the rooms that the children will have access to.

Key Term

Risk assessment

A risk is a possible danger or threat to safety. Assessment means to measure, evaluate or make a judgement. Risk assessment is therefore a case of weighing up possible dangers or threats to safety and taking appropriate action.

The Kitemark is the symbol used by the British Standards Institute (BSI) and shows that the manufacturer of the item has produced their products to high quality and safety standards.

Kitemarks can be put on items that are manufactured outside of Britain, providing that the item meets the specifications of the European Standards (EN) or International Standards (ISO).

A Kitemark in itself does not guarantee the safety of the person using the item; it just means that the item has met certain safety standards. You should always follow the manufacturer's instructions for any equipment that you use.

You must remember that making your working environment safe is not just about checking for dangers and risks. It is also about being aware of possible hazards at all times, and teaching children ways of keeping safe by setting a good example.

A room full of potential risks to children

Think about it

Look at the above picture of a typical sitting room.

How many risks to children's safety can you spot?

Can you say why each one is a risk and what you could do about it?

How might you have to adjust the environment if you were caring for toddlers, children between five and seven years and older children?

Take a walk around the rooms that the children will use. If you are caring for young children it is a useful tip to get down on your knees and look at the room

from a child's perspective – it can look quite different!

For each room complete a risk assessment exercise, listing the possible risks and asking yourself the following questions.

Why is this a danger?

What can I do about it?

You may find it useful to record this information on a table or chart.

Following is an example of a risk assessment form that the National Childminding Association (NCMA) has produced for people caring for children in a home setting.

NCMA Nanny Risk Assessment Checklist

In living, sleeping and play areas, risks to look out for include:

- banisters or railings that wobble, or with spaces where children could trap their heads or hands
- blocked fire exits
- cracked, broken or dirty toys and equipment
- dangerous items (alcohol, matches, medication, cigarettes, plastic bags, etc) accessible to children
- electrical sockets not covered
- low level glass (e.g. in windows, doors and coffee tables) that isn't safety glass
- no stairgates (if caring for babies or toddlers)
- open fires and portable heaters with no fireguards

- poisonous houseplants within children's reach
- slippery rugs and loose carpets
- radiators hot enough to burn a child
- safety catches not fitted on windows
- smoke alarms not fitted or not working
- signs of infestation by vermin
- toys and other items that don't meet current safety standards
- trailing tablecloths, blind pulls, curtain cords, etc, that could cause someone to trip.

Risks identified?	Action to be taken?	Who by?	When to be completed?
_____	_____	_____	_____
_____	_____	_____	_____
_____	_____	_____	_____
_____	_____	_____	_____
_____	_____	_____	_____
_____	_____	_____	_____

In kitchens, eating areas and utility rooms, risks to look out for include:

- dangerous items (sharp knives, cleaning fluids, matches, etc) accessible to children
- flexes trailing from kettles, irons, etc
- harnesses on highchairs broken or missing
- nappies being disposed of in kitchen bin

- no fire blanket or fire extinguisher
- pets allowed on tables and worksurfaces
- pets' food and/or litter trays accessible to children
- unhygienic dish cloths, mops and tea towels
- unhygienic food preparation or storage arrangements.

Risks identified?	Action to be taken?	Who by?	When to be completed?
_____	_____	_____	_____
_____	_____	_____	_____
_____	_____	_____	_____
_____	_____	_____	_____
_____	_____	_____	_____
_____	_____	_____	_____

In bathrooms and cloakrooms, risks to look out for include:

- dangerous items (cleaning fluids, razor blades, toiletries, etc) accessible to children
- electrical switches (should be pull-cords)

- slippery baths, shower trays and floors
- unhygienic flannels, sponges, towels or nappy-changing arrangements.

Risks identified?	Action to be taken?	Who by?	When to be completed?
_____	_____	_____	_____
_____	_____	_____	_____
_____	_____	_____	_____
_____	_____	_____	_____
_____	_____	_____	_____
_____	_____	_____	_____

This risk assessment checklist may be photocopied for non-commercial use only.
© NCMA

> CONTINUED OVERLEAF

Sample NCMA risk assessment form for nannies

In gardens, risks to look out for include:

- animal mess
- broken gates, walls and fences
- climbing frames, slides or swings broken, not securely fixed to ground, or positioned on a hard surface
- dangerous equipment (tools, garden machinery, chemicals, fishing tackle, etc) accessible to children
- garden toys and furniture dirty or broken
- loose paving stones, steps or man-hole covers

- points where children could escape from the garden
- poisonous plants accessible to children
- ponds, fountains, streams, pools, wells or water butts accessible to children
- sheds, outbuildings, greenhouses, garages and cellars accessible to children
- signs of infestation by vermin.

Risks identified?	Action to be taken?	Who by?	When to be completed?

In vehicles, risks to check for include:

- children's car seats broken, wrong size or not provided at all
- inappropriate or invalid motor insurance

- no child locks on rear doors
- no MOT.

Risks identified?	Action to be taken?	Who by?	When to be completed?

Any other risks:

Risks identified?	Action to be taken?	Who by?	When to be completed?

Signature of nanny: _____ Date: _____

Signature(s) of parent(s): _____ Date: _____

Royal Court, 81 Tweedy Road, Kent, BR1 1TG
www.ncma.org.uk

Registered Charity 295981

N11 08/04

INVESTOR IN PEOPLE

Sample NCMA risk assessment form for nannies (continued)

Keys to good practice

Safety within the home-based setting

- Never allow children of any age into any room without them being supervised (although you must respect the privacy of older children when they are using the toilet).

- Check furniture and appliances for sharp edges, such as the cooker, washing machine, table tops, shelving, and cover them if needed.

- Use short, coiled flexes on electrical equipment and fix wires and cables to walls, or to floors or skirting boards, so that they do not trail.

- Check that the plugs on electrical appliances are not cracked, and replace them if they are.

- Make sure that the wires or cables from electrical appliances are not frayed or worn.

- When checking any electrical appliance be very careful – do not put yourself at risk. Switch the appliance off at the socket before you touch it. Make sure your hands are always dry before handling anything electrical. Never put your fingers or anything other than the plug into an electrical socket.

- Fit child-resistant socket covers on all power points.

- Make sure that all sharp objects are kept out of sight and reach of children.

- Make sure that all small objects are kept out of sight and reach of children.

- Have a fire blanket in the kitchen, and ideally a fire extinguisher in another part of the house. Make sure that you know how to use them.

- Use a harness fitted securely to a highchair. Make sure that both have a British Standards Kitemark or European Safety Standards mark.

- Make sure that safety gates used across doorways and stairs are fitted securely.

- Never leave hot drinks or food unattended.

- If you use a tablecloth make sure that the edges do not hang over the table.

- Try to keep the floor space as free as possible, making sure that rugs and mats will not slip or cause a child to trip and fall. Mark big areas of glass, such as glass doors, with stickers and make sure that this glass is either safety glass or covered with safety film.

- Fit window locks.

- Make sure that there are no trailing cords from curtains or blinds.

- Make sure that all areas of the home are well lit, especially on the stairs.

- Fit a smoke alarm.

- Have a fire drill for the home and practise it regularly with the children at different times of the day.

- Buy toys and equipment that have a recognised safety symbol on them, such as the Kitemark.

How can you get the home environment ready for children and make it a safe place for them?

You need to work out a safety checklist for each room that the children will be using.

If you are caring for the child in their own home you will have to discuss safety issues with the parents and agree safe practices.

Let us start with some general suggestions on how to prevent accidents in the rooms most frequently used by children.

Safety in the kitchen

- Keep the doors to washing machines and tumble driers shut at all times.

- Keep oven doors shut. Make sure that children cannot touch the oven door if it is hot.

- Make sure that the doors to the fridge and freezer are securely shut.

- Make sure that children cannot get hold of plastic bags, cleaning materials and alcohol. These should also be kept out of sight and reach.

- Make sure that pan handles are turned away from the edge of the cooker.

- Make sure that all hot objects are positioned well away from the edge of work surfaces and kitchen units.

A safety gate for stairs

Safety in the dining room

- Avoid using tablecloths that hang down over the edge of the table.

- Never leave the children unattended while they are eating.

- Never leave a baby propped up with a feeding bottle.

- Never leave hot food or drinks unattended.

- Make sure that children can safely and correctly use cutlery. Never allow children to play with knives and forks unsupervised.

- Make sure that children can safely reach the table by using either a high chair with a harness, specially designed booster seats, or cushions.

- Do not allow children to walk while eating or drinking.

- Keep alcohol out of reach of children or in a securely fastened cupboard.

- Keep cigarettes, matches and lighters out of reach of children.

Safety in the play room or sitting room

- Keep the floor space as free as possible.

- Do not use pillows for children under eighteen months, and make sure that they sleep on a firm mattress.

- Store toys carefully (do not give children a reason to climb up and reach for things).

- Check all toys regularly for missing bits, broken pieces or sharp edges.

- Secure any doors that lead to outside areas.

Do not put anything that can be climbed upon under a window

Hall and stairs

- Use securely fixed gates to prevent children climbing the stairs unattended. It is recommended that you use gates with the safety standard number BS 4125.

- Remove any toys or objects that have been left on the floor or stairs.

- Make sure that the hall and stairs are well lit.

- Check that carpets are not frayed or loose.

- Make sure that banisters and balustrades are strong and firm, and do not have any footholds for climbing. Consider filling in any gaps between rails.

RoSPA research shows that in any one year 54,000 children aged 0–4 years have accidents on the stairs.

Bathroom and toilet

- Medicines and tablets should be kept in a high cupboard that is locked at all times.

- Cleaning materials and air fresheners should be kept out of reach of children.

- When running a bath or water for washing, turn the cold water tap on first and test the water before letting a child use it.

- The hot water temperature should not exceed 46°C. It is recommended that you use a bath thermometer.

- Use a non-slip mat in the bath.

- Wet floors can be slippery and therefore dangerous so wipe and dry floors as soon as they become wet.

Selecting and maintaining appropriate equipment

Key Term

Equipment includes all toys, utensils, furniture, fittings and materials that may be used with or by children.

The equipment that you use with children is another very important aspect of keeping children safe. It is your professional responsibility to choose equipment and toys that are safe and appropriate for the children in your care.

If you are working in the child's own home, you may want to discuss which pieces of equipment and toys are safe and appropriate with the parents. You must reach agreement on what to do about items that you are not happy to use or allow the children to have access to.

Before you buy any piece of equipment or toy it is good practice to look for one of the safety symbols or logos shown below. Some pieces of equipment or fittings in your home will have a BS number printed on the label, for example furniture that has glass incorporated into it should have a label with BS 73767 and BS 7449.8. This means that the glass has been approved to British Safety Standards.

Can you identify these safety symbols?

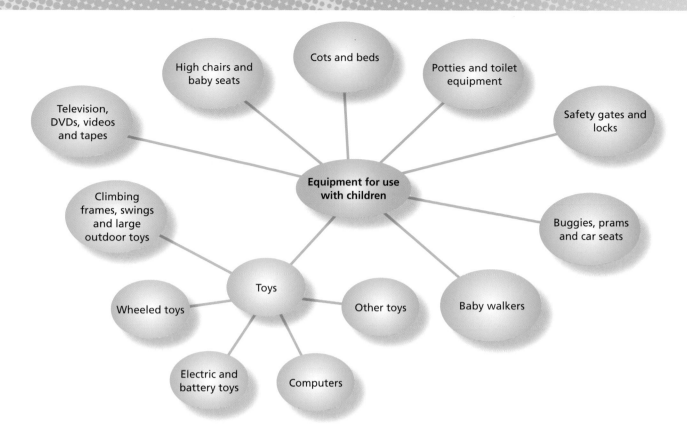

Examples of equipment that should be checked for safety before being used with children

Keys to good practice

Safety

High chairs and baby seats must have securely fastened safety harnesses. These should also be adjustable so that they can still be comfortably and safely fastened around a baby as he or she grows.

- High chairs should not wobble, the legs should be level and the whole chair should be stable. Table-mounted high chairs are not recommended as they are not stable.

- Baby seats should not be placed on table-tops or work surfaces. There should be no loose pieces of fabric, coverings or broken pieces. A young child could easily put anything small into their mouth and choke.

- Children should not be left alone in either a high chair or a baby seat.

- Baby walkers can be very dangerous pieces of equipment as babies can easily overbalance in them. There is evidence that baby walkers actually hinder children's development and home-based carers are advised not to use this piece of equipment.

- Cots and beds are potential areas for accidents, especially as children can fall out of them. Do not allow children to play on cots and beds – they should be considered as places to rest and sleep.

- Cots with sides that slide down should have secure fastenings that cannot be undone by little fingers. Beds for young children often have side rails to prevent the child falling out, but these can often be used by children for climbing.

- Young children should never be put into a top bunk that is accessible only by a ladder.

- Mattresses for cots and beds should fit snugly around the frame of the cot or bed. Look for the Kitemark or BS number on the label to check if the mattress meets safety standards. The covering and filling of the mattress must be flame retardant and should have a label to say so.

- It is not good practice to use pillows for children less than eighteen months old – a firm mattress is usually enough.

- There are many novelty potties and toilet seats available that encourage children to develop bladder and bowel control. Most of these are made of plastic, therefore you must regularly check and make sure that the plastic has not cracked or split.

- Toilet seats designed for children should fit firmly over the adult toilet seat, and do not forget that children using these seats will also need a step so that they can reach the toilet safely.

- Safety gates and locks are a very important part of equipment. Gates across doorways and stairs make it easier for you and the children to stay together.

- All gates should fit securely with the fastening being both firm and childproof.

- It is a good idea to fit window locks to all windows in the rooms that children will be using. Locks can be bought from hardware and DIY stores. Most are fitted very easily. Do not forget to look for the safety standards labels.

- Buggies, prams and car seats might not belong to you, as some parents may bring their child to you in one and leave it at your home. Even so you must check that there are no broken or damaged pieces or parts, and that the harnesses are secure and will hold the child safely. You must let the parents know if their buggy, pram or car seat is putting their child at risk because it is not safe.

- Many childcare practitioners use televisions, computers, videos, DVDs, CDs and tapes to support children they care for, both in order to help their learning and at times of rest and quiet. Electrical devices should not have trailing cables or wires and should be put where they cannot be pushed or knocked over by a child.

- Make sure that the battery compartments of any remote controls for these pieces of equipment cannot be opened. Batteries are not playthings and can be very dangerous to a child if sucked or broken.

- If you buy or rent tapes or DVDs, it is always good practice to watch or listen to them first in order to make sure that they are suitable for the children in your care.

- Toys are involved in over 40,000 accidents each year according to RoSPA. Many accidents involving toys happen when people trip over them and when babies and young children play with toys intended for older children.

- Make sure toys are safe. A European Directive was introduced into British law by the Toys Safety Regulations 1995 as part of the Consumer Protection Act 2002. Despite this, illegal and unsafe toys can still be found in many places, so shop with care. Look for the European Community (CE) symbol that means the toy meets European standards. Look also for the 'Lion Mark'. This is the logo of the British Toy and Hobby Association, and indicates that toys meet statutory safety standards. If you are using toys in the child's home it is good practice to discuss toy safety with parents.

- Toys such as climbing frames and other equipment that may be outside must be checked regularly for sharp points, edges and damage caused by the weather. Make sure that slides and swings are tough and will not collapse.

- Wheeled toys such as bikes, scooters and pedal cars must also be checked regularly to make sure that there are no loose parts, and that the toys have not become dangerously worn.

- Many toys are battery-powered, which is usually a safe source of power, provided that the batteries are used correctly. Batteries should always be fitted into the toy correctly and then covered up. Spent batteries should not be burnt, but disposed of carefully, especially smaller mercury disc batteries. These could easily be swallowed by young children or find their way into ears and noses.

- All toys should be bought or borrowed from recognised outlets.

- Try to avoid toys with loose pile fabric or hair. Young children can choke on such material.

- If there are toys with many small parts or pieces make sure that young children cannot get at them unsupervised, so keep them in secure boxes or containers.

- Beware of loose ribbons on toys and long ties on dressing-up clothes. Children can get ties and ribbons fastened tightly round their necks, with dreadful consequences.

Keys to good practice

How to keep children safe

The following 'Keys to good practice' text should also be read in conjunction with the previous 'Keys to good practice' text on safety (page 9).

- Anything that is broken, has a frayed or damaged flex, has pieces missing, or has loose pieces, should be removed so that the children cannot get hold of it.

- When something is broken you must decide if it can be repaired safely or should be thrown away and replaced. Obviously this decision will be based partly on the type of toy or equipment and the cost of either the repair or the replacement.

- You should check regularly for possible hazards, and do not forget to look at items of furniture as well as toys and equipment. Some practitioners check every piece of equipment used by the children at the end of each working day. It is up to you to decide how often you check, but remember that accidents can happen when you least expect them.

- It is far better to be constantly aware of safety issues than having to visit the accident and emergency department at the hospital. If you buy new things or the child is given anything new you should always read the labels for potential dangers and hazards, and do not forget to look for the Kitemark or European Community logo.

- It is also very important that the toys and equipment you use are suitable for the age of the children, as in the following cases:

  o high chairs, baby seats and carriers should have adjustable harnesses and should be used only for young children

  o safety gates should fasten securely and be used to stop children going up or down stairs on their own, or to stop them going into rooms alone

  o toys that are designed for older children should be stored away from younger children when not in use

  o toys with small pieces should not be within reach of young children who could easily put things in their mouths and choke.

  o electrical sockets, when not in use, should be covered with safety sockets so that children cannot investigate the holes with little fingers or toys.

  o fireguards should be securely fixed around heat sources, such as electric or gas fires. Did you know that it is actually illegal to leave a child under 12 in a room with an open fire?

You can probably think of many other examples to add to this list.

Think about it

Making sure that toys and equipment are safe

Have a look at the toys and equipment that you are planning to use.

Can you decide which things are suitable for:

• all of the children in your care

• children under two years old

• children between three and five years old

• children between five and seven years old

• children between seven and eleven years old.

• children above eleven years old

• Make a checklist like the one shown below to write down your decisions.

Toy/equipment	Age group	Safety notes
Lego	4 plus	Keep away from the babies as they could choke on the bits. Keep in a plastic tub with a well-fitting lid

This will help you to become more aware of possible dangers and will also make your personal safety checklist more effective. If you are unsure about any toy or piece of equipment, it is always good practice to be cautious, rather than to take a chance that it will be all right.

Supervising children both inside and outside of the home

Key Term

Supervision – control, management or command of a situation or other individuals.

You have responsibility for the safety and well-being of the children in your care at all times. This means that you should never leave any child, regardless of age, unsupervised at any time. Supervision of children means that you are aware of what they are doing all of the time, in other words you can see and/or hear them.

Case Study

Caitlin, a registered childminder, cares for three eight-year-olds after school. When asked about supervising older children she said that she can open a hatchway between the kitchen and playroom so she can observe the children while she prepares a snack for them. When she needs to go to the toilet, she tells the children that she needs privacy, but leaves the door slightly ajar so that she can still hear them.

Think about your own practice.

What do you do if you need to prepare snacks in the kitchen and the children are watching a DVD in a different room?

What do you do if you need the toilet?

How can you maintain constant supervision of children of different ages?

How can the practitioner in the picture on page 13 keep the children safe?

Safety outside the home

It is very important that the outside area around the home where the children are cared for is also safe. Ofsted will check the outside areas for safety and may make conditions on your registration, for example it is possible to be a registered childminder, but on the condition that you allow children to access only the inside areas of the house.

How can the practitioner supervise the children safely?

Keys to good practice

Safety in the garden

- Make sure that children do not play outside unsupervised.

- Make sure that all garden tools, equipment and any chemicals are stored away from children. These should really be in a locked shed, or garage or other building.

- Make sure that all paving slabs are firm and not loose or chipped.

- Make sure that any fences, especially wooden, are undamaged and firm.

- Children should not be allowed to climb onto fences or play equipment that is not designed for this purpose, such as playhouses.

- Make sure that tricycles, bikes and other toys are not broken or damaged and cannot harm the children. For example, check for sharp edges, punctures, loose parts and missing pieces.

- Make sure that any large play equipment, such as swings, slides and climbing frames, is set up properly and that the ground underneath has safety mats or wood chippings on it so that children do not land on a hard surface if they fall.

- Make sure that children cannot get out of the garden. Is there a secure gate or fence?

- Make sure that the children cannot get at any rubbish, dustbins, or wheelie bins.

- If there are pets, make sure that any areas where children play are free of animal waste .

- Cover or fence any areas in the garden where there is water, including water butts and ponds.

- Cover sand pits when not in use to stop animals getting into them.

- Do not use a trailing clothes line.

- Make sure that any plants in the garden are not harmful to children if touched or eaten.

If you are working in the child's home, it is essential that you discuss safety issues in the garden with the parents. They may, for example, be very keen gardeners and not at all happy about removing some of the plants that could be potentially harmful.

Think about it

Checking plants

1 Find out which plants in the garden and indoors are poisonous to children.

2 Find out which plants have leaves, sap or flowers that could cause skin irritations. Check plants that you have in the garden and also in the house.

3 Write down what you have found out and keep it somewhere safe so that you can refer to it in the future.

A good place to find out this information is at your local library, garden centre or from the Internet.

All poisonous plants in your garden and indoors should be removed. Many people find this aspect of safety a contentious issue. For instance, what can you do about any poisonous plants, shrubs and trees in a neighbour's garden that overhang into your garden? Discuss this with other course members, other home-based childcarers and the neighbours involved.

Getting out and about with children

You may have to transport children in your own car or on public transport. If you are a nanny a car may be provided for your use. You may also want to take children out in buggies or prams, or for a walk. In these cases, you could find yourself having to cope with a lively toddler and a baby in a buggy and trying to cross a busy road.

Do not forget to obtain the parent's permission to take children out; it is also good practice to tell

How can this practitioner keep the children safe?

them if you are planning a special trip or going somewhere different. If possible, it is worth getting written permission before taking other people's children out.

Think about what you need to have with you when you go out with the children. It depends on where you are planning to go and how long you plan to be out for. You should always take with you some form of personal identification, relevant emergency telephone numbers, a mobile phone, and a first-aid kit.

Taking children in your own car

If you are going to use your own car you must be aware of the following points:

- Make sure that the car insurance is valid for business purposes and that it is fully comprehensive. (NCMA can advise you on this.)
- All adults must wear seat belts in the front and in the back of a car.
- All children in the car must wear secure child restraints, which are appropriate for the age, weight and size of the child.
- Never put a rearward-facing baby seat in the front if there is a passenger airbag.
- All children should have a seat. Never allow a child to stand up in the car or sit on someone else's knee.
- Child locks should be used on the doors.
- Make sure that children get out on the pavement side of the car and not on the roadside.
- Think about how you drive, be careful and alert. Set a good example to the children when dealing with other road users.

You need to think very carefully about taking the children that you care for in someone else's car. Ultimately you are responsible for the children's safety and well-being, and if you cannot be absolutely sure that the other driver has adequate insurance in place and is a competent and careful driver, then perhaps you should decline to travel in that person's car.

Using public transport

If you use public transport you will need to:

- make sure that the children stand well back from the edge of the pavement or station platform
- make sure that young children are wearing safety harnesses (personal restraints), and that older children are taught to hold your hand
- plan your journey carefully so that you know all the details required for a safe passage. For example, where the bus stops are, which platform the train arrives and leaves from, how to get up and down stairs, or across busy roads
- make sure that when on the bus or train the children sit next to you at all times. If there are no seats left and the children are standing, make sure that they are not in danger of falling over and that if possible they can hold on to a safety rail or you.

Walking with children and road safety

When out walking with children you must be aware of their safety at all times. There are many things that you can do to teach children how to keep safe – even young children can be made aware of dangers and begin to learn about keeping themselves safe.

Think about it

Did you know that every day a child under five is killed or seriously injured on our roads? Brake is a road safety charity (www.brake.org.uk) that aims to reduce the number of horrifying deaths and injuries of young children that happen every day. They organise special events to provide young children with their first road safety lesson and raise awareness among parents and practitioners.

- It is good practice to use personal restraints on toddlers and young children. Many types are available, including reins, harnesses and straps that have a wristband at both ends for the child and the adult. Whatever you choose, it should have a Kitemark or other recognised safety symbol.

- Set a good example to the children when crossing roads. Never cross in a rush, or in a place where you cannot see traffic coming in both directions. Always use a zebra or pelican crossing if available, and show the children how to cross a road safely. If there is no crossing choose a safe place where you have good all-round visibility. A good thing to teach children when crossing a road is to Stop, Look and Listen. Only cross when you are sure it is safe, and always use a pelican or zebra crossing if there is one nearby. Never run across the road.

- Treat buggies and prams like all other equipment you use with the children. They should be regularly checked and kept in good working order, especially the brakes and folding mechanisms. They should be fitted with harnesses, which you should always use. Do not have the buggy or pram sticking out into the road while you wait to cross. It could be hit by a vehicle, and the fumes from vehicles could affect the child.

- In large open places, such as parks or even shopping centres, you should make sure that older children know what to do if you get separated. Some practitioners and children look for a prominent building or special point, such as an information desk or a park bench, and agree to meet there. Young children should always be wearing personal restraints, such as safety harnesses, so that they cannot wander off and become separated from you.

Stranger danger

Children need to know what to do if a stranger approaches them. Talk to them about 'stranger danger' and work out what they should do. Children should be made to understand that not everyone they meet, however friendly they may seem, can be trusted. They should be taught not to speak to strangers and never to go off with someone they do not know. Do not frighten or scare the children, but firmly explain to them how to cope in such situations. Remember to discuss with the children's parents what you and the children have decided in such emergencies, so that the parents can use the same tactics with the children.

Organisations such as Kidscape produce many useful leaflets and books to help teach children ways of keeping themselves safe. Kidscape has a website, details of which can be found at the end of this book. The NSPCC also has useful materials.

Case Study

Anna has been a registered childminder for six months. Apart from her own six-year-old, she has responsibility for twins aged two-and-a-half years. During the school holidays Anna and all the children often walk to the local park to feed the ducks and play in the adventure playground.

How can Anna make sure that the walk to the park is stress-free for everyone?

What can Anna do to make sure that all the children have fun, and remain safe whilst feeding the ducks?

What particular dangers should Anna be aware of in the adventure playground?

What should Anna take with her in case of an emergency?

Think about your answers and discuss them with other practitioners.

Making sure that the home is a healthy place for children

As a professional home-based childcarer you and your setting are open to scrutiny. This scrutiny may be from parents, Ofsted, the CSIW and other professionals that you could come across whilst working with children, such as health visitors, medical personnel or social workers.

It is very important that you have high standards of personal hygiene. It is also vital that your setting is a safe and hygienic environment for children and that you do everything that you can to prevent the spread of infection. As part of the registration process your workplace will be checked for its cleanliness.

The children will copy and learn from what you do and say. The way you behave, such as washing your hands after going to the toilet, covering your mouth when coughing, will teach the children good hygiene practices. You will need to establish routines that encourage hygiene and help children to learn safe ways to care for themselves.

Hand washing

Washing your hands and teaching children to wash their hands properly is one of the most effective ways of preventing the spread of infection.

- Hands should be thoroughly wet before applying soap. Ideally this should be liquid soap because soap bars have a tendency to retain bacteria if they sit in water.

- The surfaces of both hands should be vigorously massaged with the lather, special attention being paid to the fingertips, thumbs and between the fingers. If you wear a wedding ring you should wash underneath it.

- Rinse your hands well under running water and dry them with a paper towel.

The hand-washing process should take no less than 30 seconds.

It is good hygiene practice to use disposable plastic gloves when dealing with faeces, urine and blood as well as washing your hands with hot water and soap.

1 Massage palm to palm.	2 Rub right palm over back of left hand and vice versa.	3 Rub palm to palm with fingers interlaced.

4 Massage backs of fingers in opposing palm.	5 Rotate right thumb clasped in left palm and vice versa.	6 Rotate fingers of left hand in right palm and vice versa.	7 Rinse hands with water.

You should follow these steps and wash your hands thoroughly

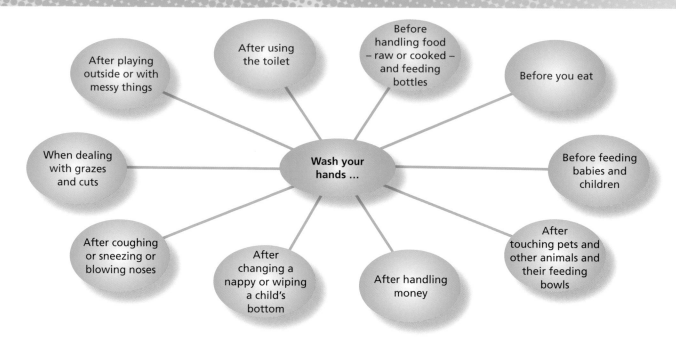

These are occasions when you should wash your hands

Find out!

When do you wash your hands?

Keep a written diary for one complete working day of how many times you wash your hands.

Then check your diary with the spider diagram above and see if there are any times when you should have washed your hands but didn't.

Key Term

Environment – the surrounding, setting or situation in which people live, in this case the one in which you work and care for children.

Keeping the home environment clean

You must do everything possible to keep the home clean and hygienic to prevent the spread of infection. Children can easily pick up infections. Touch, food, water, animals, droplets in the air, and cuts and grazes can spread infection. The kitchen and bathroom are the rooms most likely to hide germs that cause infections and as such must be kept thoroughly clean.

Keeping a clean home and workplace will stop germs from multiplying. Using everyday things like soap and water and allowing in fresh air and sunlight will destroy many germs. Cleaning products will also help you to keep the home germ-free, but remember that many of these are harmful to children and pets, and must be kept out of a child's reach at all times, even locked away if necessary when not being used.

Antiseptic cleaners and wipes are forms of weak disinfectant that help to prevent germs from multiplying. However, they do not destroy germs and bacteria, and they can be dangerous to children.

If you are caring for children in their own home you must discuss hygienic and healthy practices with the parents and make sure that the care and well-being of the children is paramount.

Keys to good practice

Keeping the home environment clean

It is good practice to clean and disinfect floors, equipment and toys regularly. Many childcare practitioners clean and disinfect kitchen and bathroom floors at least once a day.

- High chairs and changing mats need to be cleaned every time they are used.

- Indoor rubbish bins must be kept covered and should be emptied at least once a day. Rubbish bins can be a source of germs and bacteria and for this reason it is very important to keep them thoroughly clean.

- Animals and domestic pets should not be allowed in the kitchen. The much-loved family pet does not know how to wipe its feet or wash its paws! It will bring dirt and germs from outside into the kitchen no matter how careful you are.

- As well as keeping the bathroom floor clean, do not forget that germs can breed around damp towels and facecloths. It is good practice to make sure that each child has their own towel and facecloth. These should be washed frequently and thoroughly dried. Many practitioners change the children's towels and facecloths each day.

- We often think that soap is germ-free. In fact, a soggy bar of soap sitting on a washbasin can be a source of potential infection. If you and the children use bars of soap make sure that it is a clean piece and does not sit in its own little puddle of water on the washbasin. You might decide that it is better to use a dispenser with liquid soap. Remember to keep the dispensers clean as well.

- The toilet must be kept clean at all times. Children should be taught to flush the toilet each time they use it. They should also be taught to put toilet tissue into the toilet carefully before they flush it. The toilet seat needs special attention, as does the toilet bowl, both inside and out. Make sure that the toilet handle is wiped and disinfected regularly.

- If you have a carpet around the toilet it could very quickly become smelly and a source of germs. Think about the flooring in the bathroom and consider a washable mat or floor covering around the toilet.

- Nappies and other soiled clothes or products should be disposed of hygienically. You can buy specially designed covered containers that will help you dispose of nappies by wrapping and sealing each one separately in anti-bacterial film. When the container is full the bag is lifted out and put in an outside bin. On the other hand, many practitioners use plastic bags for each item, which they then fasten securely. Each plastic bag is then put in an outside bin.

- Parents may decide that they want their child to wear terry cotton, or reusable, nappies. You may need to think about the pros and cons of using reusable nappies and talk to parents about how these will be kept hygienically when soiled and how they will be washed and dried.

Find out!

Someone in your family, or one of the children that you are caring for, has developed cold sores.

How could you prevent the spread of the infection to other people and children?

Make a note of your answer, and then read through this part of the unit again to check if you have the right answer.

Key Term

Infection – a disease, illness, virus or bug.

Food hygiene

Part of your job will be to prepare and give children food and drinks. The way that you prepare, cook and serve the food will help the children you care for to learn sensible eating habits, and should also encourage them to try out various foods. If you are not very careful about how you prepare, store and handle food, you could pass many different forms of food-borne illnesses on to the children. There are some very straightforward tips that you should always follow so that you can be sure that the food you give to the children is safe.

Correct storage of food in a refrigerator

Keys to good practice

Storing food safely

- Cover all food that is left out.

- Check that the refrigerator is no higher than 5°C and that the freezer is set at −18°C.

- Make sure that air can circulate around the refrigerator, and do not try to overfill it.

- Never refreeze food that has thawed out.

- Never store raw meat next to other food. Wrap it up well and put it at the bottom of the refrigerator, preferably in leakproof containers. Raw meat can drip juices onto foods stored below them. These juices nearly always contain harmful bacteria.

- Store cans and packets in a cool, dry place. Do not store these foods above your cooker. Foods in cans should always be eaten within one year of purchase or before the expiry date on the label.

- Look carefully at the best before dates on food, and do not risk eating anything that is out of date. It is better to be safe than sorry.

- Do not store food or juices in cans once they have been opened. Once a can has been opened, air can get to the contents and affect the quality of what is in the can. It is good practice to transfer what is left from the can into a leakproof container, which is in turn covered and stored in the fridge.

- Take care to protect fruit, vegetables and salads. Many people store salads in the fridge, but what about fruit and vegetables? These are often left out in the kitchen and can be touched by anything and anyone. This is a health risk.

Preparing foods

- Be careful not to cross-contaminate food. For example, do not use the same board to cut raw meat, chop vegetables and then slice bread. The juices from the meat can contaminate the other foods. In the same way, do not use the same knives, plates or other utensils for different foods.

- Never thaw out foods on a kitchen work surface. Use a leakproof container and make sure that the food is completely thawed through before cooking.

- Plastic chopping boards are easier to keep clean than wooden ones. If you worked in a daycare centre or restaurant preparing food, you would need different coloured plastic boards for different types of food.

- You must follow the manufacturer's instructions on labels when thawing, heating or cooking food. Just as foods must be properly thawed, they must also be cooked thoroughly. Harmful bacteria are not destroyed in food until the food has been cooked to a temperature of 71°C (boiling point is 100°C).

Case Study

Jenny cares for Tom, aged five, Ahmed, aged three, and a baby of eight months. She has to prepare Tom a packed lunch for school. Tom has decided that he wants a cheese sandwich, an orange that is peeled and cut up, and a carton drink. Jenny gets her wooden breadboard and butters the bread; she uses the same knife and board to cut the cheese and the finished sandwich. She puts the sandwich and carton drink in Tom's lunch box. Jenny then wipes the board with a cloth and cuts up the orange, wraps it in plastic wrap and puts that next to the sandwich.

How many times do you think Jenny has not followed good practice?

What do you think she did wrong, and what should she have done?

- Children should never be left unsupervised when preparing food or eating and drinking.

- If you are using knives and forks, make sure that you teach children safe ways to handle and use them. Do not let children wave any eating tools around.

- Make children sit down when eating or drinking. This will reduce the chance of them choking or tripping over.

Eating safely at a table

General safety at mealtimes

Snacks and mealtimes can be very good learning opportunities for children, especially if they are involved with preparing the food. You must be a good role model so that the children will learn good, safe practice from you.

- Both you and the children should always wash your hands before eating or preparing food.

Keeping children safe around animals

You need to make sure that the children in your care are not in danger from any animals kept in the home.

- Your elderly, much loved dog might be the soppiest animal in the world around you, but might react violently to being touched by someone else when you are not there, or by being around a lively and noisy group of young children.

- No childcarer should ever have a pet in the house that is not tolerant of children.

- You should teach children how to care for animals, and encourage them, if appropriate, to clean out cages and feed the animals.

- Children should be taught to wash their hands after touching animals and not to kiss pets. It is not good practice to allow pets to lick faces.

- As with sick children, sick animals need time and special attention. You will need to consider this when caring for children. What will you do with the children if you have to take a sick cat to the vet?

- Both children and pets need fresh air and exercise, so you will need to think about whether you have enough time to walk the dog and look after the children.

- You will need to keep animal feeding bowls separated from those used by humans and will also need to wash them separately.

- Do not forget to clean up any 'pet accidents' straightaway and dispose of everything hygienically.

- If you or members of your household keep exotic pets make sure that they are securely and appropriately housed so that children cannot get access to them.

- Children should not be left alone with pets and any other animals, no matter how tame and friendly you think the animals are, or how careful you think the children will be.

There are often horrific stories in the newspapers about children who have been bitten and injured by dogs. Hamsters and rabbits can bite children too, especially if they stick their fingers through the cage. Cats will scratch if play gets too boisterous.

Animals can be unpredictable in their behaviour, especially if provoked, hurt or think that they are in danger. You can teach children how to care for and how to treat animals, but at the end of the day you are responsible for keeping the children safe.

Case Study

Jenny, Tom and Ahmed are cleaning out the hamster cage on the outside patio. The telephone rings and Jenny tells Tom and Ahmed to wait until she comes back. While Jenny is on the telephone, Tom runs in to tell her that the hamster has bitten Ahmed's finger and he is crying.

How could Jenny have prevented Ahmed being bitten?

What should she have done about the telephone call?

Think about it

The balance between safety and independence

It is not easy to get the balance between keeping children safe and allowing them to learn and develop independence. Young children love to explore – one of the ways in which they learn. Older children want to be able to go the local shop on their own, for example, and so gain confidence and independence, but you must always consult the parents and have their written permission before allowing children out alone. Children need to be educated from an early age about safety and ways to cope in emergencies. They learn about safety from you and their parents – positive role models.

Everyone in a home is relaxed, and often feels safe because they are at home. Yet most accidents happen in the home, and during the summer months. It is better to teach young children, when they are ready, a safe way to crawl up and down stairs, than have them fall down if they gain access to ungated stairs.

Key Terms

Accident – An unforeseen, unplanned mishap, calamity or mistake that may cause distress or injury to another individual.

Emergency – a crisis or situation that requires immediate action.

Independence – allowing a child to have self-autonomy, freedom, self-reliance and therefore undertaking an activity or having an experience without intervention.

Dealing with accidents, emergencies and first aid

Preventing accidents

An accident is something that happens which is not expected, or planned, and is not caused deliberately. Accidents can be prevented, or at least their effects can be limited. As a home-based childcarer your responsibility is to try to prevent accidents from happening, and if they do happen, then you must know what to do.

Did you know that RoSPA estimates that as many as 20 children die each year as a result of falling from windows, balconies or stairs, and that 42% of all accidents involve a fall.

The chart below gives examples of the most common accidents that can happen to children. It shows some possible causes of accidents and what you can do to prevent these accidents.

Remember, accidents can happen anywhere, at any time and usually when you least expect them, so be prepared

Potential accident	Possible cause	Prevention
Cuts and grazes	• Sharp objects such as scissors, knives • Sharp edges on furniture and equipment • Damaged or faulty toys • Broken glass	• Make sure that sharp objects are out of reach of children. • Protect furniture edges, especially corners. • Remove or throw away damaged or faulty toys. • Mark large areas of glass, such as patio doors, with stickers, use plastic cups for children's drinks.
Falls	• Falling between two levels, such as high chair to floor, bed to floor	• Use harnesses or personal restraints in high chairs. Fit safety rails to beds and make sure that cot sides are securely held in place.

Potential accident	Possible cause	Prevention
Falls (*continued*)	• Tripping over toys left on the floor	• Make it part of your routine to to encourage children to put away toys when they have finished playing.
	• Falling up or down stairs and steps	• Fit secure stair and doorway gates. Never let children climb up and down stairs unsupervised.
	• Falling out of windows	• Fit window locks and move furniture from underneath windows to stop children climbing.
Burns, scalds and fire	• Hot drinks being knocked over	• Do not leave hot drinks within reach of children.
	•Matches and lighters	• Keep matches and lighters out of children's reach.
	• Fires and heaters	• Fit secure guards around any heating source. Have a fire blanket or extinguisher handy.
	• Water too hot	• Domestic hot water should never exceed 54°C.
	• Kettles, irons and electrical equipment	• Fit coiled flexes to equipment and do not allow flexes to trail over the edge of work surfaces.
	• Cookers	• Oven doors can be fitted with protective guards or fitted with heat-resistant covers. Pan handles should be turned away from the edge of the hob or cooker.
Poisoning	• Cleaning materials	• Store in a secure cupboard that children cannot open.
	• Plants – both household and garden plants	• Either keep out of reach, or better still destroy poisonous plants.
	• Medicines	• Store in a locked high cupboard.
	• Cosmetics	• Keep out of reach of children.
Suffocation and choking	• Pillows	• Do not use pillows for babies under eighteen months.
	• Small pieces of toys	• Keep toys with small pieces away from small children.
	• Skipping ropes	• Discourage children from using ropes for anything else other than skipping.

Potential accident	Possible cause	Prevention
Suffocation and choking (*continued*)	• Cord and ties on clothes and furnishings	• Avoid clothes with ties. Make sure cords from furnishings and blinds do not hang down
	• Plastic bags	• Keep away from children. Store out of reach, preferably knotted, so that they cannot be easily opened.
	• Nuts	• Do not give to young children.
Electric shocks	• Electrical sockets	• Fit covers to all electric sockets that are not in use. Do not overload sockets with too many plugs.
	• Damaged electrical equipment	• Check equipment for frayed or damaged flexes and replace if necessary.
Drowning	• Bath	• Do not leave children in a bath unattended and unsupervised.
	• Paddling pools	• Do not leave children in paddling pools unsupervised.
	• Ornamental ponds	• Cover or fence all ponds.
	• Buckets or bowls of water	• Do not leave any amount of water in a bucket or bowl.

Coping with an emergency

An emergency, like an accident, is unexpected. It can involve just you or several people. Emergencies are often the result of accidents. Even though you cannot predict accidents and emergencies you can be prepared. The best way to cope is to have a personal emergency plan, so that you are prepared for the worst. Such a plan will help you remain calm and more able to cope.

You should make sure that older children know your address and phone number so that they can contact you in an emergency.

Putting together a personal emergency plan

• You will need access to a telephone, either a landline or a mobile phone. If you rely on a mobile phone, make sure it is fully charged during the times that the children are with you. Also, check that the mobile has good reception. If you do not have a telephone in your home, make sure that you know where the nearest public call box is and keep a phone card or coins handy, to be used only in an emergency. Remember that emergency services can be contacted on landlines and public call boxes by dialling 999, and many mobile phone services use 112 even when there is no signal for your network provider.

• Next, make sure that you have an up-to-date list of essential telephone numbers. This list should include:

  o the contact numbers of the parents of the children and an emergency contact number if they are not available

  o telephone numbers of the children's doctors

  o your own doctor

  o the nearest police and fire stations

Make sure you have an up-to-date list of essential contact numbers for each child

o the nearest hospital with an accident and emergency department

o the name, address and telephone number of someone who you could call to cover for you if you have to leave your home. (You will have to reassure parents that you would never leave their children unattended and, if possible, they would always be left with another registered and approved person.)

• You must make sure that your records of the children are up to date.

• When putting together an emergency plan you will need to decide what are the most important things to do first. The first actions are known as the 4Bs:

o Breathing – your first priority is to check that the child is still breathing

o Bleeding

o Breaks

o Burns.

It is very important that you do not attempt to resuscitate a child unless you have been specially trained to do so. Call an ambulance if you are in any doubt.

In case of an emergency

Mentally rehearse an emergency. This will help you plan what you need to do first and will help you feel more confident and more able to reassure the children in a real emergency.

A personal emergency plan could be something like this:

1 Do not panic, keep calm, take a few deep breaths.

2 Deal with the emergency, following the 4Bs.

3 Check if it is possible to contain the emergency without harm to you or the children, for example use a fire blanket, or fire extinguisher.

4 Check the safety of all the children and if possible remove them from the immediate area. Never leave them unattended.

5 If necessary make telephone calls to emergency services or a doctor. Make sure that you are talking to the correct person, identify yourself and explain clearly why you are calling.

6 Contact the parents of the child or children. If you leave a message, make sure that it is brief, but gives all the necessary information without causing the parents to panic. Remember to leave a contact number for the parents to get in touch with you.

A personal emergency plan is exactly that – it is personal to you and it must work for you. It is good practice to write out your personal emergency plan, so that other people could follow it if something was to happen to you. You should also look at your plan regularly and change it if necessary.

An important part of any emergency plan is keeping up-to-date records of the children. The National Childminding Association has produced a form that you and the parents can complete with details of addresses, telephone numbers, emergency contacts, medical details and other useful information. You could make up your own forms if you wanted, but make sure that you include all details about the children that you need to know in order to keep them safe.

> Sue, a registered childminder says 'I always do a fire practice at least once a term and always when a new child starts. Sometimes I tell the children that the fire is in the kitchen and we have to go out through the front door, sometimes I tell them the fire is in the playroom and we have to go out through the back. I try to make it a serious practice, not a game, because I think it is important that all the children know what to do in case of a fire.'

Why do childcare practitioners need a relevant first-aid qualification?

The most effective way to make sure that you are fully prepared for any situation, accident or emergency is to have an up-to-date and relevant first-aid qualification. It is very reassuring for parents to know that you are professional and caring enough to get as many recognised qualifications as you can. A 12-hour first-aid course is an Ofsted requirement and approved by NESTOR (the approval agency for nannies). This qualification is very important and will teach you how to deal with emergencies and some first aid. (Unregistered/approved childcarers are not inspected and so are not required to have any first-aid training.) Most qualifications last for three years, so you will need to keep the qualification up to date.

The Red Cross and St John's Ambulance run courses specially for people who work with young children. Their telephone numbers are usually in the local telephone directory, or at the library. Their addresses are at the end of this book. If you have difficulty in finding out about courses contact your local authority, or your local college may be able to help. These courses will also help you to put together your own first-aid kit. You can buy a first-aid kit from a chemist or supermarket that is already put together, however, some of the items in these kits are unlikely to suit your needs. Many practitioners make up their own first-aid kits, so that they can choose what to put in and ensure that they know how to use it.

Having an up-to-date first-aid qualification is essential for all people caring for children. However, it is important that you are aware of your own limitations and in an emergency only carry out things that you are competent to do.

In an emergency situation where you have to give first aid, follow this routine.

- Stay calm. This helps you to assess the situation.

- Deal with a dangerous situation first.

- Do not rush.

- Remove child, other children and yourself from danger.

- Talk to the injured child to see if he or she responds.

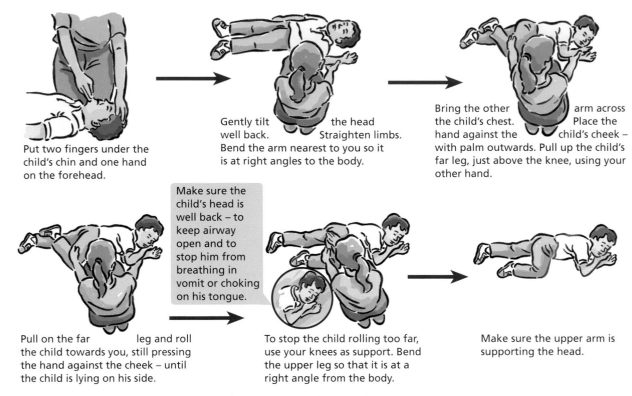

You need to follow this procedure for placing a child in the recovery position

Put two fingers under the child's chin and one hand on the forehead.

Gently tilt the head well back. Straighten limbs. Bend the arm nearest to you so it is at right angles to the body.

Bring the other arm across the child's chest. Place the hand against the child's cheek – with palm outwards. Pull up the child's far leg, just above the knee, using your other hand.

Pull on the far leg and roll the child towards you, still pressing the hand against the cheek – until the child is lying on his side.

Make sure the child's head is well back – to keep airway open and to stop him from breathing in vomit or choking on his tongue.

To stop the child rolling too far, use your knees as support. Bend the upper leg so that it is at a right angle from the body.

Make sure the upper arm is supporting the head.

If necessary, follow the ABC routine that you should have learnt on your first-aid course.

- Check the child's Airway.
- Check the child's Breathing.
- Check the child's Circulation. Is there a pulse?
- Put the child into the recovery position – see the drawing above.

Many accidents can be dealt with easily provided your first-aid box is complete and you know what to do. The chart below gives you a list of the sort of first-aid kit to carry out when dealing with some common minor accidents.

Accident	First-aid/treatment
Grazes of all kinds	Rinse the area with plenty of clean cool water to make sure the grazed area is dirt-free.
Minor burns	Run under a cold tap for at least 10 minutes; chemical burns need at least 20 minutes. Do not cover burned area.
Nose bleeds	Tip the child's head forwards and pinch just below the bridge of the nose.
Bruising and sprains	Put something cold over the area (a bag of frozen peas, wrapped in a small, clean towel is ideal). Keep the sprained area raised and try to stop the child using that part of the body.

Accident	First-aid/treatment
Head injuries	Put something cold over the injury (a bag of frozen peas, wrapped in a small, clean towel is ideal). Watch out for signs of concussion, such as headaches, drowsiness, vomiting. If in doubt seek medical help.
Objects in the nose or ears	Do not try to remove the object – get a doctor to remove it.

Think about it

Making up a first-aid kit

What would you put in your first-aid kit?

1 Make up a first-aid kit list that would be appropriate for the children you care for and for you to use.

Check your list against the one below.

2 Have you thought about possible allergies to plasters?

3 What could you use instead of plasters?

4 Have you thought about the different types of thermometers you would need, and which would be the easiest for you to use and read?

5 Have you remembered to include disposable plastic gloves, for both the children and your protection?

6 Where would you keep your first-aid kit?

7 What sort of container would you use to store the items?

8 How often would you check your kit?

You may find that your registration officer from the local authority has a list of the suggested minimum requirements for a first-aid kit, and it is well worth asking for this.

Your first-aid kit should be used only for your childcaring business. Any medication that you keep to give to members of your family should not be given to the children you are caring for. You must have written permission from the children's parents before you give any first-aid or medication. This written permission can be part of your record-keeping and included on the form mentioned earlier in this unit. Any medication that

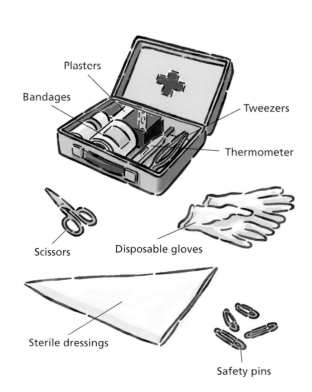

A *first-aid kit*

Every time you use the first-aid kit you should get into the habit of making a note of the items that you used and add them to your shopping list if necessary, doing a quick check to see if everything you need is still there and usable. You could stick a list of the contents of the kit on the lid of the container, and then simply do a quick check against the list.

you have been asked to give to a child by parents must be kept out of the reach of children, stored at the correct temperature (read the label), and disposed of carefully when the course of treatment is finished. You should also record all accidents or incidents with the date, time, the child/children involved and what action you took. Parents should be shown this record and sign it to indicate that they have seen it.

Giving medicines or prescribed drugs to children

Key Terms

Medicine and **prescribed drug** – a remedy, tablet, pill, lotion or liquid that can help alleviate a medical or health problem.

Before you can give a child any form of medication, injection or invasive procedure, it is essential that you have undertaken any appropriate and up-to-date training that enables you to do such things competently. You must be trained by an appropriate medical practitioner who can provide you with written confirmation of your competence. Never give a child medication unless you have the written permission of the parents. Once you and the parents have agreed that you can give their child medication you will need to know the following points.

• Exactly when the child needs the medicine or medication, for example if before eating, how long before. Some children who take insulin injections for diabetes need to be injected about half an hour before eating.

• What the point of the medication is, in other words what it is supposed to do. If you do not have this information, you will not know if the medication is working properly.

• The correct dose for the child.

• What to do if the medication does not seem to be working.

• How the medication should be stored.

• The particular way to give the child the medication.

• What you should do if you forget to give the child their medication.

• If there are any side-effects.

It is important that you have a positive attitude when giving children medication. Some children do not like taking any form of medication and may resist. They will need gentle, but firm persuasion. You could make taking medication into a fun experience, or offer something that the child likes, such as a favourite drink or an activity immediately afterwards. Help the child to associate the medicine with good things, not unpleasant ones. Remember to record when you gave the medication, how much you gave and any reactions.

Link to assessment

Unit 1 is assessed through a series of multiple-choice questions. Help and further information on multiple-choice questions can be found in the study skills section at the end of the book on page 277. Examples of these questions relating to establishing a safe and healthy home-based childcare environment are given below.

These multiple choice questions assess your knowledge of Sections **1a**, **1b**, **1e** and **1f** of the syllabus in your CACHE candidate handbook.

1 **What is the maximum temperature for hot bathwater?**

a. 50°C.

b. 56°C.

c. 46°C.

d. 53°C.

2 What is the purpose of a Kitemark?

a. The equipment has been checked by the manufacturer.

b. The equipment is safe.

c. The equipment can be used outside.

d. The equipment meets British Safety Standards.

3 What is essential when transporting children in a car?

a. Child locks are used on all doors.

b. Children are seated comfortably.

c. Children can see out.

d. Child locks are used on the back doors.

4 What is the correct action for dealing with nappies and soiled clothes?

a. Keep away from children.

b. Dispose of hygienically.

c. Put in plastic bags.

d. Put in the bin.

5 What are the correct temperatures of a fridge and freezer?

a. 4°C and –18°C.

b. –5°C and –19°C.

c. 5°C and –18°C.

d. 4°C and –19°C.

Answers to these questions can be found at the end of the book on page 294.

Establishing routines for home-based childcare

In any business, time management is something that should be thought about very carefully. If not planned carefully, a lot of time can be wasted, or not used well. If you are caring for other people's children in your home you are running a business. It is unlikely that you will employ large numbers of people, but nevertheless, how you manage your time is very important if you are to be successful and enjoy what you are doing. Even if you are caring for children in their own homes, time management is equally important. One way for all home-based childcarers to manage their time is to establish routines.

What are routines?

Key Term

Routine – a custom, scheduled event or activity that is usually planned with regularity.

Routines are everyday events and activities that happen regularly in the home setting. Routines can be set up for daily, weekly or monthly activities and events. They are usually planned things, such as watching a favourite television programme, having a haircut, collecting children from school at the same time each day, or the activities around a child's care, such as nappy changing and sterilising bottles. Daily routines often happen at roughly the same time each day, such as getting meals ready and going to school.

The importance of establishing routines

Routines can sound rather dull, repetitive and sometimes boring, especially for adults. However, this is not the case for babies and children. Routines provide security and stimulation. Care routines such as nappy changing are excellent times for stimulating a baby. Routines can provide consistency and continuity for both the children and for yourself. They can help children feel secure. Children who feel secure, having consistency and continuity in their lives, tend to develop well, especially emotionally. An established, well thought out routine can help a child settle with a new carer or into their new care environment, and can also help promote emotional well-being.

Routines provide continuity and security

Daily routines give structure to the working day, so that both you and the children know what is going to happen and what you are expected to do. They can help you cope better with a busy, hectic working day or week.

> Bea is a nanny to Thomas, 10 months, and Bethany, four years old. She says 'We have to have a routine in the morning or else we wouldn't get to nursery on time. Bethany has a chart that we made together with her routine on it so she knows what is going to happen next. Even Thomas knows that after he has got dressed he has his breakfast.'

Routines can also be to do with physical care, such as having meals at certain times, care of the teeth and teaching children about hygiene. A good routine, for example when sterilising bottles, can help you make good use of your time to allow you more time to spend playing with the children. A routine for nappy changing can make sure that you spend time talking to the baby as

well as allowing them the freedom to kick and stretch their legs, both important aspects of their development.

It is impossible to describe routines in a general way because each routine will depend on individual circumstances, such as the ages and number of children being looked after, the needs of the parents, your own family, and personal likes and dislikes. A routine should be planned to help you. It should make your working day easier and, within reason, should be flexible. For example, you may have to decide whether it is more important to go outside to play with the children during a dry spell on a wet day or to prepare vegetables for the evening meal, because that is what your routine normally consists of at this time. Routines also need to change as children grow and develop. Remember, whatever routine you plan, it must be right for you and the children in your care.

You should try not to change your routine too often. If you do regular activities, such as getting ready for a meal, a different way each time or with no set pattern, then the children may become confused. They may not be able to predict what will happen next and this, together with feeling confused, could affect their emotional development and possibly their behaviour. Obviously there will be times when you will change things with good reason, and you need to be flexible enough to accommodate these cases. However, there is a danger that if you change your routines too often, or make them too flexible, you could become overwhelmed by events and will lose control. Some routines should not be moved around, such as sterilising bottles, as you could put the health of the children at risk.

Remember – you should be managing your time and activities, not letting activities control you.

Being a professional childcarer is a busy and demanding job. If you can establish routines for daily, weekly and longer events, you will hopefully make your life run more smoothly.

Routines also play a part in establishing good standards of care and hygiene, and teaching children to look after themselves, such as going to the toilet and helping them become independent. You should discuss your routines with parents and make sure that you take their wishes into consideration. This is especially important when establishing care routines such as feeding and changing as it will ensure continuity for the young child and will therefore make them feel more secure. Making sure that you meet parents' wishes will be discussed in more detail in Unit 4.

If you are caring for a child in their own home and do not have experience of care routines, then you must make sure that you spend time with the parents to learn from them, and also check your knowledge from recognised publications and texts. It is always good practice to try to follow as closely as possible the routines that the parents have already established.

Why routines need to change as children develop

If you start your childcare career caring for a baby and a toddler, you will probably have planned care routines for such activities as sterilising bottles, nappy changing and cleaning potties, as well as other routines that allow enough time for play and rest. As these children grow and develop you will find that bottles will be used less and less, and there will come a time when the routine for sterilising bottles will not be needed. It may be replaced by another care routine that is more suitable for the age and needs of the children. You may find that your daily routine will include one quiet time for rest and sleep. In the same way, you may find yourself caring for a child who goes to a morning pre-school session, so your daily routine will be planned to fit in with taking and collecting this child.

There will come a time when children start at school, at which time your daily routine will have to change. Older children in your care may join after-school clubs as they become more independent, and this could also affect your daily and weekly routines.

As children develop and grow they will want to help you or do things for themselves. It is often quicker to put a child's coat on yourself; however, letting the child do it for themselves will help the child to learn how to do fastenings or zips and so learn independence. Allowing the child to do things independently will probably take longer, so you will have to adjust your routine for that, but it is good for the overall development of the child. Again, a child might want to help you prepare food or help find things in the supermarket. This is valuable learning experience for a child. However, it takes more time, and you will have to remember this when planning your day.

Think about it

Think about your own daily routine.

List three things that are part of your routine today that will have changed by this time next year.

Why will they have changed?

What impact will these changes have on other daily events?

If you are caring for children in their home your routine will be different. You may have more contact with the parents and more demands on your time, for example you may have to get the children up, washed and dressed, then sort out breakfast and get to school on time.

All children benefit emotionally from structure and routine regardless of their age. Older children are gaining in independence and this needs to be encouraged. They need opportunities to make responsible choices about what, when and how they do things. However, the duty of care still remains with the childcarer and older children may find this restrictive at times, especially if you are caring for younger children as well. The practitioner has to be sensitive to the needs of older children whilst allowing them independence and privacy at times.

Routines for arrivals and departures

It is good practice to encourage the parents to develop a routine for saying goodbye to their children. This is something you should raise at the first meeting. Parents should work out their own special routine of saying goodbye. Encourage the parent to make their goodbyes quite short and to

say the same thing each time they leave. By doing this the child will begin to understand what to expect and what is going to happen next. They will then settle into your care better, and will feel emotionally safe and secure. If young children are showing signs of being distressed at being separated from their parent, some childcarers suggest that the parent leaves a small personal item with the child when they leave. It is hoped that by doing this the child will understand that the parent will come back to collect the item and therefore also the child.

Long, drawn-out goodbyes can be stressful for everyone. They take up more time than necessary, and if a child is already unsure about their parent going, delaying the actual parting will not help. Parents should remember to give their child a kiss (assuming the child wants one that is).

Keep It Short and Simple – KISS

A suggested routine for settling a child into a home other than their own and saying goodbye could be something like this:

A mother says goodbye with a comforting smile

- parent and child arrive at the house

- you greet both child and parent as they both come in

- parent removes child's outdoor clothing

- if appropriate, both you and the parent take the child through to the room that they will be in

- parent says that they are going now and that they will come back at lunchtime or teatime, or at another agreed time in the day

- parent and child say goodbye in their own special way

- you pick up the child or hold their hand, or whatever is appropriate

- go with parent to the door

- child and parent wave goodbye to each other

- close door and immediately start to occupy the child with an activity.

A routine for parents leaving and arriving when a child is cared for in their own home is equally important. Parents should be encouraged to have a leaving routine as well as one when they return.

Case Study

Emma is employed by working parents to care for three children, a baby of 12 months, a boy of five years and a girl of seven years. The girl goes to gymnastic classes twice a week from 5 to 6pm. The boy is sometimes invited to play with at his friend's house and needs collecting at around 6pm, but also at this time the baby is starting to get grumpy and tired. Emma has the use of a car and drives the children to their activities.

How can Emma make sure that the needs of the baby are met?

How can Emma organise the pick-up times of the older children so that nobody is left waiting and possibly put at risk, or misses out on part of an activity?

This will benefit the child, the parents and the home carer. It is important to remember that some parents may need some space when they arrive home and the initial greeting might be quite brief.

The time of day when parents return to their child is very important. It is a time for exchanging and sharing information. Sometimes we can all be tired and a bit grumpy at the end of the day, both adults and children, so it is important that you have a routine which allows you and the parents time to talk, and time for the children to talk to their parents as well. Some childminders find that their routine is to welcome the parents and then let the parents talk to the child before there are any exchanges of information. One nanny recounts how in her workplace the routine is for the children and the nanny to have their tea when the mother returns home. Mum gets changed, by which time the children have finished their tea and then they all spend time together.

Routines for taking children to and from school and playgroup/pre-school

It is important that you establish routines for these events to make sure that everyone has plenty of time to be prepared and there is no last-minute rush. Remember, some things take much longer than you expect and there is always the possibility that you may become harassed and forget something. Make sure that everyone has time to go to the toilet if needed, get their coats and any equipment that they may need for school or pre-school. Before leaving, check one last time that the children have got everything they need for the day ahead. If by chance something is left behind at home in the early morning rush, reassure the child and if needed speak to the teacher to let them know.

Try to make time to talk to the child about their day ahead, and it is good practice to remember what you talked about, so that you can ask them about it when you next meet them. Do not rush or hurry the child. Help them to start the busy day ahead in a calm and relaxed way, in other words be a good role model. Use care routines for washing hands and cleaning teeth before leaving for school.

Children of school age need to learn how to become independent while still remaining safe.

The walk or journey to school is a good time to talk about 'stranger danger' and road safety. Children may also want to talk about problems that they have at school with friends and peers. Listen to what the child says and if you have any concerns speak to their parents.

It is quite possible that school-aged children will only be in your care for a relatively short time before school, and it is likely that this will be a very busy time for you. You may have other children to care for, parents arriving and leaving, and possibly your own children to consider.

Each child in your care has an equal right to your care and time. Even if a child is older and perhaps more independent than others, they still need your time and care. Do not leave school-aged children to fend for themselves before school because you are too busy dressing and sorting out younger children or talking to parents.

If it is appropriate and does not distract you when you are driving, or from caring for other children, you could use the journey to school to play 'mind games' such as 'I-spy' with the older children, or you could just talk to each other.

If you are walking with the children remember to take this opportunity to reinforce road safety and stranger danger.

Case Study

Tina has to walk to school with her own two children, a toddler in a buggy, and then take a three-year-old to nursery. At 11.30am she collects the three-year-old and another three-year-old. At 3.00pm Tina, the two three-year-olds and the toddler in the buggy go to collect her own children from school.

Tina has been asked to care for another child after school, but one that goes to a different school from her own children. She has had to turn this job down as her routine did not give her enough time to get to two different schools.

What would you have done in Tina's position?

Routines for snacks and mealtimes

All mealtimes should be social, happy times and a positive experience for all. It is important to teach all children good personal hygiene when handling food and eating.

It is more than likely that the mother will have established some sort of feeding pattern for her baby. This can be varied, from feeding whenever the baby is hungry or at set times of the day. Whatever pattern has been established by the mother you should not try to change it without talking to her first.

If the baby is still being breastfed you will need to make sure that your routine considers the needs of the mother. You may have to help the mother and baby transfer from breast to bottle and later you may have to wean the baby on to solid foods. Routines will help you manage all these things better.

Case Study

Ruksana has agreed to care for a three-month-old baby boy from 8.30am to 5.45pm for three days each week in the baby's home, because his mother has returned to work. The mother has breastfed her baby and has tried to gradually introduce him to formula milk and bottles over the last three weeks. At the moment the baby has a combination of formula milk and expressed breast milk at different times of the day when he is hungry. He is beginning to get colic, often cries, and you feel that he is not as content as he could be.

What would you suggest to the mother that you could both do to try to sort out these problems?

What else might be causing the baby distress?

Toddlers will be fully weaned and many will have made serious and determined attempts to feed themselves. Most toddlers eat a normal balanced diet and drink from a cup or training cup. It is also quite normal for toddlers to still have a bottle, especially just before a nap or bedtime. Bottles and training cups should still be sterilised, following the routines that you have established for babies.

At this age toddlers can be taught when their hands need washing. They can learn a lot by watching other children and you will begin to understand what is acceptable and what is not.

Toddlers are very active and use up a lot of energy. Boys usually need more calories than girls to keep up their energy levels. It is good practice to give children regular small meals or snacks every 2–3 hours rather than three big meals, for example children could have breakfast quite early before coming to you and will be ready for a mid-morning snack and drink. All children should be able to have drinks of water whenever they are thirsty, especially in hot weather or after physical, vigorous play activities.

Routines for rest and sleep

All babies are different in their needs for rest and sleep and in the ways that they settle to sleep. You must ask the parents how much sleep their baby needs during the day, what position they are put in, and how they are settled. These questions should be part of your first meeting with parents, especially if you are not caring for the baby in their own home. It is important that you follow the routine that has been established by the parents for rest and sleep, but at the same time be flexible. By the time a baby is about nine months old a routine or pattern for rest and sleep should have been established or else it might be difficult for you to settle the baby.

Find out from the parents where they put the baby to sleep during the day, and if possible use the same piece of equipment, such as a cot, Moses basket, or baby seat.

A quiet moment before going to bed

Find out from the parents how they settle their baby. This could be cuddling or rocking, using comfort objects like a blanket, special toys or soothers, making a special noise or playing music.

As babies get older they will begin to learn the sequence of some events in their lives, for example they will get to know that after eating they will have a nappy change and then go to sleep.

It will help you and the other children if you can establish a pattern for rest and sleep times. Babies who are over-tired are often difficult to settle and can become distressed. This could upset and distract older children. When a baby is asleep during the day, do not creep about and prevent other children from making any noise. Carry on as normal because the baby should be able to sleep through a normal level of noise.

Many young children still need to take a nap at some point during the day, often up to the age of four. Toddlers are very active and need time to recharge their batteries. Some children do not want to sleep, but you should still encourage them to rest and be quiet. Establishing a routine for naps or rest and quiet will help parents, as their toddler should then be ready for bedtime at home.

It is good practice to establish a routine of a calm and quiet time before you expect a lively toddler to sleep. This could be sitting down together to read a book, listening to music and quietly talking together. Many childcarers practise this routine in the room where they want the toddler to sleep.

Routines for children's play and activities

These routines could be part of your daily routine in that there will be set times for meals, feeding, collecting other children from school, so play and other activities will fit in around these events. Some practitioners work out a timetable for the day so they can plan in advance how long they will have for certain activities. For example, it is not worthwhile starting a cooking activity that will take about 45 minutes when in reality you have only 30 minutes before you have to collect a child from nursery.

One of the main benefits for a home-based carer is that you can be flexible and spontaneous, and whilst planning your day's activities can be very useful, it is also important to remember that there will be times when you will want to drop your planned routine and take your cues from the children. For example, it has started to snow and you had planned to do finger painting but it is much more fun for the children to go outside and feel and experience the snow.

Routines for taking children out and about

The safety of the children at all times must be your major concern. It is very important that older children have an understanding of road safety and stranger danger. You should have routines that make sure all of the children are safe, for example if you expect children to hold either your hand or on to the handle of the buggy when walking down the road, be firm and do not compromise. You can use these events very effectively to teach road safety and establish a routine for crossing a road safely. You need to establish a routine procedure for what to do if children become separated from you. Some practitioners suggest that they and you look for a prominent landmark, for example a well-known shop in a shopping centre or a large building in a park, and children are taught that the routine if they become separated is to head for the agreed place.

Your routine should also include a personal safety check, for example have you got a first-aid box, emergency phone numbers, is your mobile phone fully charged and have you got a signal? You need to get into the habit of regularly checking your car tyres, lights, oil and battery if you are planning to use it for transporting children, or ask someone else to check it for you if you do not feel competent enough to do so.

Routines for after school

At the end of the school day many children are tired. Their concentration and energy levels will be lower and they may not want to talk or be bothered by other children. On the other hand, some children will come out of school bursting to tell you about what they have done. However the child behaves, you must respond appropriately.

For the quiet child, allow them time to recover, sit quietly and perhaps play a game that does not require much effort. Do not push them into doing an activity if they are clearly tired, as this will only lead to upset and possible confrontation.

For the talkative child, give them your attention and let them tell you what they have been doing. Do not just 'hear' what is being said, actively listen, by giving eye contact, nodding affirmatively and not doing anything else while the child is talking.

Most children come home from school hungry so you will need to give them a healthy snack and drink. Many parents like children to change out of school clothes into something more casual; this is a good time for the quiet child to have their own space while they change their clothes independently. Many children will have homework to do and you should agree with the parents when this is to be done. If it is your responsibility to make sure that homework is started then you will have to provide the child with a quiet place to work but where you can still supervise them.

Many children attend after-school or early evening activities. It could be part of your job to take the child to these activities, so you will need to adjust your routine in order for you to do this. It could be that taking a child to an early evening activity will affect the pick-up times and collection of other children. You will then have to decide what is most important or arrange with other carers or parents also going to the same activity to car share if possible. If this is what you decide, you must get the parents' written permission for someone else to take their child. If there is an accident and you have not got this permission, you could be held responsible for whatever happens to the child.

Routines for school holidays

School holidays should be fun times for children. It is important that all children have a structure and routine to their day at any age. You will still need to have routines for care and mealtimes during school holidays as well as routine times for rest, sleep or quiet activities.

Older children can be given responsibility for planning their own day and building into their plan routines to encourage good personal hygiene, for example children can also use charts to help them plan a week's activities by drawing or writing daily details. This helps them to develop a sense of time as well as giving them independence and responsibility – both important aspects of a growing child's emotional development.

Link to assessment

Unit 1 is assessed through a series of multiple-choice questions. Help and further information on multiple-choice questions can be found in the study skills section at the end of the book on page 277. Examples of these questions relating to establishing routines for a home-based childcare environment are given below.

These multiple-choice questions assess your knowledge of Sections **2a** and **2b** from the syllabus in your CACHE candidate handbook.

1   **Care routines are good opportunities for:**
a.   Making sure that the baby or child is clean.
b.   Stimulating the baby or child through play and talking.
c.   Checking that the child is not ill.
d.   Meeting the child's needs.

2   **Why is a routine for parents leaving and arriving important?**
a.   It helps the child feel emotionally safe and secure.
b.   The parents can get away more quickly.
c.   It helps to develop relationships with parents.
d.   The children do not like long goodbyes.

3 Routines for rest and sleep should:

a. Always be the same.

b. Be at the same time of day.

c. Be discussed with the parents.

d. Be rigidly kept to.

Answers to these questions can be found at the end of the book on page 294.

Providing play and other activities for children in a home-based setting

What is play?

To play can mean amusing yourself, having fun either on your own or with others, and sometimes just 'messing about'. You can probably think of other meanings. Some educationalists and theorists believe that it is one of the most complicated ideas to try to understand. Friedrich Froebel (1782–1852) set up the first kindergarten in Germany where he was able to test his ideas about play. He believed in outdoor and indoor play and is recognised as inventing finger play and many songs and rhymes. Many of Froebel's ideas still influence modern-day thinking about play.

The importance of play

Play is one of the most important ways that children learn. Some people think that children play naturally, but in fact they learn how to play. Children will learn from their parents and family members, from you, from older children, and from doing the same things over and over again. We all like to play, whatever our age. It should be fun and can be relaxing as well as stimulating, and is a very important part of children's lives. When children play they are in control, they can put right their mistakes and can experiment and explore.

How the home-based childcarer can help children play

To help children get as much as possible from play you must understand how valuable it can be. You will need to know how to plan and organise play opportunities for all children, and you can get involved with those activities. As a childcarer you should give all of the children in your care activities that they will enjoy, that will stimulate them and thus help them to learn. You will have to plan opportunities and time to play into your routines and, sometimes, things to play with and the space to play. You will also have to learn when to become involved in the children's play and when to step back and let them get on with it. Planning appropriate play activities will be looked at in greater detail in Unit 5, page 251.

Think about it

In 1979 the United Nations produced the Declaration of the Rights of the Child. In this important document, Principle 7 states:

'The child shall have full opportunity for play and recreation, which should be directed to the same purposes as education; society and the public authorities shall endeavour to promote the enjoyment of this right.'

Children have a right to play and as a professional childcarer you have a duty to support and encourage that right.

Think about the different ways that you can support and encourage that right for children:

• under two years

• between two and four years

• between five and eleven years

• over eleven years.

How might your practices have to change to meet the needs of different aged children?

Helping with a jigsaw

Remember, children need:

• play mates

• play time

• playthings

• play space.

Promoting development through play

All children play in some way whatever their age, whether it is the latest toy or their own fingers and toes. Some experts say that a baby's first toy is the mother's breast because the baby becomes familiar with the smell of the mother's skin, learns to find the nipple, suck and get satisfaction whilst being fed. When children play they behave in different ways. Sometimes their play will be noisy and energetic, sometimes it will be quiet and thoughtful. Occasionally children will describe what they are doing, then discuss and plan how to play and what to do next.

Key Term

Development – ways in which children grow and acquire skills and competences. Areas of development are sometimes categorised as physical, intellectual (or cognitive), language, social and emotional. All of these areas are interrelated and interdependent.

Playing with a baby gym is more than just fun!

Playing with a baby gym on the floor will help a baby learn to control their arm muscles so that they can pat at the objects hanging down. This is a new physical skill. A child playing with a bat and ball will learn how to coordinate their movements and hit the ball. This can be developed so that they can play a sport, get greater control of their movements and become more physically skilful.

Think about it

If you learnt to drive a car, can you remember how many times you practised reversing around a corner before you could do it without touching the kerb? In the same way, children need to do things over and over again until they are truly capable. This practising of skills is part of play.

Think about a play activity that children do repeatedly.

What physical skills are the children using?

How might these skills be developed?

Skills can be developed in many different ways when a child is playing. For example, if a baby has learnt how to control the muscles of the arm to pat a dangling toy, they can extend that skill so that they can grasp and hold the toy. A child who has learnt how to fit two construction bricks together can use that skill to build a bigger model.

Children need to learn about their world and the people in it; this is part of their social and emotional development. They need to understand how they fit into society and the roles of other people. Communicating with other people is part of language development. Children can develop these skills through role-play, dressing up and pretending to be somewhere or somebody else.

Exploring is part of learning. Children can find out a great deal from playing in water, in sand, feeling different materials, helping you cook and looking at changes and differences. They will be using language and probably asking questions; these are aspects of cognitive and language development. All of this can come from play activities that you provide.

Children's development will be looked at in greater detail in Unit 2.

Learning about children through observations of their play

Making specific time to observe and watch children is very important. We all watch children play and observe them, sometimes in a formal way, but often intuitively. You may, for example, notice that a child can complete a 10-piece jigsaw puzzle very quickly, so it is obviously time to introduce a 15-piece puzzle. These kinds of observations will help to plan appropriate play activities that will stimulate and extend a child's development and learning. It can help you identify particular strengths or weaknesses, or perhaps confirm your suspicions if you think that there may be cause for concern. Information that you get from watching children can be passed on to parents, keeping them informed of their child's progress and development.

Think about it

Look at your daily routine (you may already have written this down as one of the activities suggested earlier in this unit).

Can you identify specific times when you can watch and listen to the children? (These times do not have to be very long; it is better to observe for frequent short sessions of 5–10 minutes that one long session.)

Can you identify one specific skill, or aspect of development that you could focus on for each child that you care for?

It is good practice to get into the habit of having a pen or pencil and notebook or post-it notes to hand so that you can make quick jottings to be referred to later.

Kath says, 'When it was suggested by my tutor that I did observations of the children I thought that I would never find the time, but I do, I am watching them all of the time. Observations are now something that I do all of the time.'

Using observations to develop your understanding of children is looked at in greater depth in Unit 5.

Case Study

Marie, a nanny, lives in the family home and cares for a nine-month-old baby and Daisy aged two years ten months. Daisy loves to dress up and pretend to be a princess, queen, or a fairy. Marie listened carefully to Daisy's language when she was playing and realised that in some ways her vocabulary was quite limited.

Marie decided to look for books and DVDs in the library that were linked to Daisy's interests but would at the same time introduce new situations and extend her vocabulary. Marie did not think that she would have been aware of Daisy's limited vocabulary if she had not made a conscious decision to observe her.

Can you suggest possible reasons for Daisy's limited vocabulary?

What else could Marie do to extend Daisy's vocabulary?

Planning play, including routine domestic activities

Play is all about encouraging the children that you care for to develop and learn in every way possible. Play can be spontaneous and require little or no planning or preparation. On the other hand, it may be necessary for you to plan ahead for some play activities, to make sure that you have appropriate resources.

Imagine that you are caring for two three-year-olds and a six-year-old during the school holidays. You think that a play dough activity would be appropriate for all of the children, and plan to let the children measure out the ingredients and mix the dough first.

Think about:

• where you will do this activity

• what you will need to do beforehand

• what resources and equipment you might need

• what areas of development could be stimulated

• how long it will take

• who will clear up afterwards

• what you might do if the children are not interested.

It is not necessary to buy expensive toys and play equipment to encourage development. There are many things around the home and routine things that you do that will help children of all ages develop through play. You must remember that whatever you give the children to play with must be safe and not be likely to harm them in any way.

All of the activities in the table below are things that you probably do every day in the home. They are also excellent play activities and opportunities for children's development. The list could be extended – only the main ones have been included here.

Setting the table for a meal

Routine activity	Learning opportunities for young children	Learning opportunities for older children
Cooking	• Sequencing – cognitive • Counting, measuring, weighing – cognitive • Using a range of tools and utensils – physical • New words, and asking questions – language • Awareness of healthy diet – cognitive • Sharing, taking turns and playing in a group – social • Having fun – emotional	• Sequencing – cognitive • Addition, time, weighing, measuring – cognitive • Science, how things change – cognitive • Greater fine motor control, coordination – physical • Vocabulary development – language • Understanding a healthy diet – cognitive • Sharing, taking turns and playing in a group – social • Having fun – emotional
Preparing food	• Counting, matching, sorting – cognitive • Colours – cognitive • Sensory development • Using tools – physical • Likes and dislikes – emotional	• Understanding of quantities – cognitive • Awareness of needs of others, diets and allergies – social and cognitive • Using tools – physical • Personal preferences – emotional
Setting the table	• Counting, matching, sorting, patterns – cognitive • Following instructions, new words – language	• Developing independence – social and emotional • Understanding house rules – social and cognitive
Getting dressed	• Learning names of different parts of the body – language and cognitive • Developing fine motor skills – physical • Self-help skills – physical and social	• Making choices and decisions – emotional and social • Developing independence – social and emotional
Helping to tidy up	• Counting, matching, sorting, patterns – cognitive • Developing an understanding of house rules – emotional and social • Developing an understanding of caring for equipment and toys – social	• Awareness of needs of others – social and emotional • Understanding house rules – social and emotional • Understanding how to care appropriately for toys, resources and equipment – social
Washing hands and face	• Developing an understanding of good hygiene practices – physical, social and cognitive • Self-help skills –physical and social	• Understanding good hygiene practices and preventing the spread of infection – physical, social and cognitive
Making shopping list	• Understanding that symbols carry meaning – language and cognitive • Memory skills – cognitive	• Writing for different purposes – language • Memory skills – cognitive • Valuing opinions of others – social and emotional

Routine activity	Learning opportunities for young children	Learning opportunities for older children
Making shopping list (*continued*)		• Making choices and decisions – social and emotional • Developing independence – social
Putting shopping away	• Counting, sorting, matching – cognitive • Recognising different shapes and colours – cognitive • Following instructions – language and cognitive	• Developing an understanding of safe food storage – cognitive and social • Developing independence – social and emotional • How to dispose of packaging and waste – cognitive and social

All the play activities above can be fun and enjoyable for all children. None of them need special or expensive equipment, but they are still play activities. It is up to you to make the play activities experiences from which the children can learn and develop.

Think about it

Some childcarers think that getting children to help sort clothes before putting them in the washing machine could be unhygienic, but it is a matter for discussion and also depends on what you are planning to wash. Others may think that getting children to help with domestic activities is almost like making them into domestic workers.

Can you think of some other domestic routine activities that might be contentious?

Play activities outside the home

The play activities that can be found outside the home depend very much on where you live.

When the weather is fine, most play activities can take place outside. As well as being able to run about and let off steam, playing outside can help children develop and learn in many ways. Playing outside allows children to use up energy, stimulates the appetite, aids circulation and digestion, helps them to sleep and generally makes them more able to fight off infection. In other words, playing outside is good.

Travelling by bus or train can be a learning and play experience for children. It can give them a different perspective of the world, for example sitting on the top deck of a bus looking down on people and cars will let children see different things.

If you are driving with children in the car, you must make sure that any games being played do not distract you. Cassette tapes and CDs can be used to entertain children in a car, leaving you free to concentrate on driving safely.

When caring for children during the school holidays you may want to take advantage of play schemes in your area. These can be excellent social opportunities for older children, where they can experience play activities that you may not be able to provide in your setting, or in their own home or garden. Remember that you will need the parents' written permission before children become involved in such activities.

Outside play activities in the garden

Earlier in this unit we looked at making the garden safe for children to play in. The children's safety must always be your first thought. Sandpits can provide lots of good play opportunities, but remember to cover the sand when it is not in use.

Playing out of doors

Climbing frames and other outdoor equipment can be expensive and is not essential, but can be beneficial if it can be afforded. Children will get lots of fun and exercise from running around outside. Think of the garden as another room in the house – there are very few activities that you do inside that cannot be done outside.

Visits to friends

You should make sure that your work takes you and the children outside the home. Some childcarers get together in each other's homes, or at a community centre, local leisure centre or any other safe venue. These can be very useful occasions, when you can make new friends, get new ideas, and share worries and concerns without breaking confidentiality.

If you are working as a nanny, the parents may have enrolled their children for classes such as music, swimming and ballet, or you may wish to suggest this to them. These provide opportunities for the children to play and to learn new skills.

Find out!

Find out whether there is a childcarers' group in your area that organises 'drop-in' sessions. NCMA or your local children's information centre can give you this information.

The children will also make new friends whilst playing with different people and different things. They will learn how to get along with people and new games to play. These times can benefit everyone.

Going for walks and trips to parks and sports centres

The local park will provide many opportunities for children to play and learn. The large open space enables children to run about, and there are many other chances for children to play. For example, you could organise a hunt in the park for different shaped leaves or different coloured flowers, children could draw their favourite thing in the park, or they could learn how to care for living things by watching the people who work in the park.

However, you might not have a park near your workplace. In that case, just walking along the street can provide good play opportunities. Play 'I-spy' as you walk along, and make up word or number games for older children using the registration numbers of cars that pass by. For example, see who can add up the numbers on a car number plate the fastest, who can make a word from the letters or who can suggest another word that begins with the same first letter.

Remember that you must always have the permission of the parents of all children before you take them outside of the usual setting.

Taking and collecting other children from school

This can be an opportunity for children to learn about road safety. They can be given the responsibility for stopping, looking and listening, then deciding if it is safe to cross the road. Traffic lights can help children learn colours and sequencing. As well as playing 'I-spy' and other games, younger children can look for different coloured doors, shapes of signs, or jump over cracks in the pavement. This is also an opportunity for older children to learn more about personal safety.

Shopping

When toddlers throw very noisy temper tantrums in supermarkets, their parents or childcarers may quietly vow that they will never take that child into a supermarket again! However, there are some things that you and the children can do to make the experience better for everyone. Several large supermarket chains provide child-sized trolleys that children can push around and collect items from a specially made up shopping list. You can set older children challenges to find certain foodstuffs or products, or add up how much things cost. It is in no way intended that home-based

childcarers, with the children that they are caring for, undertake a 'family-sized' shop, but buying a few things for lunch, a picnic or a cooking session can be very good learning opportunities. Shopping in small local shops can also be fun as children can learn to ask for things themselves, learn social skills, how to handle money and find out more about the world around them.

Visits to health centres

If the parents are unable to do so you may need to take children to health centres if they are feeling unwell, or need to have routine health checks or injections. Again, you must make sure that you have the permission of the parents to take their child. If the child is unwell they will probably not want to play games, but you could share a story together whilst you wait.

Think about it

Some activities with children

Make a note of short activities that you and the children could do together, such as sorting the washing or setting a table for a meal. These are ideal opportunities for learning and playing.

Decide which activities need planning beforehand and which could be spontaneous.

You could make a game of sorting washing by colour and 'accidentally' put a red sock in with whites, before washing of course! Children love to point out your silly mistakes, so as well as helping them to recognise colours, doing something like this is fun and helps to build their self-confidence.

Extending your play equipment

No one can expect you to have every toy, book and plaything for every situation. There will be times when you may only want to have a plaything for a short time and for a specific purpose. For instance, you may be caring for a child with a special need and so require specially adapted toys. A child in your care could be going into hospital, so you could get storybooks about hospital visits and stays from your local library. You may want to have a dressing-up area of uniforms worn in hospitals and have play stethoscopes, and so on.

For situations like this, toy libraries are invaluable. They will lend toys and equipment to childcarers for agreed lengths of time at a nominal charge. In most cases you have to collect and return the toys to the library. Toy libraries also have toys that are more accessible for disabled children. Ask your local Children's Information Service or library if there is a toy library in your area. If you have difficulty contacting them, their addresses are at the end of this book.

As well as toy libraries, some childcarers share toys and equipment informally between themselves. This is another good reason to meet up with other childcarers in your area. Some groups of childcarers have got together and successfully applied for funding from the National Lottery to set up their own toy libraries. Again, the addresses should be available through your local library and are at the end of the book.

Some local libraries give special tickets to professional childcarers so that they can borrow larger numbers of books. Ask in your local library for this service.

If you are caring for a child with special or additional needs, the relevant association can sometimes offer advice and support about playthings. Some of the larger organisations have regional offices that run their own toy libraries. It is a good idea to ask the parents of the child if they are members of the association. If they are they could give you a contact name and number, which always makes it easier. Alternatively, at the end of this book are the names and addresses of some of the organisations for children with special or additional needs.

Link to assessment

Unit 1 is assessed through a series of multiple-choice questions. Help and further information on multiple-choice questions can be found in the study skills section at the end of the book on page 277. Examples of these questions relating to providing play and other activities are given below.

These multiple-choice questions assess your knowledge of Sections **3a**, **3b** and **3d** from the syllabus in your CACHE candidate handbook.

1 **How can the practitioner encourage children to join in a play activity?**

a. Provide them with resources and equipment.

b. Insist that they take part.

c. Make sure that the activity is attractive and interesting.

d. Provide only one activity.

2 **Why is outside play beneficial for children?**

a. It helps them to explore.

b. Children enjoy being outside.

c. It helps stimulate the appetite, circulation and digestion.

Case Study

Tracey is a registered childminder who, as well as looking after her own two young children, has three eight-year-olds to supervise after school. The older children have told Tracey that they are learning about the Egyptians at school and have homework to make a model of an irrigation tool. Tracey does not have any books at home to help with this so she goes to the local library where she is able to borrow five books linked to this subject to help the children with their homework.

What other sources of information could Tracey have used?

What would you do in such a situation?

d. It gives the practitioner a chance to tidy up inside.

3 Which cooking activity will help a child aged six develop an awareness of science?

a. Choosing equipment.

b. Freezing ingredients.

c. Weighing ingredients.

d. Talking about recipes.

4 What is the main aim of providing play for a child aged four years?

a. It is enjoyable.

b. It provides social experiences.

c. It keeps them occupied.

d. It stimulates learning.

Answers to these questions can be found at the end of the book on page 294.

Introducing children and their families to your childcare service

The importance of working in partnership with parents for the well-being of the child

Parents and primary carers, such as grandparents or foster carers, are the most important people in young children's lives. It is from them that children will learn about their family cultures and religious beliefs. Parents and primary carers know their children very well, probably better than anyone else. They are a child's first teachers and can hugely influence the child's attitudes and development.

In recent years there has been a distinct shift in attitudes towards the role of parents in the education and care of their children. The Children Act 1989 gave parents definite rights, such as being able to express a preference about which school their child should go to and the right to information about their child's progress and achievements. Most educational establishments and childcare settings have established policies that aim to make parents partners in the care and education of their children. As a home-based childcarer, you may not have a 'parents as partners' policy, but it is essential to establish positive relationships with parents from the first time you meet. The relationship between home-based childcarers and parents is often a close one. Parents come into a childminder's home regularly, and a private nanny may live in the family home, so they get to know one another very well.

It is important that you consider and respect parents' wishes in all aspects of the child's care and well-being. For example, it is important that you make sure all of your routines fit in with the wishes of parents. This does not just mean rest and sleep times, but could include how much time is allowed for watching television and what programmes are suitable. One of the main reasons parents choose home-based childcare is because they want their child to be cared for in a home that is as much as possible like their own home. You will need to think about the different cultural practices that may be involved within the care of children. It may be that some compromises will have to be discussed and agreed upon in order to meet the needs and wishes of several different families.

You may need to think about how you prepare food for some children. Some cultures have clear guidelines on handling and storing food, and what meats are excluded, whereas others have no rules as to what people can or cannot eat. Do not assume that everyone eats what you do or that your way is necessarily right or better than the ways of other people. At the end of this book (page 295) there is a table of common dietary habits that you may find useful.

If you care for African-Caribbean children you could find that their hair and skincare is very personal so your routine must take this into consideration. Some cultures have strong views about modesty and this could affect clothing worn by children when playing, or using the toilet.

Speech bubble: Is there anything that Anita does not eat?

Working in partnership with parents is an important part of childcare

Again, your routine must show that you have thought about these things.

Case Study

Paul and his wife are registered childminders. They have only one son, who is eighteen and still living at home; he is a full-time student at the local college. They live by the coast and often take the children to the beach, especially in the summer.

At the moment Paul and his wife care for four children each day. The youngest child is three months old and the oldest one is eight. The others are four and seven years old. They have been asked to care for twin girls aged eighteen months, whose parents are Trinidadian.

How might the routines need to be adjusted to care for the twins. Give good reasons why the changes are needed?

Do not assume that because a family is part of a particular culture or group that they follow all the practices of that culture. The only way to make sure that your routines give the child the care that the parents want is for you to ask them. You may have to reach a compromise with the parents, especially if certain aspects of a routine could affect other children. If you do reach agreement in such cases, you must stick to it.

The importance of sharing information with parents and ways to do this

It is important to share information with parents effectively if you are to establish a positive working relationship. Older children often tell their parents what they have been doing and how they feel about their day. They can also tell a home-based childcarer what they have eaten and what they might need for their day at school. Younger children are not able to do these things yet so it is essential that there are systems in place for parents and childcarers to exchange information.

Many registered childminders find that an information sheet with a brief résumé of their service is a useful starting point following an enquiry from a parent.

Angie said, 'I found that to give parents an information sheet about my childminding business was a good opening because they could take it away with them. I put my name and telephone number on it, along with brief details of my experience, qualifications, when I was working and my charges. Later on, when a new family started and we began to discuss the contract, I gave them my welcome pack which was more detailed.'

A welcome pack is a good starting point for exchanging essential information. The idea of a welcome pack is that parents can take it away with them and keep it as a reference. Some nannies use their CV, with additional notes and letters from previous employers to help new employers find out more about them.

Some childminders make a booklet about their business. What you give to parents is up to you, but ideally it should include the following points.

- Your full name.
- Your full address including postcode.
- Your telephone number/s, both landline and mobile if you have one.
- Details of the days and times when you are able to care for children, including details of your holidays.
- Details of your charges for a full day, part-time/sessional, holidays and additional hours. Include exactly what parents will get for their money. Will your charges include nappies or food and drinks if you are caring for the child in your home? Do not forget to include any extras that you may wish to charge for and make it very clear who will pay for such things as pre-school sessions and after-school activities.

- A brief outline of how you plan to organise your day. This helps parents know where you are likely to be if they want to get in touch with you.
- A brief outline of some of the activities that you plan to do with the children.
- Brief details of when you were registered and inspected last.
- A detailed registration document to be completed before you start to care for the child, for example a contract form.

Much of this information will have to be regularly revised and kept up to date, for example your own holiday dates.

Think about it

Compiling a welcome pack

Start to make your own welcome pack.

Think what you are going to include.

Think about how you will make it. Can you use a computer to compile it, or to devise your registration form?

Will you use a form that is already made for you, such as the one produced by the NCMA?

Parents will want day-to-day information about their child. This can be done face to face when the parent leaves the child in your care either at the beginning or end of the working day. It is important for you to know, for example, if a baby or young child has slept well the night before. It is also important for a parent to know how much food, drink and rest their child has had during the day. However, you must remember that the start of the working day can be a busy time for parents, and they may well be tired at the end of the day. Some childminders use a home/setting diary where they record important information for parents to read at home, and parents can also include information for the childcarers. Some nannies find exchanges of information happen after the children have gone to bed, often through telephone calls and emails from the parents during the day.

Case Study

Sara is a nanny for two children, a girl aged two years and four months and a boy aged six years and eight months. Both parents are doctors, working full-time and shifts. Sara lives in the family home. She realises that it is important to share and exchange information with the parents, but sometimes they leave or return from work when the children are in bed. They have worked together to establish regular opportunities for passing on information when they cannot meet face to face. They all have mobile phones and find short text messages very useful; Sara and the older child also check the family's email account before he goes to bed and he sends messages to his parents. It has been agreed that post-it notes on the fridge door are used for important messages.

How can Sara and the parents make sure that the younger child is not left out of these exchanges of information?

Can you think of more ways that Sara and the parents could use to pass on important information?

The effects of the transition from the family home to another childcare setting or carer

In any new situation that we face there are bound to be insecurities and worries. They may be about things that seem to be relatively minor afterwards, but at the time seem very important. You can do several things to reduce your worries. For example, when starting a new job, you could do the journey from home to work before you start, so that you know how long it will take, where to park or which bus stop to get off at. It then becomes one less thing to worry about.

Settling any child into a new place or with a different carer takes great care and thought. It should not be rushed and you should allow the child and parents to set the pace. Having established routines can help to settle a child because they can quickly learn what happens at certain times of the day.

Babies and young children develop strong emotional bonds with their main carer, usually a parent. These bonds are referred to as attachments and are crucial in helping how a child develops other relationships later in life. Very young babies can develop attachments indiscriminately, usually with anyone who meets their needs. As they get older they begin to discriminate more and the attachments are with the main person or carer in their lives. After about eight months babies can form multiple attachments depending on where they are and who they are with.

Key Term

Attachment – a strong bond or link between a baby and an adult, usually a parent.

As children become older it is usually easier for them to leave their parents because they have formed multiple attachments, and they have learnt that when their parents leave them, they will come back. However, some babies and young children can experience separation anxiety when separated from their main carer.

Separation anxiety and attachment will be discussed in greater detail in Unit 2, page 152.

Many parents can find this a very distressing time and will need your support and understanding.

It is good practice to discuss changes with older children and explain to them what may happen. Allow them to ask questions and express their concerns. Do not assume because children are older that any changes will not affect them. Children often become quite anxious at the start of a new school term; amongst other things they have to begin to build a new relationship with a different teacher and will probably be in a different classroom. In the same way they can become anxious about changing carers, which can also affect their behaviour. They may lack confidence, become withdrawn, attention seeking, there could be a range of behavioural changes. Some children have expressed fears that their parents love them less because they leave them with someone else, and some children think that their parents will forget about them.

Parents may also experience a range of feelings. Some may feel guilty that someone else is caring for their child, others may feel relief. Some parents become very anxious about the quality of care given to their child and it is not unheard of for parents to have webcams in their home so that they can regularly check on their child and carer whilst at work. Many text or call the carer throughout the day to check on their child. Modern technology can be used in a positive way to help allay parents' fears and worries.

Separation can be a distressing time for both parent and child

The importance of preparing the child and their family for change

The first thing to consider when preparing a child and their family for a change in caring arrangements is your relationship with the parents or carers. It cannot be stressed how important this is for you, the parents and the child. This relationship should be initiated at a planned first meeting – the start of your professional relationship with the parents. You should spend some time getting to know each other, a quick telephone call in response to 'have you any vacancies' or 'can you care for my children' is not enough. It is good practice to talk to parents face to face and spend time answering their questions. Mothers returning to work after the birth of their first child are often very anxious about leaving their baby, so your job is to be as reassuring as possible.

Sometimes home-based childcarers can start to care for a child at short notice so the first meeting and preparations could be rushed. In such cases you will need to think of ways, such as making a 'must do' list, to make sure that all the important points are covered and all essential information is exchanged.

The first meeting

For childminders it is always good practice to invite the parents and the child to visit you in your home before the child starts coming to you. Nannies should visit the family in their home, preferably when the children are there.

- First impressions are very important so you should be professional and welcoming.

- Agree a definite time for the first meeting. This means that you can organise your day so that you have the time to give to the parents and the child.

- If you have other children, including your own, or other family members, do not forget to tell them that you have parents coming to visit.

- Offer the parents tea or coffee if appropriate.

- Start off by talking about everyday things such as the weather or something that is in the news that day. This helps to put people at ease and build confidence.

- Be businesslike but at the same time friendly.

- Childminders could show parents the rooms that the children will be using and also the garden if the children will be playing there.

- Nannies can ask which rooms the children have access to, then ask to see them, making sure that the outside area is included.

- Explain what kinds of activities you will be doing during the day.

- Ask the children what activities they like to do, finding out their likes and dislikes.

- Show the parents your business documents such as certificates, registration and insurance documents.

- Explain to parents why you need them to complete specific information about their child and give them your information sheet or welcome pack.

- Agree what would be good times for you to share information about the child. Not every parent, nanny or childminder has time at the end of the meeting to chat. Some practitioners give parents a brief outline of what the child has been doing during the day. This is especially useful for parents of babies and young children as it can give information about what they have eaten, and when, how often they have had a soiled nappy or how successful the toilet training has been that day. This also provides parents, children and you with common information and helps to build good relationships.

Preparing yourself

As well as having to cope with parents feeling anxious and perhaps guilty about leaving their child, you will feel certain emotions yourself. Childminders will be concerned about the other children that they care for and their own children if they have any. You will need to think about how a new child could affect them, or about what strangers will think about you and your home. You may worry that you will not like the new child. Nannies may worry that they might not be able to cope caring for children that they do not know very well in an environment that they also do not know very well.

All of these worries are perfectly normal, but being able to recognise your own concerns and do something about them will in the end make you more professional and more able to offer a high-quality home-based caring service. You should remember that you can learn from parents. Not every parent will bring his or her children up in the same way as you, if you have any. You must respect each parent as an individual and recognise that although their ways could be different from yours, they are often equally valid. Be open to new ideas and different ways of doing things.

Think about it

Think about the sort of questions that you will need to ask the parents about their child.

Write down your questions, so that you will not forget anything important.

Write down the answers too, in order to avoid any future misunderstanding.

Registered childminders should think about how they will introduce the new child to the other children that are cared for and also to the other people that live in the house. Do not forget to introduce the parents too.

It is good practice to make all of your introductions clearly, do not rush your words, and take your time. Allow the child time to hear the name of the person being introduced, to think about it, and possibly repeat it before moving on to the next person. Be consistent in your introductions, for example do not ask one child to say hello, another one to say hi, and then have your partner say good morning.

Strategies to prepare and support the parents and the child during the settling-in period

One of the best ways to cope with new situations is to plan ahead as much as possible. When you are caring for children for the first time, it is important to remember that they could be feeling just like you did when you started school or a new job. Just as you could have done certain things to reduce your own concerns, there are things you can do to help a child to settle, support the parents and make the change of circumstances easier to deal with.

Practical ways to prepare and support a baby and their parents

In many ways it is easier to settle a young baby than an older child. However, you still need to plan carefully.

- The first visit is always very important. Babies learn about the world through their senses and will build a mental picture of you through the smells, sounds and shapes they experience if you are caring for them in your home. During the first visit they will be bombarded by new smells, sights and sounds; the next time these will not be so new.

- The first visit is the time to ask questions about the baby, such as their feeding pattern, the way they sleep, what types of nappies are used, the comfort objects they have.

- It is also very important that you and the parent care for a small baby together at the beginning. This helps the baby to get used to being handled by different people. It also reassures the mother that you are capable of caring for her baby. If the baby is being breastfed it will give the mother time to adjust, perhaps by expressing milk for you to store and give to the baby, or to wean the baby on to a bottle and formula milk.

- You may have to adjust your routine to cater for both the mother and new baby as well as the needs of other children if you are caring for them in your home.

- When a baby is about eight months old, it will have become aware of strangers and will start to miss its mother. This can make the baby feel unsure and upset about being left by the mother.

- You may need to prepare the parents by warning them that their baby may be distressed at first at being left by them, so you should be very reassuring to both the parents and the baby.

Practical ways to prepare and support a young child and their parents

If possible parents should be encouraged to stay with their child for a while, especially during the first week, but this obviously depends on their work commitments.

A child may need the comfort of something familiar

- As both the child and the parents become more confident and reassured, the length of time that a parent stays can gradually be shortened and the child can be left for short periods during this settling in period.

- If you are a childminder and parents cannot stay with their child, do not let them just drop the child off and go, especially at the beginning. Suggest that for the first few days they can bring their child a little earlier so that they can come into your home and help to settle the child.

- Once parents decide that they are going, make sure that the goodbyes are not long, drawn-out affairs, as these can be distressing for everyone concerned.

- Encourage the parents to develop a routine for saying goodbye and ensure that they stick to it.

- Parents should not leave suddenly when the child is not looking as this can lead to insecurity and distrust in the child. Children tend to be more clingy and insecure when parents disappear suddenly.

- Once the parent has gone you should try to give the child as much attention as possible. If you are a childminder with other children you may need to adjust your routine to allow you to spend more time with the new child.

- It is a very good idea to give the child an activity to do immediately after their parent has left. This should be something that they are familiar with. Any activity that you offer should be fairly straightforward and one that does not involve too much concentration.

- Some homecarers find it very useful if a child keeps a special toy with them that both of you can play with during this time.

- Do not force them to play or join in play, let the child set the pace at the start.

- A child who is distressed might need cuddles, or their comforter. Remember that some children only like close contact with their mother and you should always take your cues from the child.

Practical ways to prepare and support an older child and their parents

Older children are more able to understand what is happening, but this does not mean that they will not experience difficulties in adjusting. The way that children and their parents adjust to changes in care depends largely on their past experiences; however, all children need time to settle. Older children may start to express strong feelings about changes in their care and may feel that their established friendships will be threatened.

- If possible children should be with friends or children and adults that they already know.

- It is good practice to introduce children to other children who you know are willing to include another in their group.

- Take your cues from the child, do not force them to make friends.

- Listen to their fears and concerns, value and respect what the child or young person has to say.

- Talk to the parents about their child's concerns, but also include the child in your discussions.

The importance of effective communication with parents and children

The key to any successful relationship is communication.

Communication in any form is a two-way process that requires time and effort from both sides. Lack of communication can lead to misunderstanding and misinformation. You must think about the communication needs of both the parents and the children. An adult or child whose home language is not the same as yours may need you to simplify your words or use visual clues. An individual with speech impairments may need more time to respond.

Effective communication takes time and effort. It is not acceptable for you, the child, or the parents to rely on snatched exchanges at the start or end of the working day. This can lead to frustration and misunderstanding.

There are skills that you can learn which will help you become a more effective communicator, not just with parents, but also with the children that you care for and indeed all the other people that you come into contact with in both your professional and personal life. Communication skills include listening, speech, body language, including facial expressions and gestures, and written communication. These will be looked at in greater detail in Unit 4 (see page 223).

Case Study

Alia is a registered childminder and cares for two children after school. The children's mother has a hearing impairment and can lip-read. Alia makes sure that when she is talking to the mother she faces her, so the mum can read her lips. She also has the mother's mobile phone number and uses text messaging to contact her instead of speaking on the telephone.

Alia also has a policy of giving all parents a written monthly update on the service she offers.

Think of the ways that you communicate with parents. Are they effective and do they meet the needs of all parents?

Unit 1 is assessed through a series of multiple-choice questions. Help and further information on multiple-choice questions can be found in the study skills section at the end of the book on page 277. Examples of these questions relating to introducing children and their families to your childcare service are given below.

These multiple choice questions assess your knowledge of Sections **4a**, **4d** and **4e** from the syllabus in your CACHE candidate handbook.

1 One of the main reasons parents choose home-based care is:

a. Because it is cheaper than other forms of childcare.

b. Because parents want their child to be cared for in a home environment.

c. Because it is near to where they live.

d. Because they know the person has had a police check.

2 How can a parent best prepare a child aged two years old when starting in a childcare setting?

1 Visit the setting with the child.

2 Leave quickly after taking the child.

3 Watch the child play.

4 Phone the setting to see if the child has settled.

5 Stay to settle the child in.

a. 1, 2 and 3 are correct.

b. 2, 3 and 4 are correct.

c. 3, 4 and 5 are correct.

d. 1, 3 and 5 are correct.

3 What does the role of the home-based childcarer involve when settling a child into the setting?

a. Helping the child to accept separation from their parents.

b. Helping the child to be with other children.

c. Telling stories to the child.

d. Being with the child all of the time.

Answers to these questions can be found at the end of the book on page 294.

Managing children's behaviour in the home-based setting

Key Term

Behaviour is the way in which an individual acts or responds to a certain situation.

Every society has its own rules and social boundaries, with behaviour that is considered to be either acceptable or not acceptable. Each family can also have its own rules and boundaries; for example, some families always expect children to ask before they leave the table after a meal, in other families this would be unnecessary.

You will have your own views on what is acceptable behaviour and what is not. These views will have been formed by your upbringing and culture and may have changed over the years, or may have been altered by where you live and who you live with. However, deciding what is acceptable behaviour is not easy and we must remember that it is important to accept different types of behaviour from different ages of children.

Children are not born with an understanding of what is acceptable behaviour. This is something they learn as they grow and develop. Adults play a very important part in helping children to learn acceptable forms of behaviour that will help them become useful members of our society. In the past adults often expected children to obey without question and be compliant to their requests. Children's behaviour was managed through control with little or no consideration of children's rights or their needs. Today we manage behaviour by recognising that children have rights and are entitled to be valued.

Understanding more about children's behaviour is covered in Unit 2.

Factors influencing children's behaviour

There are numerous factors that can influence a child's behaviour. Some influences are relatively short term, such as feeling under the weather, whereas other factors can be long term, such as the effect of abuse.

Overall development

A child might behave in a certain way because they have emotional difficulties, or because some aspect of their development is delayed. It is often the case that children with some form of developmental delay will show behaviour that is not normally associated with a child of a certain age.

Self-image

The way a child feels about themselves can affect the way they behave. Their self-image is in turn affected by many things shown in the diagram.

The way in which a child's self-image is affected

Changes in a child's life

A change in a child's circumstances is often shown by a change in their behaviour. These changes can immediately affect the child or have an effect on their family.

The changes can be:

• the birth of a baby

• the death of a family member, close friends or pets

• moving house

• illness within the family

• divorce or separation of parents

• work pattern of parents or unemployment

• adapting to a stepfamily following the remarriage of one parent.

A child's personality

Think about how a child's personality develops.

A child's school

School, nursery or pre-school groups will have behaviour expectations that the child will have to adapt to. This can affect how they behave before or after attending the school. Children who have been inactive and quiet for a period of time in school will use up surplus energy when they get to your house.

Peer group

Some peer groups will set their own rules and expectations for behaviour, which can have both positive and negative effects on an individual child. The influence of the peer group and the need to belong is very strong in older children. The desire to fit into the group can bring a child into conflict with their carers and parents at times.

The influence of the media

Children may copy the behaviour of people they see on television regardless of whether or not it is right or wrong. Examples are the way famous footballers spit during the games, or argue with the decisions of the referee. A child who sees the way that these famous people behave may believe this kind of behaviour to be acceptable and so copies them.

We must also remember that young children can be influenced by the way that the media reports world tragedies, such as the Asian tsunami in December 2004. How do you know if the children are frightened or worried by such events? Sometimes how the child feels can be reflected in the way that they behave.

The importance of consistency of care between the home-based practitioner and the parents

When you first meet a family and the children you will need to ask about their views on behaviour. If you are a registered childminder you may well include aspects of your policy of managing children's behaviour in your welcome pack, or discuss the contract at the meeting.

There are several family structures and traditions that may influence the way in which parents manage the behaviour of their children. It is important that you respect and understand these differences. This will be looked at in more depth in Unit 4.

It is in the best interests of the child that home-based childcarers, be they nannies or childminders, and parents try to have a consistent approach to managing behaviour. When this does not happen children will get mixed messages and can become confused. Parents should be seen as the main educators of their children, and home-based carers must work with parents to help manage their behaviour.

Case Study

Adie throws toys across the room narrowly missing her baby brother. Jenna, her nanny, tells her to stop, but Adie carries on throwing the toys. Jenna asks her to stop again. Jenna realises that Adie gets attention when she throws toys. Adie has learnt that behaving in this way will get her attention. Jenna discusses this with the children's parents and they realise that they too give Jenna more attention when she does something that they consider unacceptable. Jenna and the parents agree that they will praise Adie and give her attention when she is playing well.

Why do you think Adie needs to seek attention in this way?

What would you do in this situation?

How to develop and share a framework for children's behaviour

It is important to establish a framework for what you consider to be acceptable behaviour in the home very early on in your career. You will probably base your framework or house

rules on things that are important and matter to the children, their parents and you, for example most people believe that keeping children safe is very important, so your framework could focus on preventing children hurting or injuring themselves.

Part of your framework could be:

- Children are not allowed in the kitchen unless I am in there as well.

The second part of your framework could be:

- Children are not allowed to open the gate.

You may not write down this part of your framework, but it will become part of the everyday things that the children learn whilst in your care. You can discuss this with older children as well as their parents, talking about why these things are important and what may happen if they do not agree to the framework.

Other things that you could base your framework for behaviour on are:

- preventing children from doing anything that is dangerous, offensive or hurtful to other adults and children

- doing things that will not make them welcome in other people's homes or things that other people would find unacceptable

- doing something that could cause damage to other people's possessions.

You could write down a few short simple sentences about your framework for behaviour. This will be your behaviour policy, which you could give to parents and discuss with them at your first meeting. Developing and sharing your framework will help children feel secure and they are more likely to conform once they understand what the 'house rules' are and why they are there.

An example of a framework for behaviour, or behaviour policy, is shown below. Hayley includes this in her welcome pack for parents and reviews and discusses it with parents and children.

**HAYLEY SMITH
REGISTERED CHILDMINDER**

I have very few rules in my childminding business, but I do expect all children that I care for in my home to learn to accept these rules.

My rules are:

- we will not be hurtful, offensive or dangerous to another person

- we will take care of another person's things

- we will all care for each other.

I believe that if children know what the boundaries are for their behaviour, they feel more secure.

I will not use any form of physical punishment. I will not humiliate, restrain or isolate a child. I will be firm, consistent and fair.

I will discuss any concerns that I have with you.

I will praise children when they behave well and will provide a positive role model.

If you would like to talk to me about any part of my framework for behaviour then please do so.

Tel: 01234 567890
September 2005

may have no restrictions on going into the kitchen. It is therefore very important that you explain to children clearly and simply why you have that rule. You might say something along these lines:

'I want to make sure that you, and all of the other children, are safe and not in any danger. There are things in the kitchen that could hurt you, such as the electric kettle, the oven and the cupboard doors. I do not want anyone to be hurt so we all go into the kitchen together, then we can make sure that we are all safe.'

A nanny may have exactly the same house rule – that a child is not allowed to go into the kitchen without an adult present – and the reasons for it are probably very similar to those of the childminder. When the child's parents are at home, the child may not have any such limits. If explained simply and fairly to the child it will appear reasonable and consistent.

Children need to know and understand that your rules and boundaries will not keep changing. It is very important that you are consistent and firm in applying your boundaries for all children, because if a child is not dealt with in a consistent way it can lead to difficulties in behaviour. Knowing what the rules are and that boundaries are set helps to make children feel secure.

For childminders it is inevitable that the rules, boundaries or framework that you establish in your home may be different from the accepted rules in the child's own house. For example, you may not allow any child to go into the kitchen unless you are also in there, but when at home they

Think about it

Creating a behaviour policy or a framework

Try writing a framework, or behaviour policy, for your work setting.

If you already have a behaviour policy or framework, have another look at it. You may have written it some time ago.

Ask yourself the following questions.

- Does it really say what I, the parent and the children understand?

- Is it positive?

- Does it work?

If you answer no to any of these questions you need to review your framework or policy.

It is good practice to review all your policies at least once a year. Some childminders review their policies every three months.

Establishing your behaviour framework

Establishing your personal behaviour framework as early as possible is very important for you, the children, the parents and, if you are a childminder, other members of your family. It will mean that everyone will know what is expected of them and will lead to a consistent approach.

Your framework will consist of boundaries that set limits on behaviour and are simple rules which children will learn must not be broken, for

Case Study

Jane, a registered childminder, has recently started to care for three-year-old twin boys. They often jump on the chairs and sofa. Jane explains to the boys that they could fall and hurt themselves and that she does not let other children jump on the furniture. Jane explains to the boys why she does not want them to do this and that they can climb and jump outside in the garden. The boys tell Jane that their mummy lets them do it at home. Jane arranges to talk to the mother and explains that she fears the boys could fall and hurt themselves if they jump on the furniture. She also explains that she does not let other children behave in this way. Jane reminds the mother about her framework of behaviour that was discussed at their first meeting. The mother agrees with Jane that the boys should do as Jane asks when they are in Jane's home. She agrees to talk to the boys and explain that they must do what Jane asks them when she is caring for them.

Do you agree with what Jane did?

Are there any other ways of handling this situation?

What would be your reaction if the boys' mother felt that Jane was making a fuss over nothing and that it didn't matter?

How should I handle this?

Managing children's behaviour in the home-based setting

example 'You must not go into the kitchen on your own'. When you start to establish your boundaries there are certain things that you should do.

- Help children to learn the rules by reminding them whenever appropriate, for example in response to a request for a drink you may say 'Yes, you can have a drink when I go into the kitchen'.

- Explain why you have rules – children are much more likely to remember your rules if they know why you have them.

- Use simple, clear language when managing children, for example 'It is time to come in now'. Saying something like, 'It is almost time for us to collect your sister from school, so we must start to put the toys away soon', is confusing. What is it you are asking the child to do?

- Explain in simple, clear language what will happen if your rules are broken. You could say, 'I may have to put that game away'.

- Some rules or boundaries can be written down. This is especially appropriate for school-aged children who often quite enjoy doing such an activity. You could get the children to produce a poster or chart of 'The rules of the house'.

- Always praise and encourage children when they do follow your rules and at times when they are playing well and happily.

Strategies to promote positive behaviour and respond to challenging behaviour

There are numerous strategies that can be employed to promote positive behaviour. Some strategies will be very effective for one child but completely ineffective for another, so it is important that the strategies you use are appropriate for each child's individual needs.

Our response to a child's behaviour, whether unwanted or not, will send a message to that child. You should aim to send positive messages to children at all times. It can be very difficult to be positive when managing children whose behaviour is challenging. However, it is good practice to try to turn around anything that you say into a positive statement; for example, instead of saying, 'Do not do that,' try to say 'Let's do this.' Rather than saying, 'Do not leave those toys there,' try saying, 'Let's put these toys in their box together then we will not trip up over them.'

There will be times when you will say 'do not' or 'no' to protect a child from a potential hazard or danger. In such cases you want the child to respond immediately. If you use words like 'do not' and 'no' frequently there is the possibility that the child will not respond quickly, or may even ignore you.

It is very important that you discuss any concerns you have about a child's behaviour with the parents. You should tell the child that you and their parents are going to talk; sometimes the child will be included as well. This should not be regarded as a threat, but should be seen as a consistent approach by the child. For instance, 'If you do not stop hitting I will talk to your parents,' is much better when replaced with, 'Let's all sit down and talk about what happens when you play with other children and how you feel,' which comes across as far more positive and respectful of the child's needs.

Sometimes concerns do not arise over one aspect of behaviour – there may be several things that cause concern. Decide upon the most important thing to tackle first, for example you may be caring for a child who is biting other children and cannot share. It may be they are too young to understand what sharing means, but you should still try and stop the child biting and hurting others.

- Use a positive approach to guide the child, to distract them and so avoid situations where the chances of the unwanted behaviour happening are increased.

- Be firm and consistent. If you say no, mean it, and make sure that your framework, goals and boundaries are firm, consistently applied and not altered.

- Avoid confrontation. Distract the child, or gently remove them from the situation. Offer an alternative play activity or toy with a positive statement.

- Show your disapproval. Children naturally want to please adults, so showing your disapproval of their unwanted behaviour can be a powerful reason for them not to behave in that way again. However, do not show your disapproval by humiliating or embarrassing the child.

- Explain why the behaviour is not acceptable, and if the child is old enough also explain the possible consequences of their behaviour.

- Be a positive role model. Children learn by imitating and copying the actions of adults and others around them. If you use a loud voice and inappropriate language when you are angry, children will think that it is OK to do this when they are cross.

Try to create an environment where children have opportunities to be in control of situations. This is usually referred to as empowering children. You could, for example, give children more choices about what they do, or different ways of doing certain activities. Children could be given special achievable responsibilities which are rewarded with lots of praise and thanks. This not only empowers the child but also helps to build up their self-confidence and self-esteem.

Link to assessment

Unit 1 is assessed through a series of multiple-choice questions. Help and further information on multiple-choice questions can be found in the study skills section at the end of the book on page 277. Examples of these questions relating to managing children's behaviour in the home-based setting are given below.

These multiple-choice questions assess your knowledge of Section **5a**, **5b**, **5c** and **5d** from the syllabus in your CACHE candidate handbook.

1 How do boundaries help manage children's behaviour?

a. The practitioner knows what to expect from the children.
b. Children feel emotionally safe and secure.
c. Parents know what to expect from the children.
d. Children know what they can get away with.

2 A child aged three years is showing behaviour that causes concern. What is the best way to deal with this behaviour?

a. Praise the child's good behaviour.
b. Withdraw the child for a short time.

c. Tell the child off for behaviour that causes concern.
d. Give the child more attention.

3 A strategy to promote positive behaviour is to change the child's routine. Why is this often a successful strategy?

a. Acceptable behaviour is reinforced with attention, so the child might be confused.
b. Changing a routine provides security for the child.
c. The child can play out any worries or fears.
d. The trigger for unwanted behaviour may be removed.

4 Why is it good practice to have a behaviour policy or framework?

a. It helps the practitioner to be fair and consistent.
b. Parents will know that the practitioner is professional.
c. It will make sure that the practitioner is a positive role model.
d. It is a requirement of registration.

Answers to these questions can be found at the end of the book on page 294.

Inclusion and anti-bias practice

The importance of valuing each child as an individual

It is a requirement of registration for all childminders that they comply with the Children Act 1989 and its guidance. The Act has the requirement 'to treat all children as individuals and with equal concern'. Anyone who offers home-based childcare should comply with the Children Act.

Treating children as individuals is not the same as treating all children in the same way. This is impossible to do, as all children are different. What is important is that practitioners understand how to treat all children and their families with respect in a fair way and do not discriminate.

Recognising children's individuality is the basis of anti-bias practices and should underpin all of your work with children and their families. Inclusion is often used in combination with anti-bias practice, and in the case of home-based care, should mean an environment where everyone is welcomed and respected.

Key Term

Inclusion – the process of recognising, understanding and overcoming obstructions or barriers to participation.

All children are unique, they have different personalities, needs, interests and abilities. They should be valued and respected for who they are. Children who feel valued will enjoy being in your company, and will respond positively to you. Home-based carers should always try to meet children's individual needs and develop positive relationships with children based on trust and respect.

Understanding that children develop and learn as individuals

All children will pass through the same stages of development but the rate at which they develop will vary according to each child. On this basis it is can be misleading to say, for example, that all babies can sit without support at eight months. Some will, some will sit at seven months and some will do it at nine months; when they can do it depends upon many factors. All of these babies are developing quite normally, but differently and in their own individual way.

It is important that children know that you respect them as individuals regardless of their strengths and weaknesses.

One very positive way of helping children understand that you respect them as an individual is to use their name. Make sure that you pronounce the name correctly and when writing a child's name make sure that it is spelt correctly.

Case Study

Chris is a private nanny and has just started to care for twin girls aged seven and a three-year-old boy. Chris notices that the parents rarely use the twins' individual names, referring to them collectively as 'the twins'. They talk about their son as 'the twins' brother' to other people. One of the girls can be quite defiant at times and Chris wonders if she might feel resentful.

Why do you think the girl might be feeling this way?

What could Chris do?

The effects of prejudice and stereotyping on children

If you hold prejudicial or stereotypical views you may find that these will affect your work practices. Prejudicial attitudes and stereotypical views can be obstacles to children reaching their full potential.

Prejudicial views are often based on incorrect judgements and in many cases lead to stereotypical assumptions, for example 'looking after children is not a proper job'. Prejudice and stereotyping lead to discrimination. This may not always be obvious, but may result in children's and parental rights being ignored. The view that childcare is not a proper job could result in the carer giving a poor quality service because they do not feel valued or respected.

Key Term

Prejudice – narrow mindedness, bigotry, unfairness, discrimination.

Key Term

Stereotype – to label, put into artificial categories, to typecast.

Stereotyping gives people labels, which in itself is a form of discrimination. Stereotyping is a fixed way of thinking about people and can stop children reaching their full potential. Sometimes our ways of thinking are not based on our past experiences but on stereotypes. Many people hold stereotypical views in some form or other, some are learnt from the media, some from our peers or what we may have learnt.

A helping hand

Think about it

Do you have different expectations of what girls and boys can achieve?

Do you provide different activities for girls and boys?

Do you think that some activities are more suitable for girls than for boys?

The importance of the home-based practitioner being a positive role model to the children

One very effective way to encourage children to develop positive attitudes and respect for other people is from your own example. Children notice how you behave and react towards others and will take their cues from you. You should give each child equal opportunity to develop and grow in their own unique and individual way. It is essential that you are able to make adaptations to your work practices so that children can be treated according to their individual needs.

Children learn how to behave, react to others and manage their feelings from the adults around them. If children see adults behaving in an aggressive way towards each other they will think that such behaviour is acceptable. If at all possible children need to see adults managing their feelings appropriately and understand that feelings can be talked about and shared.

> ## Think about it
>
> You are driving your car along a busy road, with children in the back. The driver in front of you does not indicate that they are turning left. What do you do?
>
> - Shout at the driver about their bad driving, even though they cannot hear you.
>
> - Say nothing, but just shake your head to show your disapproval.
>
> - Do nothing.

Children need to have accurate information about every aspect of their learning and development, with honest and truthful answers.

Being a positive role model means that you do not pretend differences do not exist, but instead talk openly about them and encourage children to do the same.

Being a positive role model does not mean that you will be perfect all of the time – everyone makes mistakes. Being a positive role model for children means that you will admit to your mistakes and learn from them. In this way children see that you are open-minded, treating children and their families with respect and care.

Creating an environment in which all children feel welcomed, respected and included

An effective way of encouraging children to develop positive attitudes and respect for other people is to create a positive learning environment in your setting. You should have materials, toys and resources that reflect the diversity of our society, but which are also inclusive.

There is a danger that some home-based childcarers may inadvertently provide children with materials and images that do not accurately reflect other cultures. For example, giving the idea that all Inuit people live in igloos, when in fact many live in towns and cities. In the same way, having a length of material in the dressing up box and calling it a sari does not show respect or understanding of women who do wear this form of clothing. How you use and work with your equipment and resources is very important. Adults should avoid the potential dangers of presenting children with a stereotypical image of any given culture. It is like believing that British culture is only about Big Ben and Christmas, in that everyone uses Big Ben to set the time and celebrates Christmas.

During your childcare career you will care for children from a wide variety of backgrounds. You need to show that you value and respect each family and, if appropriate, should ask parents to help you acquire suitable resources and toys. This could include sharing a new song, rhyme or story or trying a new recipe together. This will not only make individual children feel welcome and valued by you, but will also extend the knowledge and understanding of other children that you care for.

Think about it

It is possible to buy small-scale toys of people in wheelchairs, on crutches and with physical impairments or disabilities. Ask yourself, do these help make children with disabilities and impairments more welcome, included and feel more respected?

Link to assessment

Unit 1 is assessed through a series of multiple-choice questions. Help and further information on multiple-choice questions can be found in the study skills section at the end of the book, on page 277. Examples of these questions relating to inclusion and anti-bias practice are given below.

These multiple-choice questions assess your knowledge of sections **6a**, **6b**, **6c**, **6d** and **6e** from the syllabus in your CACHE candidate handbook.

1 When children are playing what should the practitioner make sure of?

a. That boys and girls play together.

b. That boys and girls take turns to play with the toys.

c. That all children use a range of play resources.

d. That younger children have first choice of the toys.

2 What is the main purpose of anti-discriminatory/anti-bias practice?

a. It shows that the practitioner can work without cultural and gender bias.

b. It shows that the practitioner can meet the needs of individual children.

c. It encourages boys to play with dressing-up clothes.

d. It encourages all children to help those with disabilities.

3 How can the practitioner encourage children to respect and value each other?

a. Involve children in looking after pets in the home.

b. Involve children to play in groups.

c. Encourage children to bring items that they value.

d. Listen to what the children have to say.

4 How can the practitioner ensure inclusive practice?

a. Ensure all children can play with everything.

b. They cannot refuse to care for a disabled child.

c. It will make sure that you are a positive role model.

d. Engage in the process of recognising, understanding and overcoming obstructions and barriers to participation.

Answers to these questions can be found at the end of the book on page 294.

Child protection in the home-based setting

Throughout this unit it has been stressed that you should do everything you can to make sure that the children in your care are safe at all times. You will have looked at the possible risks and hazards in the home and garden and thought about the ways that your practice ensures children are protected.

However, there could be times when, despite all your good practices, children may need protecting from harm and ill-treatment. It is important that you have a basic knowledge of types and signs of abuse and that you know what to do if you suspect that a child is in need of protection. Many practitioners find dealing with any issue about child protection very difficult, so it is important that you know where you can get support and help.

Child protection issues will also be discussed in Unit 3.

Definitions and types of abuse

It is generally accepted that there are four forms of child abuse.

The four types of child abuse

Neglect

To neglect a child is to fail to give them proper care or attention. A neglected child does not receive the appropriate care that they need to grow and develop – they are literally abandoned to look after themselves. It can be that the child does not receive medical care and attention when they need it, or that they are not given enough food, appropriate clothing or kept clean. Parents that leave children unattended can be considered to be neglecting their child. They are therefore abusing that child.

Parents of neglected children often have personal problems which can have a negative impact on the overall well-being of the child. Many parents of neglected children love their offspring but are unable to care for them adequately.

Physical abuse

Physical abuse can occur when an adult injures a child by hitting, shaking, using excessive force, burning with cigarettes or giving a child something that could harm him or her, such as alcohol or drugs.

Smacking

There is a very fine line between smacking a child in order to discipline them and physical abuse. A gentle smack on the hand could be considered acceptable by some people, whereas hitting a child with an object would be regarded as a criminal offence. In recent years there has been much controversy about the rights of parents to smack in order to discipline their child. In some countries, such as Sweden, parents are not allowed to use any form of physical punishment on children. Many educationalists and childcare experts believe that smacking a child is an ineffective form of discipline. They feel that it teaches children to be violent and makes them more likely to believe that it is acceptable to deliberately hurt another person.

At the present time, parents can still use 'reasonable chastisement' to discipline their child.

Sexual abuse

Whenever an adult uses a child for their own sexual gratification they are said to be sexually abusing that child. This can be anything from rape and full sexual intercourse, fondling the genitals and other parts of the body, to involving children in pornographic material, videos, Internet sites, photographs or showing such material to a child. Most cases of sexual abuse of children are by people that they know. It can begin gradually and develop over a period of time. Sometimes children who are sexually abused believe that this is a way of pleasing adults and so gain their love and approval.

Emotional/psychological abuse

When an adult fails to show a child love and affection, the child will lose confidence and can become withdrawn and nervous. This is a form of emotional abuse. In the same way, continually threatening, verbally abusing or shouting at a child can have long-term damaging effects. It is very difficult to assess this form of abuse and it is only recently that emotional abuse has been considered as a form of abuse.

Bullying is also a form of abuse and can be physical, emotional and psychological.

Common signs and symptoms of possible abuse

There are definite indications of abuse. Sometimes practitioners suspect that a child is in need of protection without having seen any physical signs of abuse. This could be through a child's behaviour, such as becoming withdrawn or distressed for no apparent reason. It is important that you are alert to changes in a child's behaviour, as well as being aware of the physical signs of abuse.

If you suspect any form of abuse, you must proceed with care, caution and be certain of your facts. It is not good practice to question a child or probe into what has happened, instead you should gently encourage them to talk about how they could have been hurt or how they are feeling. Take your cues from the child. If you suspect that they need protection you should make a written record of any conversation that you have with a child, and also make a note of any signs or symptoms. Be factual and precise, never make assumptions, for example do not assume that because a child has a black eye they have been hit by someone, they may well have hit their head on the edge of a cupboard.

In all cases of abuse the signs and symptoms fall roughly into two categories: behavioural and physical.

Signs and symptoms of neglect

1 Behavioural

- Parents can be difficult to contact or fail to make appointments.
- Children tell you about looking after younger siblings and taking on responsibilities not normally expected of children of their age.
- Children talk about being left alone.

2 Physical

- A generally unkempt and uncared for appearance, perhaps dirty, unwashed clothes.
- Underweight.
- Always hungry.
- Frequently tired due to lack of sleep and regular sleeping habits.
- Lots of accidental injuries that could be caused through being unsupervised or left unattended.

- Lots of minor infections and ailments that are not treated, such as colds, coughs and earaches.

Signs and symptoms of physical abuse

Most children will at some point in their life suffer an accidental injury. In the normal rough and tumble of everyday activities and play children can fall, bump their heads, become bruised and grazed or cut. These are accidents, and while you should offer sympathy and support, you should not necessarily become concerned.

The time to become concerned is when the injuries are frequent, do not have an acceptable explanation, or if the part of the body that is affected is not where you would normally expect a child to have an injury, for example bruising on the back or stomach.

1 Behavioural

- Being withdrawn and quiet when in the past the child has been sociable.
- Aggressive play, often towards other children and in role-play.
- Aggressive responses to the childminder.
- Messages from parents asking that the child is not changed or undressed for any reason.
- Unable to sit comfortably or sitting with unusual stiffness, and reluctant to join in vigorous play.

2 Physical

- Unexplained bruises, cuts and grazes.
- Unusually shaped bruise marks.
- Frequent broken bones.
- Unusual scalds and burns such as cigarette burns.
- Bite marks.

Parents feel under tremendous pressure at certain times in their lives and having a small baby or child can add to their stress. A baby who is difficult to feed or cries incessantly at night can put some parents under an intolerable level of stress, especially after a long day at work. At such times an adult may physically abuse a child or baby.

Such adults may lose control of their actions, and often feel they are also losing control of other aspects of their lives. They may lose control to the point that they violently shake their child. Shaking a young baby can cause a great deal of internal damage, and damage to the brain alone can be much the same as dropping a baby head first onto a concrete floor. The symptoms of this type of brain damage can be:

- loss of vision

- loss of hearing

- fits

- lack of response.

If you know that the parents are under stress, you should offer support and advise them to seek help from appropriate organisations and other professionals. You should be concerned if a child or baby starts to show the following signs:

- not interested in feeding

- unable to settle to rest or sleep

- unusually tired and not interested in what is going on around them

- poor muscle tone.

Remember that these signs could also indicate that the child is not well, possibly in the first stages of an illness or infection. However, it could be related to physical abuse such as shaking.

Signs and symptoms of sexual abuse

It can be very difficult to notice any signs or symptoms of sexual abuse. Sometimes there are no visible marks, especially in the case of showing pornographic materials to children or involving them in pornographic materials. Sexual abuse in children is easier to detect by looking at changes in behaviour rather than physical signs.

1 Behavioural

- Using sexual language and knowledge of sexual behaviour not normally associated with a child of that age.

- Showing insecurity.

- Clinging to trusted adults and at the same time indicating an unwillingness to be in the company of particular adults.

- Immature actions for their age, such as comfort habits like rocking, thumb sucking, wanting a comforter.

- Using imaginary play to act out sexual behaviour.

- Undressing themselves at inappropriate times or exposing the genital area.

- Drawings or paintings of a sexual nature.

2 Physical

- Injuries such as bruises and scratches that are non-accidental, especially around the genital area.

- Bloodstains.

- Vaginal discharge.

- Difficulty in urinating or having a bowel movement, or frequent 'accidents'.

- Difficulty in sitting down or walking.

- Frequent urinary and/or genital infections.

- Showing distress or signs of fear when needing to pass urine or have a bowel movement.

Signs and symptoms of emotional/ psychological abuse

Emotional abuse is the relentless mistreatment of a child until their emotional development suffers. When an adult fails to show a child love and affection, or has unrealistic expectations of a child's abilities, the child may lose confidence, have a poor self-image and can become withdrawn and nervous. In the same way, continually threatening a child, causing them to feel in danger or frightened, and verbally abusing or shouting at them can have damaging long-term effects. These are all forms of emotional abuse. It is very difficult to assess this form of abuse because the signs are not always straightforward.

It can be very difficult to see any signs or symptoms of emotional abuse, especially physical signs. Children who are subject to this form of abuse are very vulnerable. They lack self-esteem and crave attention. Children who are subject to emotional abuse will have a very low opinion of themselves, very poor self-worth and very little confidence.

1 Behavioural

- Attention-seeking, such as deliberately being uncooperative, troublesome, telling lies or clinging to an adult and craving attention.
- Inability to accept praise or trust people.
- Immature behaviour, such as tantrums at an age when normally they would not behave in that way.
- Poor social skills with children of their own age.
- Frequently anxious, perhaps trying too hard to please another person.

2 Physical

In older children the signs may be:

- Extreme eating habits and dieting caused by very low self-esteem and self-worth.
- Deliberately hurting themselves to gain attention.
- The development of sudden speech disorders.

Understanding the nature and extent of child abuse

It is very difficult to get accurate figures about how many children are in need of protection at any one time. Charities, such as the National Society for Prevention of Cruelty to Children (NSPCC), work unceasingly to protect children and raise awareness, but children are still abused. When it was suggested by the NSPCC that as many as one in six children may have been abused, some people felt that this was overstating the true picture. Many children who are abused, or in need of protection, do not talk about their experiences. The abuse may not be obvious to other people that they come into contact with so it can be very difficult to do anything about it, sometimes until it is too late.

Every childcare professional, in whatever capacity, has a responsibility to put the child's needs and welfare first. It therefore follows that if you suspect that a child is in need of protection you must do something about it. Rather than regarding child protection as something that you will hopefully not have to deal with, it should be part of your everyday practice to protect children.

Abuse can have long-term effects. Children who are subjected to repeated abuse can suffer severe psychological damage and be seriously affected for the rest of their lives. Many adults who suffered abuse as children or young people have great difficulty forming relationships and can have problems parenting their own children.

Abuse can happen in any family, whatever the family structure or parenting style. It does not only happen to children in poor families, or in single-parent families, and can happen to any child. Practitioners must not assume that children of 'respectable' families will not be abused.

Empowering children to protect themselves and to understand that they have rights

Empowering children is about teaching them the skills to take control and management of their lives. Children who are empowered feel good about themselves. They have a high level of self-confidence and esteem and are assertive and self-aware. These positive attributes can be developed through an environment that makes sure children feel safe and protected, where they have opportunities to talk freely and develop independence, have positive role models and caring sensitive adults who show respect and tolerance of the children.

Key Term

Empowerment – to give strength, confidence or power to someone.

Considering child protection from the standpoint of children's rights should mean that every practitioner supports the development of those rights.

Children's rights are considered in more detail in Unit 2, page 95.

Every child has the right to be protected from abuse, to be treated as an individual according to their needs and to be taken care of in appropriate ways when abuse is recognised. It is for these reasons that practitioners must be aware of the issues and factors that can have an effect on a child, for example the environment in which the child is living and relationships within their family.

Bullying: recognition, prevention, supporting children and taking appropriate action

Bullying is abuse and can take many forms, such as:

- name-calling, sarcastic comments, spreading rumours

- fighting, physical attacks or the threat of physical attack

- not allowing a child to join in play activities or games with the peer group, excluding them

- racial remarks

- torment or ridicule.

There are many other forms of bullying, but all usually result in distress and emotional problems for the child concerned. It is also important to note that a child can be bullied through emails and text messages on mobile phones.

The distress of bullying is often shown by changes in ways a child would normally behave. You are very well placed to be able to spot changes in behaviour. Look for things like:

- a child suddenly not wanting to go to nursery or school

- a child making up illnesses to avoid going to school, for example an unexpected stomach-ache or headache

- fall in academic achievement

Bullying can take many forms

- crying a lot

- coming home with unexplained injuries or ripped clothing

- a child who starts behaving in an aggressive way, or bullying other children when in your care

- parents telling you about disturbed sleep and possibly bad dreams or nightmares

- running away

- depression and indicators of low self-esteem and worth

- attempts or threats to commit suicide.

You must always tell parents if you suspect that their child is being bullied. With the parents' permission you should also pass on your concerns to the school.

Together with the parents, you need to ensure that help is given to the child. It is important that the true facts are established in a calm way and that the child is given comfort and reassurance. However, you should not take matters into your own hands in such situations. Always work with the parents and the school.

The children's charity Kidscape has developed excellent programmes and strategies to empower children who are bullied or abused. Many of these work on the basis of building and developing confidence and communication skills. Children are encouraged to play games such as 'What would you do if someone asked you to keep a secret?'. Such games put the child in control and empower them to come up with solutions and suggestions, to decide upon strategies. Kidscape's details can be found at the end of this book.

Children can also be supported in other ways. They can be encouraged to share their worries with a trusted friend or adult. If a child begins to talk to you about bullying, remember to:

- listen carefully to the child

- be patient, calm and show sensitivity

- try not to show shock, anger or doubt

- do not ask direct questions, let the child talk at their own pace

- reassure the child that they are doing the right thing by talking to you

- do not promise to do anything that you cannot fulfil, for example do not promise not to tell anyone else.

Older children can be given information on services such as Childline and the NSPCC helpline.

Key Term

Disclosure occurs when a fact, especially a secret, is revealed. For instance, if a child has told an adult or another child what has been happening to them.

Your responsibilities if you suspect that a child may have been abused

There are very clear procedures for responding to suspected cases of child abuse. The Local Safeguarding Children Board (LSCB) is a multi-agency body working within each local authority. The LSCB has the responsibility for producing child protection procedures. These are based on the 'Working together to safeguard children' (Department of Health 1999) guidelines based on the principles of the Children Act 1989.

Many practitioners have great concerns about reporting suspected abuse. They may think that they have made a mistake or that the parents will retaliate in some way. They may feel that the child will suffer even more and could be removed from their homes and parents. However, it is every practitioner's responsibility to be objective and keep the best interests of the children in mind.

If you suspect that a child is in need of protection then you must contact your local LSCB officer, social services or the NSPCC. You must also keep dated, written records of what has been disclosed to you, or evidence of physical harm. It is up to the LSCB team and/or social services to contact the parents and other professionals.

Case Study

Kerrie is a very experienced registered childminder with extensive experience of living with children who have been abused because her mother is a foster carer. Kerrie suspected that one of the children in her care was being sexually abused and found this very distressing. Kerrie sought advice and reassurance from her mother, also a registered childminder and her college tutor, both of whom advised her to report her concerns. Kerrie was very careful not to breach issues of confidentiality when seeking advice. Kerrie said later that this was the most difficult telephone call she had ever had to make.

How do you think you would feel in such circumstances?

Do you know who to contact in the case of suspected abuse? (If you answer no to this question, then find out!)

The vulnerability of practitioners to allegations of abusing children, the importance of keeping records of incidents and where and how to seek advice

Child abuse is an emotive topic. It is likely that if you are working with children who have been abused, or suspect that a child is being abused, you will experience a range of emotions and feelings. This could be anger at the abuser, shock at what has happened to the child, a feeling of helplessness, or feeling that you have failed the child because you did not notice that something was wrong sooner. All of these feelings are perfectly normal. You may of course react in different ways.

It is important to remember that you should not expect to deal with all of these emotions on your own. You should not try to pretend that you do not feel angry, frustrated or have a sense of failure. The most professional way to act is to recognise your feelings and seek the support of another adult. It is essential to remember that you must maintain confidentiality at all times, so select your supporting adult with care.

There have been cases of childcare practitioners being accused of abuse. This can be a most distressing time and experience for all concerned. If this happens to you, you must remain calm and professional. Keep records of all conversations that you have regarding the accusation, and keep copies of all letters that you write. It would be sensible to seek legal advice because once an accusation is made there is a legal requirement that it be investigated. Organisations such as the NCMA offer legal help and advice to its members, or you can seek independent advice from the Citizens' Advice Bureau.

Where to seek support for yourself

Childminders who are working in a community childminding network may be asked to care for children who are already on the at risk register or subject to a protection order. In such cases there will be a range of other professionals that you could turn to for support, such as:

- social workers
- general practitioners or local doctors
- health visitors
- child protection police officers
- network coordinators.

If you are working as part of a childminding network, your network coordinator could initially offer you support and put you in touch with other professionals as necessary.

Organisations such as the NSPCC and Kidscape will often lend a 'listening ear'. The contacts for these organisations are at the back of this book. The NCMA will also support and offer advice in such situations.

How to protect yourself

All childcare practitioners are in positions of trust and great responsibility, given that they care for other people's children. In such positions they are vulnerable to allegations of mistreating children and accusations of abuse. In this respect, childminders and nannies are no different from other childcare professionals. In some ways you are even more vulnerable as you can be working alone and may not have the support of working with other people.

There are things that you can do to protect yourself from false allegations. It is essential that you keep accurate, written records so that reporting of suspected abuse is based on factual, observed evidence and not rumour or gossip. It is vital that these records are kept securely and confidentially at all times and disclosed only to the appropriate professionals.

How to protect yourself from allegations of abuse

- Maintain confidentiality at all times.

- Make sure that all your records, registers, incident report forms, accident forms and other documents relating to the children in your care are kept up to date and are stored in a safe place. You should get into the habit of completing records for each child every time that you care for them.

- Any suspicions that you have about ill-treatment or abuse of a child should be reported to the Local Safeguarding Children Board, formerly known as the Area Child Protection Committee (ACPC), or social services and you must keep a written record of your conversations or contact, including the name of the person you spoke to, the date of the conversation and what was agreed.

- Make sure that you tell parents about every incident, accident or event that has happened to their child which could result in a mark or injury on the body, regardless of how insignificant it may seem. Keep a written record of such conversations and record the incidents or accidents and get parents to sign that they have seen what you have recorded.

- Make sure that you tell the parents if the behaviour of their child changes, such as playing or speaking about things in a way that causes you concern.

- Never leave the children unattended or in the care of unauthorised people.

- Encourage the children to be independent as soon as they are able, especially when carrying out personal tasks.

- Make sure that you do not handle a child roughly when managing unwanted behaviour.

- Make sure that you always use appropriate language when with the children.

- Take your cues from the children and do not ask for cuddles and so forth if the child is reluctant to respond.

- Be open and honest with the children and do not ask them to keep secrets.

- Help children to learn how to protect themselves.

- Attend child protection courses, keeping yourself well informed and up to date.

Link to assessment

Unit 1 is assessed through a series of multiple-choice questions. Help and further information on multiple-choice questions can be found in the study skills section at the end of the book on page 277. Examples of these questions relating to child protection are given below.

These multiple-choice questions assess your knowledge of Sections **7a**, **7b**, **7c** and **7f** from the syllabus in your CACHE candidate handbook.

1 Which of the following may be a sign of physical abuse?

a. Bruising of both sides of the body.

b. A grazed knee.

c. A bruise on the leg.

d. A bump on the head.

2 Which agency would usually investigate a suspected case of child abuse?

a. The Local Safeguarding Children Board.

b. The Department of Social Security.

c. The District Health Authority.

d. The Children's Services Authority.

3 Where can the practitioner seek support?

a. From a friend.

b. From a social worker.

c. From other home-based childcarers.

d. From the NCMA.

4 What is a symptom of physical abuse?

a. Child becomes withdrawn.

b. Child doesn't join in familiar activities.

c. Child has bruising to the inner thighs.

d. Child is unkempt.

Answers to these questions can be found at the end of the book on page 294.

three or more families, in which case they should be registered with Ofsted. However, there is a voluntary approval scheme for nannies that can provide evidence to prove that they:

• have relevant qualifications or have attended an approved induction course in childcare

• have a valid first-aid certificate suitable to the care of babies and children

• have an enhanced Criminal Records Bureau (CRB) disclosure

• are over 18 years old.

> ## Key Term
>
> **Ofsted** – the Office for Standards in Education (England). The governmental department responsible for the inspection of childcare, schools and local education authorities.

Starting a home-based childcare service

It is important that you start your childcaring career as you mean to continue and that you take a professional approach to your work from the very first day. You need to keep up to date and informed of current changes in legislation and professional development issues.

Current, relevant legislation and the role of regulatory bodies

Childminders must be registered with Ofsted before they can care for other people's children in their own home (or the CSIW in Wales). At the time of writing, nannies and childminders who just look after children aged eight and over do not have to be registered unless they work for

At the present time a nanny will have to pay £96 annually to become approved. The benefits of this scheme are that parents may be able to get some financial support to help pay for nannies. In addition parents do have some reassurance that the person caring for their children has the relevant qualifications to do so.

The approval scheme for nannies will not determine the level of your qualifications or the experience that you may have. For example, if a nanny has an NVQ at Level 3 in Early Years Care and Education, and a CACHE Diploma in Childcare and Education or equivalent, they will be seen as being approved.

Further information on the Childcare Approval Scheme is available at www.childcareapprovalscheme.co.uk or on their telephone helpline, 0845 7678111.

From September 2001 the National Care Standards for Under Eights Day Care and Childminding state that anyone who applies to become a childminder must undertake a training course within six months of registration (England only). In the past, many local authorities used the CACHE

Level 3 Certificate in Childminding Practice, Unit 1 'Introducing Childminding Practice' as the training course to comply with this regulation. This will be replaced by Unit 1 of the Diploma for Home-based Childcare in 2006 and it is intended that nannies seeking to join the approval scheme will also complete this unit.

In October 2005 Ofsted introduced new childminding and daycare application packs that are in line with the changes to home-based childcare regulations and inspections implemented in 2005. The documents from the pack can be completed electronically and can be accessed from www.ofsted.gov.uk

For childminders, and nannies working for three or more families, the registration and inspection officer from the Early Years Directorate of Ofsted (England only) will carry out certain checks on you and the home before agreeing to your registration. These are based on the National Care Standards for Under Eights Day Care and Childminding.

- A police check (CRB) on everyone over the age of sixteen years who lives in the childminder's house. This is to safeguard and protect the children that you intend to care for. The police check will look for convictions of abuse, child pornography, paedophilia and any areas related to childcare. Any outstanding, unproven accusations may be uncovered and offences of violence and dishonesty are checked.

- A medical check to make sure that you are in good health and do not have any infectious illnesses or diseases that could be passed on to the children.

- A social services check to make sure that you are not known to that department in relation to the care of children. For example, if your own children had been taken into care because you could not cope as a parent, this could affect your registration as a childminder.

- A dog check to make sure that any pet dogs you have are not considered dangerous. You may be asked to provide a vet's certificate that your dog is fit and healthy.

- You will be asked for two references from people who know you well and will vouch for your character. The people who give the references cannot be related to you.

- Checks will be made on your home. Sometimes registration and inspection people may visit your home two or three times before agreeing to your registration. The number of children that you intend to mind will be discussed, as will your routines for making sure that your home is safe and hygienic. These visits will also check whether you are able to offer the children stimulating activities in a warm and safe environment.
- In some cases checks are also made by fire prevention officers and environmental health officers.

It is always very good practice to enrol on a first-aid course specifically aimed at practice with children and gain a recognised qualification. This is a condition of registration.

You will also have to show that you have public liability insurance cover and are committed to providing a service that respects individuality and is non-discriminatory.

This may seem like a daunting number of checks and things that you have to do. However, you must remember that all these checks are to safeguard both you and the children that you intend to care for, so it is in your best interests to think of them positively.

Once you are registered you will receive an annual visit from a registration and inspection officer, who will continue to check that all the things required for registration are still in place. You must also inform Ofsted (or CSIW if you live in Wales) of any significant changes or events which may affect the safety and welfare of any child in your care. Such changes could be:

- structural changes or alteration to your home
- in the rooms used for caring for the children
- outside your house such as building a pond or greenhouse
- a new assistant or co-childminder
- to people living or employed in the home
- a serious illness or accident to you or a child in your care
- police or social services involvement with you, or anyone else who lives in the home.

All registered childminders in England are now required to display their registration certificate during their working hours. It is not sufficient to keep your certificate in an information file, but you can take down your certificate if you are not working.

Kath, a registered childminder spoke very positively about her Ofsted inspections, 'I was very nervous as lots of people had told me about bad experiences, but that wasn't the case at all. The inspector was very friendly and supportive and we talked about my work in great detail. I only had one recommendation and after she had gone I felt really good about myself and my childminding business.'

The importance of effective record-keeping and the information that needs to be kept

Regulations set out in the Children Act 1989 state that certain records must be kept on the childcare premises and some must be retained for a period of two years. This would include a daily record of children being cared for, their hours of attendance at a childminding setting and names of the carers, accident and medication records. National Standard 14 requires that certain records are kept, such as an accident book which complies with National Standard Health 7.11. There is no common agreement about the length of time that other records should be kept for but judgments by the European Court of Human Rights suggested that it should be as much as 21 years. This in reality poses huge storage problems for home-based carers and it is up to each individual to make up their own minds as to how long records are kept. You might want to consider:

- the requirements of other organisations such as HM Revenue and Customs

- other requirements such as child protection
- the long-term welfare of the child, such as medical or behavioural information which may help in the future.
- which records you will give to the child and their family when they leave and which ones you will keep, such as registration information
- records that might be needed in the future to protect yourself.

Records should be regularly maintained in order for them to be beneficial to you, the child and the family. Records you will need include:

- the name, address and date of birth of each child
- the name, home address and telephone number of each parent
- the name, home address and telephone number of the registered childcarer and any other adult regularly in contact with the children
- a daily record of names of children cared for and hours of attendance
- a record of accidents
- a record of any medicinal product given to a child plus written parental consent, also records of any medical product that a child may administer themselves, such as insulin
- fire safety information
- vehicle records with written parental permission to transport children in said vehicle
- a record of compliments and complaints
- daily records of food intake, nappy changing, rest and sleep – especially for babies and young children.

How to negotiate and agree a contract with parents

A contract is an agreement between two parties, in this case between you and the parents. A contract should make your responsibilities and those of the parents very clear. There should be no ambiguities, or words that could be misinterpreted. The agreement between you and the family is about the care and well-being of the child, the most important reason for having the contract.

Most childminders have written, or computer-produced, contracts for each family that they are involved with. NCMA produce contracts that are comprehensive and have clear guidance notes on how to complete them. The NCMA contract has three copies, one for the practitioners, one for the parents and one for any agencies involved, such as Social Services in Community Childminding Schemes. Contracts should be signed by both parties and dated. Contracts, like policies, should be reviewed regularly, and especially when circumstances change, for example you might have agreed a contract to care for a child three days per week, then the mother increases her hours of work and asks you to care for the child five days per week. In this case you will need a new contract to reflect the new circumstances. Contracts need to be agreed, signed and dated regardless of the number of days, hours or period of time that you will be caring for the child, whether it is only one day, one week, or for the foreseeable future.

Reasons why you and parents need a contract

1   Having a written contract for parents is a professional and businesslike way of conducting your childcaring affairs. It should give parents a good impression of your professionalism.

2   It makes clear exactly what you are willing to do and so prevents misunderstandings.

3   Each contract can be personal to each family, to take into account the individual needs of that family and the child. However, at the same time the contract can have standard clauses that apply to all families, such as details of fees, pick-up and drop-off times.

4   Contracts that are signed and dated by both parties are legally binding. This could be very important if you have problems later on.

You will need to make time to discuss the contract with the parents before you agree to take on the child. Make time to go over it and explain, if required, each part of the contract and make sure that the parents are in full agreement with all aspects of it. Do not be pressurised into agreeing to something that will have an adverse effect on either you or the other children that you care for. Be firm and use your communication skills to explain to the parents why you have written the contract in the way that you have. Make sure that both you and the parents are very clear about what will happen if the contract is broken.

Case Study

Mike is a registered childminder and cares for two children, Liam and Kerry, as well as his own baby. The contract that Mike has with both sets of parents clearly states that payment will be made weekly on the last day of care. In the case of one child, Liam, this is Thursday morning. For the first six weeks, Liam's father gave Mike either cash or a cheque. On the seventh week the cheque was returned by the bank and Mike had to give it back to the father, who was very apologetic and gave Mike the cash the next week. The following week, Liam's father said that he had forgotten his cheque book, the next week Liam was dropped off by his grandmother, who said that the parents were busy, and the payments were nothing to do with her.

Mike felt that he was being put in a difficult position, especially as his own partner felt that the parents were taking advantage of Mike's goodwill – his childminding was a business and not a charity. Mike recognised that he had to do something as this family had broken their contract. Mike decided to telephone the father and ask him to come a few minutes earlier as he wanted to discuss things with him. The father did not keep this appointment. Mike felt that he had no option but to write to the parents giving

them a week's notice that he would not be able to care for Liam unless they paid him the outstanding fees. The result of this was that Liam's grandmother gave Mike cash for the outstanding fees and said that her son had decided that he would care for Liam himself. Although Mike was sorry that his relationship with this family had not been very good, he did acknowledge that he could not afford to offer a free childminding service, and taking positive action meant that he had less worry and stress.

In your view, did Mike do the 'right' thing?

Was there anything else that Mike could have done?

Sharing information, confidentiality and data protection

You should regard all information that you have on a child as confidential, which should be shared only between yourself, the child's parents and the child. There may be times when some children need support and help from other professionals, such as speech therapists. You must seek parental permission before you disclose information about a child. The only exception to this may be in the case of child protection, when telling the parents might endanger the safety of the child.

Many practitioners keep information and personal details about children and families on their personal computers, plus records for their business. All such information should be kept in a secure place, or in the case of computer data, be password protected.

Financial planning in setting rates for childcare services

The income from home-based childcare is governed by the number of children that the registered person is allowed to look after (set by

Ofsted) and fees that can be charged. In the case of childminders this is often an hourly rate.

There are no set rates of how much can be charged but surveys by both NCMA and many local Early Years teams can give guidance. It is also very helpful to talk to other home-based carers in your area to get an indication of fees, which can vary from £2.50 per hour in some areas to £6 or more.

If a home-based childcarer could guarantee that their provision would always be full, then financial planning would be relatively straightforward. In reality many childminders find that over a year they operate on 75% capacity. Also, it must be remembered that a childminder's own children under eight years old count in the set numbers and, as such, can reduce earnings.

In order to achieve any income there must be children to care for. It can take up to 12 months from registration for a childminder to build up a client base and earn a reasonable income. Advertising locally, in health centres, schools, gyms and shops can help you to establish a business. It is also useful to go to 'drop-in' sessions for children and their carers, which will help to get 'your face known' and can often result in other practitioners passing on your details to parents.

How to maintain accurate financial records, including deductible costs, to meet statutory requirements

NCMA produce an accounts book and an attendance register which are good ways of recording income and expenditure on a weekly basis. Some practitioners prefer to keep their accounts on a computer using a program such as Excel. However, NCMA have agreed with HM Revenue and Customs that the format of the cash book is an adequate record of trading. NCMA have also agreed with HM Revenue and Customs some expenses specific to home-based childcare.

- Heating and lighting – 33.3% of costs.

- Water rates – 10% of costs.

- Council tax – 10% of costs.

- Wear and tear – 10% of gross income.

Other allowable expenses are those similar to any other business:

- stationery and printing

- telephone

- vehicle expenses

- insurance

- professional fees

- subscriptions.

You will also be allowed to claim for:

- additional food (if providing breakfast/lunch/dinner/snacks)

- toys and books

- outings

- safety equipment

- cleaning/hygiene

- nappies.

This list is not exhaustive, but HM Revenue and Customs may still refuse the allowance if the cost is not 'wholly, exclusively and necessary' for the purpose of the business. Larger items such as buggies, car seats and high chairs will be treated as assets of the business and would be subject to capital allowance, that is, the costs of the assets would be spread over a number of years as an allowable expense. (It is interesting to note that home-based carers who are not members of NCMA may find that HM Revenue and Customs may not accept those allowances that have been agreed with NCMA.)

In April 2005, under the Childcare Approval Scheme, families with a combined family income below £59,000 became eligible for working tax credit support for childcare in their own home. Parents on the lowest income will receive the most with support decreasing towards the higher end of the scale. The financial support will cover 70% of childcare costs up to £175 per week for parents with one child and £300 for two or more children. This support will increase to 80% in April 2006. Child Tax Credit can be claimed by anyone whose joint income is below £59,000, so newly registered home-based childcarers should consider claiming as it can help with cash flow in the first few months of trading.

Since September 2003 you (registered childminders only) may have been contacted by HM Revenue and Customs asking for your help to confirm that you provide childcare for families claiming the childcare element of the Working Tax Credit. This help will now extend to other approved childcarers.

You must register with your local tax office as a self-employed person, which will affect your National Insurance contributions. There are different charges for National Insurance and, depending on what rate you decide to pay, your entitlement to certain benefits will be affected, such as sick pay or maternity pay. You should contact your local tax office for advice and help.

The importance of having written policies if required by law, sources of help and guidance

Ofsted do not specify any particular policies but do expect to see:

- children's personal details such as full name, address, date of birth, emergency contact number
- parents' names, addresses and contact details
- attendance register
- accident and medication records.

Some local authorities suggest that home-based childcarers develop policies on:

- child protection
- behaviour management
- lost children
- nappy changing.

Some also suggest that home-based carers develop an initial letter, leaflet or welcome pack for parents.

Childminders who become part of a network may be asked to develop policies on:

- health issues
- safety
- behaviour management
- equal opportunities, anti-bias/anti-discriminatory practice
- child protection
- confidentiality
- admissions
- special needs.

The importance of having adequate public liability insurance cover

It is important that every home-based carer is fully insured; public liability insurance will protect against unforeseen comebacks and is a requirement of the National Care Standards. Public liability insurance will provide you with legal liability cover against:

- accidental injury or death to any person, including the children that you are caring for, caused by your negligence or activities
- any damage that may be caused to other people's property by the children that you are caring for.

Many companies will arrange public liability insurance but costs vary considerably. NCMA has arranged with leading insurance company public liability insurance for home-based carers. At the present time this costs £19.75 per annum to NCMA members. (NCMA membership is currently £52.50 per annum).

It is also important to consider your house, contents and car insurance policies. Many insurance companies do not cover childminder households. Again, NCMA has a specialist house and contents insurance which costs around £28 per month. Car insurance is slightly different because many insurance companies will insure you provided you let them know that the vehicle is to be used for business – the nature of the business does not matter. However, it is good practice to let your insurance company know, in writing, that you offer home-based childcare, to avoid any comebacks.

How to market your childcare service effectively

Many home-based carers do not have to advertise or market their services. They are in an enviable position. Some find that word of mouth and personal recommendations of parents are effective ways of filling vacancies. The Children's Information Service in each local area keeps lists of home-based carers which can be accessed by parents from the Internet. If you do decide to advertise then you need to consider where the best places to put your adverts are. These should be places parents and children frequent, such as health centres, leisure centres, local libraries, schools and educational establishments, churches and other places of worship. Many supermarkets have advertising boards. Remember that you do not have to put your full address in these adverts – your name and a contact telephone number should be enough to protect you from unwanted visitors and callers.

Recently, NCMA has been working with care-4, one of Britain's largest providers of childcare vouchers, to develop 'Childcare Places' – a new website to help registered childminders fill their vacancies. Care-4 provides childcare vouchers to many of the UK's leading employers, and from January 2006 parents employed by companies in the care-4 scheme will have free access to the Childcare Places website and will be able to search for an NCMA home-based childcarer who lives locally and can meet their family's particular childcare needs. NCMA members should indicate on their membership or renewal forms that they want to be part of the childcare vacancy scheme, and then when you log on to the Childcare Places website you need to register with your name, postcode and NCMA membership number. The website is secure and password protected.

Think about it

You are offering a professional service and should remember this when you are considering how to fill vacancies. A tatty bit of paper stuck in a shop window will not give a very good impression. You can advertise very successfully in local shops, but you need to make sure that your advert is legible, clear and written or printed on a cleanly cut piece of card or paper.

Think about it

Bran is a registered childminder. He has a vacancy for a child over two years old for five mornings each week (maximum of four hours). Bran's childminding business closes on Bank Holidays and for three weeks in August. He charges £5 per morning, including a mid-morning snack and a light lunch. His telephone number is 01230 567890, and there is an answer machine.

Using the above information design a small advertisement, about the size of a postcard, that could be put on the notice board of the local health centre.

Sources of support and information on setting up and running your childcare service

All practitioners, regardless of how professional they are, will find that at some point they need support and information. Childcare is a very demanding job and being self-employed can be quite isolating, especially as far as adult company is concerned.

Local childcare groups

Many childminders set up local groups so they can meet one another socially. Sometimes they can meet in each other's homes, depending on the numbers, or in local amenities, such as a sports centre. These groups can be great fun and sources of support. Sometimes people of your own profession are the only people who can really understand some of the issues involved in childcare. The local groups also provide the opportunity to share information and ideas, and to generate new ideas for activities. In many areas nannies set up groups for themselves for support purposes, and social activities for themselves

and the children. Remember that you must never discuss personal information about the children or families that you work with.

Network coordinator

Childminding networks are growing all over the country and these can also be valuable sources of information and support. Each network has a coordinator who will be able to tell you what training and courses are available in your area.

NCMA

The National Childminding Association (NCMA) is the only organisation in England and Wales specifically for childminders and other home-based carers. It is committed to promoting quality home-based care and improving the status and conditions for home-based carers, children and their parents. NCMA has a national network of development workers and support staff. It is also very effective in liaising with government departments on issues concerned with childcare and home-based childcare in particular. Practitioners who join NCMA are provided with a wealth of information, free legal advice,

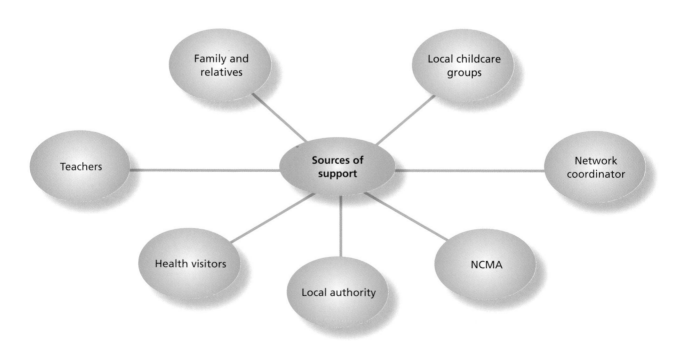

Sources of support and information on setting up and running your childcaring business

Adults supervising safe outside play

special offers for insurance; as well as training opportunities and the chance to purchase useful publications and stationery, such as account books and sample contracts.

Local authority

In recent years all local authorities have set up Early Years Development and Childcare Partnerships (EYDCP). Many of these teams have employed development officers with special responsibilities for home-based carers. These people can put you in touch with other home-based childcarers and also provide information about courses that are being run in your area. Your development officer can be a very useful source of support and help. They can often put you in touch with other local authority personnel and social services staff, such as child protection officers.

Health visitors

Health visitors, either your own or those of the children that you mind, can be a valuable

source of support and help. Health visitors have a good understanding of children's growth and development, which they often gain through carrying out child health surveillance and developmental checks. They can also put you and parents in touch with other professionals, particularly in the medical world, if they think that there may be a problem. You should contact a child's health visitor only if you have the written permission of the parents to do so.

Teachers

More and more childminders are getting accredited as part of NCMA's quality assurance scheme, Children Come First, and so are able to accept nursery education funding. This means they must offer activities to four-year-olds that are part of the stepping stones on the Foundation Stage Curriculum in England or Desirable Learning Outcomes in Wales. Teachers can be an invaluable source of support and advice for childminders offering this service and many good professional relationships can be developed along with an exchange of ideas and activities. Teachers can also be supportive with children's learning difficulties and emotional and behavioural problems. It is likely that a child who has problems at the practitioner's home, or their own home, will also have them in school. You should work with the parents and teachers to support the child and hopefully deal effectively with a difficulty or problem.

Family and relatives

Before you started your business you should have discussed it with your family, partner, children, and anyone else who could be affected, such as elderly relatives. Hopefully they will have supported you in your new venture, otherwise you could have problems.

Anyone who works full-time and has family responsibilities and commitments can find, at times, that it is difficult to meet all the demands placed on them. It can be difficult to balance the needs of your family against the needs of your professional life. This may be more difficult for childminders as they are working in their own homes. Many self-employed people work from home, but often have a separate work area, so that their business life does not encroach into their family life. This is not the case for most childminders. There will be other children and partners in their home. There will be changes in the family routine and your working hours may mean that you have less time to spend with your own family. These issues should have been thought of and discussed with your family before you started your business.

If your family understand the demands of your business, then it should not be unreasonable to expect them to support you. This might mean taking a greater share in the running of the family home, such as doing the weekly family shop, or doing the running repairs and DIY around the house that will be incurred with having more children around.

Case Study

Ameera has decided to become a registered childminder. She stopped working following the birth of her one-year-old son and she has another child who is at school. Ameera and her husband live with his parents. The house has a large garden at the back that is accessible through a conservatory. Ameera plans to use the conservatory as a playroom for her business and will use the big kitchen to serve the children's meals. There is a downstairs bathroom with separate toilet.

At first, her in-laws think that the house will be full of other people's children, it will be noisy and they will lose their privacy. Ameera tries to reassure them that this will not be the case and agrees that the children will not have access to any of the rooms upstairs or the family sitting room. Her in-laws agree to see how things go for six months.

Ameera meets an experienced childminder at the pre-registration meeting. She explains her concerns to the childminder. The childminder suggests that Ameera brings her in-laws to see how she runs her business, and hopefully that might alleviate their concerns. Ameera and her in-laws visit the childminder's house and they see for themselves that it is possible to run this kind of business and at the same time keep areas of the house private.

A few weeks after Ameera was registered, she noticed that her father-in-law would often be about as the children were leaving making a special point of using their names when he said goodbye. Her mother-in-law began cooking a few extra sweetmeats 'for Ameera to share with the children'. Ameera now felt confident that she had the support of all of her family, thanks in part to the help of an experienced childminder.

Information about continuing professional development, training and quality assurance

Being professional involves continuing to learn, develop and extend your skills and knowledge, keeping up to date with current trends and thinking. Childcare is a profession that requires people to be lively and self-motivated. There is always something new and different to learn and read about, and there are literally dozens of courses and training events that you can attend. It is so easy to say to yourself, 'Well, I've done my pre-registration course, I have got two children of my own so I do not need to do anything more.' This attitude does little to raise the professional status of childcare and nothing for the person who thinks in this way.

Ways to update and develop your knowledge and skills

There are many courses and training qualifications available to home-based childcarers, just as there are hundreds of books about children, their care and development, as well as many magazines.

Courses and training

Local authority early years teams offer many training events which may or may not lead to a qualification. However, they are an excellent way of meeting like-minded people, sharing ideas and opinions and extending your knowledge.

The CACHE Level 3 Diploma in Home-based Childcare has five units. The first unit is assessed through multiple-choice questions, whereas the others are assessed through written assignments. This qualification is specifically for home-based carers. It has been developed by NCMA and CACHE (Council for Awards in Children's Care and Education) and is nationally recognised and offered by colleges, NCMA and by distance learning through the National Extension College.

Some practitioners go on to NVQ (National Vocation Qualifications) Level 3 in Early Years Care and Education, once they have gained the full CACHE award. The new Early Years Foundation degrees will be accessible to people with a Level 3 qualification and will include the opportunity for distance learning.

CACHE also has professional qualifications in Playwork and Professional Development, such as Supporting Children and Families in Toy Libraries, Working with Children and Young People with Special Needs, and Protecting Children. CACHE's

---

Think about it

1 Some years ago it was common practice to cover up a burn or scald. Today we know that the skin and tissue under the burn or scald can go on being damaged for some time after the heat source has gone. Burns and scalds are now treated by putting the injured part under cold running water for several minutes. In such a case if you do not keep up with your first-aid qualifications and read articles, you could do more harm than good.

2 Children with a disability were often referred to as handicapped and people felt sorry for them. Today, disabled children are encouraged to lead full and active lives, and society is starting to see the child first, not the disability. If you were not aware of how attitudes have changed over recent years you could not offer a non-discriminatory childcare service, where every child is respected as an individual.

These are just two examples of the ways in which attitudes and care for children have changed in recent years. Unless practitioners keep up to date they will not be offering a professional service.

Several years ago a group of childminders agreed to become 'guinea pigs' for a pilot course that was being developed by NCMA. All were registered with their local authority and had many years of experience minding children. However, many of them had not set foot in a classroom for a very long time, and one had no formal 'paper' qualifications. But with tutor support every member of the group successfully completed their written assignments and became the first group of childminders in the country to gain what was then known as the Developing Childminding Practice 2 (later known as the ECP) qualification.

Several of the group 'got the learning bug' and within a short space of time they had gained an NVQ Level 3 in Early Years Care and Education.

Some went on to gain a recognised qualification for teaching adults so that they could spread their enthusiasm and professionalism to other childminders in the area.

address is at the end of the book; you should contact them or your local college for more information about these and other awards.

Publications

If you become a member of the NCMA, you will receive a copy of their magazine, *Who Minds*, at least four times a year. This will provide you with relevant and useful articles on every aspect of childminding, from insurance to planning activities to stimulate and interest children on a wet afternoon.

Another useful magazine is *Nursery World*, a weekly magazine written for people who care for young children. There are often very good articles on child development and health issues, as well as up-dates on the latest government initiatives.

Practical Parenting is a magazine written mainly for parents, with very helpful and useful articles on health and development issues. Also worth looking out for is *Practical Pre-school*, another very useful magazine. *Practical Professional Childcare* is a relatively new publication for all practitioners, with pull-out pages on specific topics for future reference and information.

Quality assurance

Quality assurance schemes are offered by local authority early years teams and also by NCMA. NCMA Quality First has been awarded a DfES Investors in Children Kitemark. Practitioners who participate in these schemes are required to develop a portfolio of evidence which shows that they meet high quality standards in their practices. Some of the areas that are considered are health and safety, interactions and relationships, the learning environment and working with children of different ages from birth to 16 years. These schemes offer assurance to parents that they are leaving their child in the care of a professional who has high standards.

Link to assessment

Unit 1 is assessed through a series of multiple-choice questions. Help and further information on multiple-choice questions can be found in the study skills section at the end of the book on page 277. Examples of these questions relating to starting a home-based childcare service are given below.

These multiple-choice questions assess your knowledge of sections **8a**, **8b**, **8c**, **8d**, **8h** and **8k** from the syllabus in your CACHE candidate handbook.

1 Why is it good practice to have three copies of the contract with parents?

a. The practitioner might lose a contract.

b. The parents might lose their contract.

c. The practitioner always has a spare copy.

d. Copies are available for the practitioner, the parents and for any other agency involved with the child.

2 Confidentiality is most important to:

a. Protect children and their families.

b. Keep information about children inside the workplace.

c. Be sure that children are not compared with each other.

d. Avoid some children having all the attention.

3 Public liability insurance provides legal cover against:

a. Accidental injury.

b. Death caused by negligence.

c. Damage to property caused by the children.

d. Accidental injury, death by negligence, damage to property incurred during normal working practice.

4 Why is continuing professional development important?

a. It makes the practitioner's CV look better.

b. It helps the practitioner to meet like-minded people.

c. It helps to develop knowledge and skills.

d. It is a requirement of registration.

Answers to these questions can be found at the end of the book on page 294.

Childcare and child development (0–16) in the home-based setting

In order for you to be inclusive and promote children's rights, you will need to have an understanding of children's development. Through this understanding you can plan and provide appropriate activities and experiences that will meet individual needs whilst stimulating and promoting development and growth.

The rights of all children are paramount and it is essential that all home-based childcarers protect and promote those rights. It is also important that your setting is an inclusive environment, where everyone is welcomed.

This unit is assessed by one assignment which can be presented in a variety of formats. It will be marked by your tutor and then externally moderated by CACHE.

This unit will teach you about:

- promoting children's rights
- working with disabled children and their families
- children's development and well-being.

Promoting children's rights

What are rights?

To try to explain what a 'right' is people sometimes talk about the difference between 'wants' and 'needs'. 'Wants' are idealistic things that are not vital to our lives, such as a plasma screen television, whereas 'needs' are things that we must have in order to live, such as clean water. Rights are similar to needs in that they are the basic standards we must have in order to live a healthy and secure life. To violate someone's rights is to treat that person as though they were not a human being.

The government has the responsibility to make sure that people's rights are met, and also has a responsibility to help parents, childcare practitioners and guardians to meet young people's rights and needs.

The United Nations Convention on the Rights of the Child and its relevance for home-based childcare

The United Nations Convention on the Rights of the Child (UNCRC) was drawn up in 1989; the UK is a signatory and the Convention was approved in 1991. It protects the rights of children and young people under the age of 18. All children are covered by the 54 articles contained within the UNCRC which essentially states that all children must be shown respect and their interests are of the utmost importance.

Of the 54 articles there are five which primarily affect childcare practitioners.

- **Article 2** states that children have a right to be protected from all forms of discrimination.

- **Article 3** states that the best interests of the child must be the primary consideration in all activities and actions concerning children.

- **Article 12** states that children have a right to express their views freely and that their view is to be given appropriate weight in accordance with the child's age or maturity.

- **Article 13** states that children have a right to freedom of expression and the exchange of information regardless of frontiers.

- **Article 28** states that children have a right to education with a view to achieving this right progressively on the basis of equal opportunities.

These articles are relevant and important for home-based childcarers because they should make us think about the way we relate to children, how we listen to them and respond to their comments and views. These articles should reinforce the fact that all children are special and each one is unique, and as such all children are entitled to be treated with dignity and respect.

The historical and legislative background

In the past children were regarded as different from adults only in that they were smaller. They were dressed in smaller versions of adult clothes, worked alongside adults and effectively belonged to an adult society. Children's care and education was not seen as being of benefit to the child, but more as a means of providing skills to enable the future adult to take their place in society. Furthermore, children who were considered to have behaved in antisocial ways, such as those who stole, were dealt with under the same laws as adults. Children could be imprisoned, sentenced to death or sent to penal colonies abroad. *Oliver Twist*, written by Charles Dickens between 1837 and 1839, gives us a very graphic image of how children could be treated by society.

The Education Act 1902 attempted to formalise education in Britain by the training of teachers. The Children Act 1908 was possibly the first public recognition of children as individuals in their own right and one of the consequences of this Act was that children under the age of fourteen years could not be sent to prison.

Eglantyne Jebb, who founded Save the Children in 1919, worked tirelessly for the universal recognition of children's rights. In 1923 she set out a summary of some of the essential rights of children for the first time and these became the Declaration of the Rights of the Child. This declaration was agreed upon by the General Assembly of the International Save the Children Union in 1923. A year later the declaration was adopted by the League of Nations and became known as the Declaration of Geneva. However, this declaration was not given the legally binding status that could have forced governments to make it law. Still, it represented a movement in attitudes towards children.

The Education Acts in 1936 and 1944 came about at a time of great social upheaval and were more concerned with administrative issues, rather than children's rights and needs.

The Plowden Report of 1967 was not a piece of legislation but set the scene for the empowerment of children. There have been several important pieces of legislation that have recognised the rights of children and their families since this report. These are summarised in the table below.

Legislation	Focus of legislation
Sex Discrimination Act 1975	Supported by the Equal Opportunities Commission to ensure that individuals are not discriminated against upon the grounds of their sex.
Race Relations Act 1976, amended in 2000	Equality of opportunity must be promoted and settings should develop a policy which is monitored and assessed.
Education Act 1981	First official recognition of: • parental rights regarding children's education • special educational needs.
Education Reform Act 1988	National Curriculum introduced into schools.
United Nations Convention on the Rights of the Child 1989	A formal statement agreed by many nations stating that all children have specific rights such as: • a right to good food • a right to education • a right to shelter • a right to play.
Children Act 1989	First acknowledgement in UK law of children's rights, encapsulated by the phrase 'the needs of the child are paramount'.
Education Act 1993	Secretary of State required to publish a code of practice for children with special educational needs. The parents of children under two years of age have the right to ask for their child to be formally assessed.
Disability Discrimination Act 1995	Aims to ensure that rights of disabled individuals are met in England, Scotland, Wales and Northern Ireland.
Education Act 1997	Incorporated all Acts since 1944 into one. Set a time-frame on the legal process for identifying and assessing a child's needs as set out in the Code of Practice.
Human Rights Act 1998	Became legal in 2000, the result of requirements laid down by the European Convention on Human Rights.
Code of Practice for the Identification and Assessment of Children with Special Educational Needs 1994, revised in 2001	Guidance on the responsibilities of local education authorities and governing bodies of schools towards children with special educational needs.

Legislation	Focus of legislation
Data Protection Act 1998	Prevents confidential and personal information being passed on without a person's consent; in the case of children the consent must be given by the parents.
National Standards for Under Eights Day Care and Childminding 2001	All early years childcare practitioners must meet a set of 14 standards concerning children's rights, care and education. Monitored by Ofsted.
Special Educational Needs and Disability Act 2001	Protects children from discrimination on the basis of disability and settings must make reasonable adjustments to their provision to meets the needs and rights of the child.
Birth to Three Matters – a Framework for Effective Practice 2002	Not legislation, but aims to support, inform, guide and challenge early years childcare practitioners.
Children Act 2004	Arose from the Green Paper 'Every Child Matters', and identifies five outcomes for all children: • be healthy • stay safe • enjoy and achieve • make a positive contribution • achieve economic well-being.

The law relating to children and young people in the UK

As can be seen in the table above there are numerous laws aimed at protecting the rights of children and young people in the UK. The most influential of these is the Children Act 1989, which was built on the principle that children and their families needed to have their rights more clearly protected and defined within the law and legal processes. In divorce or formal separation proceedings this Act requires that the welfare of the child be considered, which means that when deciding where a child should live they must be consulted and have their needs taken into account. The Children Act clearly states that an individual child's race, culture, language and religion must be respected. All home-based childcarers are legally obliged to conform to this and have a responsibility to make sure that their practices treat all children with equal concern.

The National Standards for 2001 require that all childcare practitioners promote the welfare and development of the child in the setting, while working in partnership with parents and, where applicable, other professionals and parties. All registered home-based childcarers have to comply with all 14 standards, which are monitored by Ofsted.

The Children's Rights Director of England has responsibility for campaigning for the rights of children who are getting any form of help or support from Social Services. The Children's Rights Director spends a lot of time listening to what children and young people have to say, and passes their views on to the government and inspectors. Children who want to have their say can contact the director at www.rights4me.org.uk

Despite recent laws and much recognition of children's rights there are still some gaps in legislation, in particular in some aspects of equality. Some local authorities will refuse to register a childminder on grounds of age – this is a form of discrimination.

In December 2005 the rights of gay and lesbian people were recognised through legislation which allowed them to enter into civil partnerships, giving gay and lesbian couples the same rights as heterosexual couples with regard to pensions and other social benefits.

Inequality and the effects on children and their families

As a home-based childcarer your aim should be to promote children's development and learning. To do this you must match the quality of your provision to the needs of the children and their families. However, there are several factors that may affect access to provision for many children and their families. Despite legislation the lives of many children and their families are still impinged upon by discrimination. Children and their families or childcare provision should never be excluded from your setting because they belong to a different race, culture, religion, gender or age group.

Poverty is one of the biggest causes of inequality in the UK and children living in poverty are often unable to access quality childcare services due to practical problems such as lack of transport or lack of money to meet the additional costs of childcare. It is important to remember that parents cannot move out of poverty and into work or training without affordable childcare services.

In recent years Sure Start initiatives have done much to lessen the impact of inequalities and poverty on families and their children. Programmes have been established to advise families on health, nutrition and early education. Many Sure Start centres also run childcare facilities supported by community-registered childminders.

Conflicts, chronic social instability and preventable diseases such as HIV/AIDS threaten children's rights. This is because children can face discrimination and unfair treatment. In many respects the abuse of rights is worse for girls because of the discrimination they can face in all sectors of society in every country.

The negative effects of discrimination and prejudice on all children

Stereotypical attitudes, labelling individuals and prejudice will all lead to discrimination with negative effects on children and their families. Labelling takes away a person's individuality, for example saying that all football supporters are hooligans does not take into consideration the many families and children who regard supporting their local football team as a great way to spend time together.

Kath, a registered childminder, believes that she has encountered negative discrimination and remembers one parent in the school playground asking her in front of other children, 'Are you going to get a proper job now that your youngest has started school?' Kath says, 'One of the other children asked me later why I wasn't doing a proper job and was quite upset about it.'

How is this discriminating?

Think about it

Try to describe yourself in terms of categories, such as age, gender, position in the family, marital status, occupation, nationality and so on.

How do these 'labels' make you feel?

Do you feel different from other people because of the label or does it make you feel that you have something in common with others?

One of the most significant effects of discrimination can be a lack of self-esteem. Individuals who have low self-esteem may find it difficult to handle pressure or establish relationships. Children with low self-esteem think of themselves and what they may achieve in a negative way. They may think that they will never get anything right and so may be reluctant to respond to challenges. It becomes a self-fulfilling prophecy and the child fails because they do not expect to succeed. Parents with low self-esteem will find it very difficult to motivate their children, so their feeling of low self-esteem will be passed on to their children.

Discrimination is not always obvious and people's rights can sometimes be ignored as a result of negative assumptions that may have been made. For example, a registered childminder planned for the children to make Christmas cards, but didn't provide an alternative activity for non-Christian children.

Many forms of discrimination are at the root of violations of children's rights, when specific children face discrimination on account of their sex, colour, race, religion, political or other opinion, national, ethnic and social origin, disability, birth or other status. For example, gender discrimination keeps young girls from school in some communities and also, when older, from active and equal involvement in their community. Another example is when disabled children are excluded from mainstream schools. Children of minority, indigenous or migrant backgrounds face discrimination in a number of ways, and are less likely to gain access to a relevant, high-quality education.

Discrimination can sometimes result from a group or an organisation treating people differently from others, for example in the workplace. A company would be discriminatory if they advertised for 'an active and fit' person for a job that is desk-bound, because people with some disabilities could be perfectly capable of doing the job.

Equal opportunities and anti-bias practice in home-based care

One of the ways that children learn is through watching the reactions and behaviour of the people around them. It therefore follows that children will learn about prejudice and stereotypes from you. Children need to have accurate information about every aspect of their learning and development, and an understanding of equal opportunities and anti-bias practice is no different. They need honest and truthful answers to their questions. They need to learn that differences in people are interesting. Home-based childcarers should not pretend that the differences do not exist but need to talk openly about them and encourage children to do the same.

You will have to be very careful that you do not make judgements based on your particular views;

for example, your ideas on parenting may be very different from the life and parenting styles for some of the families that you work for. There is no such thing as an average family, and we should value and respect the differences between family types.

Link to assessment

E2 Describe the role of the home-based childcarer in meeting the individual needs of all children.

Hint

It is important that you can show how you implement children's rights in your work setting and meet individual needs.

Write a reflective account which takes into consideration:

- your understanding of children's rights
- how you find out about children's needs, such as by talking to parents, other professionals, doing observations
- how you seek and respect the views and preferences of all of the children in your care
- how you adapt your practice to meet the child's needs, age and abilities
- practical examples of how you do these things.

D Explain how to implement children's rights in the home-based setting.

Hint

This criterion is an extension of **E2** above. You could write about:

- how and why you give children choices
- how you respect and value diversity and the range of needs and abilities of the children in your care
- the different ways that you may communicate with the child and their family.

Think about it

Have a look at the books in your home setting that are available to the children that you care for.

Do they reflect the cultural diversity of today's society?

Do they have stereotypical characters or story lines?

Do you know where you can get a wider selection of books?

Strategies for challenging prejudice and discrimination

There are still many groups of people in our society who are discriminated against, so it is important that home-based childcarers have strategies that challenge prejudice and discrimination and, in doing so, teach the children in their care to be fair and non-discriminatory in their dealings with other people.

Keys to good practice

Practical things you can do

1 Make sure that within your framework for managing children's behaviour you include rules or guidelines about children playing together and not excluding another child for any reason.

2 Get immediately involved if you hear a child make a discriminatory or prejudicial remark and talk to the child who made the remark about the hurt and distress that they could have caused.

3 Comfort any child who has been on the receiving end of a discriminatory remark. Make sure that they understand that you will care for them unconditionally. Help the child to respond positively to such remarks.

4 Be aware that sometimes children repeat things that they have heard adults say. When discussing what children have said, do not devalue or undermine the child's parents or family members. It is better to explain that everyone has different views and opinions, and without being judgemental try to explain to children how you wish them to behave when they are in your care. Hopefully the good example that you set will help the child form positive attitudes themselves.

5 Be brave and protect the children in your care from prejudice and discrimination. Point out that prejudice and discrimination are hurtful and politely give accurate information to any individual who makes a prejudiced or discriminatory remark.

6 Answer all children's questions about why some people look different, wear different clothes or behave differently from them, with accuracy and honesty. Do not ignore their question or change the subject.

7 Think before you speak! Use language that is positive and does not give stereotypical impressions. For example, get into the habit of saying 'police officers' rather than policemen.

Developing your own policy in relation to inclusion, diversity and equality of opportunity

Many registered childminders, especially those involved in networks, will develop and write an equal opportunities policy for their business. Your policy for equal opportunities has to show that you will treat all children with equal concern – this is a basic requirement. It is also important that any policy you have takes the wishes of the parents into consideration and shows respect for different styles of parenting. This is of course much easier said than done! However, if you become a member of the NCMA you will have to agree to uphold its equal opportunities policy, which opposes all forms of discrimination. Even if you do not become a member of NCMA, a policy which opposes all forms of discrimination is a good starting point for you to write your own policy.

Every policy that you have in your business should be regularly reviewed and, if necessary, revised. An equal opportunities policy needs revision and will probably develop as your business develops. However, it is essential that your policy is in place and working for you from your first day in business.

Remember that having a policy is to follow a course of action or to produce a written statement about your intentions. Bear these words in mind when putting together your policy. It is something you must actively follow and believe in, not just a piece of paper that is filed away and brought out only to show your inspection officer or prospective parents. Many registered childminders produce a short leaflet for parents to explain their views on equal opportunities. It does not matter how you present your ideas as long as you are clear in your own mind about how you will treat the children in your care and their families.

Your policy might include, if appropriate:

- how you will care for children's skin and hair

- details of the language that you will use and expect the children to respond to.

- brief details of your own feelings and acknowledgement that you will not know everything, but are prepared to seek assistance and help from parents and other people, if required, in order to treat children with equal concern.

As with any policy, it is your working document, so it must work for you.

Keys to good practice

- Make sure that the language you use is non-discriminatory and not judgemental.

- Try to stress similarities, not differences.

- Show that you are genuinely interested in other people, their beliefs, protecting and promoting their rights.

- Think about your routines.

- Think about how you ensure that all children have opportunities to reach their full potential through the activities and experiences that you offer.

Nannies and other childcare practitioners working in the children's own home may think that they do not need to have a policy for equal opportunities. Whilst it may not be strictly necessary to have a written policy, it is of great importance that you have given careful thought to how you will make sure that your practices are non-discriminatory and inclusive, and how you will deal with prejudice and stereotypical attitudes. It is important that you are aware of children's rights and the ways in which you can protect and promote them. You are a role model for the children in your care and it is essential that you have positive and non-discriminatory attitudes.

Things to consider when writing your policy statement

Below is a list of things to cover in an policy statement for your business.

- Issues about religion.

- Issues about race, including colour and language.

- Different cultural practices, including food and diet, clothing, hair and skin care, parenting styles.

- Language used in the childminding setting.

- Stereotypical attitudes, including issues about gender.

- How your approach to managing children's behaviour encourages inclusion.

- How your routines promote children's rights.

- How parents can make a complaint (although some home-based childcarers have a separate policy to cover disagreements, concerns and complaints).

- Parental or marital status.

- Sexual orientation.

- Disability.

- HIV / AIDS.

This is not a complete list. You can probably think of many other things to add to it.

Within Ofsted inspections there is a good deal of importance placed on actual and missed opportunities for developing and improving children's learning experiences. All childcare practitioners should think about what factors may have an impact on the equality of opportunities offered to the children in their care.

This may involve us thinking about our own value judgements and understanding.

Think about the following points.

Do we really understand what we mean by 'opportunity' when caring for children?

What opportunities are accepted to be equal?

Do these opportunities concern and involve the children in home-based settings?

Do we offer different opportunities to children based on their gender, their parental expectations or any other judgement?

Working with disabled children and their families

Increasing numbers of home-based childcarers are working with disabled children and their families, especially in the context of community childminding networks. Every year 1,500 babies born in the UK are affected by cerebral palsy, which is equal to one in every 400 births, so knowing how to care for a disabled child is something that every home-based childcarer should consider. It is estimated that

It is important to engage disabled children in play

up to 20 per cent of children have a disability or impairment. These disabilities could include:

- a wide range of physical and sensory impairments
- a range of learning difficulties
- a range of medical conditions
- behavioural and emotional problems
- a combination of any of these.

It is important that the difference between disability, impairment and difficulty is understood and that we consider disability equality issues. To develop your understanding and knowledge you need to think about your own and other views of disability, and people with disabling conditions. Having a kind and sympathetic nature is a very good quality to have, but it is not enough. It is important that you are able to consider wider issues, such as the importance of the Disability Discrimination Act 1995 and the Education Act of 1996 (or the Disability Strategies and Pupils' Educational Records Act of 2002 in Scotland) when caring for children who may have additional needs.

The importance of understanding disability equality issues

Key Term

Inclusion – the process of understanding, identifying and breaking down obstructions to belonging and participation.

Inclusion means that all individuals with disabilities and/or learning difficulties have the opportunity to be integrated into mainstream society. For home-based childcarers to promote inclusion you must treat all children as individuals and support their needs. Sometimes a child with a physical disability may also have a learning difficulty or special educational need and vice versa. However, some children with severe medical conditions such as asthma or arthritis may not have learning difficulties but may have rights under the Disability Discrimination Act.

If home-based childcarers, or indeed any setting, treats a disabled child less favourably than another child because of a disability, they may be breaking the law.

Case Study

A registered childminder has told the parents of a girl with epilepsy that she cannot be cared for in the registered childminder's home unless her fits are controlled.

A nanny with a child in a large modified buggy is refused entry to a 'play warehouse' as staff say that the buggy is a health and safety issue.

Do you think that either situation is defensible?

What would you do as a home-based childcarer?

Definitions of impairment and disability

An impairment can become a disability, but not always. For instance, a child with a hearing impairment might be able to wear a hearing aid which will allow that child to function normally and enjoy their life. In this case the hearing impairment is not a disability. Impairments and disabilities should not be stumbling blocks to meeting a child's needs.

Key Term

Disability – a physical or mental condition that limits a person's movements, senses, or activities, for example limited mobility due to cerebral palsy.

Key Term

Impairment – a condition that negatively affects the ability to hear, see, walk or coordinate actions.

The value of the social model of disability compared to the medical model

The medical or individual model (also referred to as the medical/individual view)

An impairment is viewed as the 'problem' of the individual person. If this viewpoint is taken to a logical conclusion, it could be argued that any disability or impairment is the cause of one person's problems. Therefore disabled people should try to be as able-bodied as possible. Furthermore, a solution to their problems will be found only through medical treatment. Medical people and other professionals often make decisions about the disabled person's life, such as which school they should attend. The focus for support tends to be on care needs rather than what the person concerned wishes. The focus is therefore shifting away from the person and onto the impairment; some argue that this infringes an individual's rights. The situation that the disabled person finds themselves in is regarded with pity and often they are encouraged to make the best of the situation, being brave and courageous. Some people feel that this view is encouraged by the idea of giving awards to disabled people, especially children, for bravery.

The social model of disability

The social model of disability sees the problem being with society, the environment and negative attitudes. This viewpoint gives children and people with impairments exactly the same rights as anyone else and is non-discriminatory. The social model aims at changing society, the environment and attitudes, so that the impaired person can have as full a life as anyone else. The medical model aims to 'normalise' the person with the impairment or disability. Most disabled people favour the social model.

Childcare professionals could make statements such as, 'I cannot take Jodie out because her adapted buggy is too big for my car.' This is viewing disability from the medical/individual model – the problem is seen as Jodie and the buggy, regardless of what reason there is for her needing the buggy. A social model of the same situation could be, 'The boot of my car is too small. I need to find other ways of Jodie and me getting out.' In this statement the 'problem' is not Jodie, but the design of the car.

If you are going to actively combat and challenge discrimination it is essential that you work from the viewpoint of the social model.

Think about it

Look at the following statements and then decide which fits the medical/individual model or the social model.

- Anna can't go to the pre-school group because her walking frame won't fit through the door.

- The door on the village hall can't be altered so that Anna can get in with her walking frame.

- Your child can't hear me so I can't care for him.

- The gap between the station platform and the train is too wide so he can't use trains.

Case Study

Alastair has hearing difficulties and as a result has delayed speech and difficulty communicating. The nanny who cares for Alastair has learnt Makaton so that they can communicate. It has also been possible for the nanny to attend the pre-school group with Alastair to support him, and one member of the pre-school staff has also started to learn Makaton.

What other opportunities can be provided to help Alastair achieve his full potential?

The significance of images and language

The words we speak and the images that surround us in daily life are both very powerful and effective ways of communication. They can combat and challenge or promote discriminatory attitudes. It is important to consider very carefully the words that we use in all contexts. The use of language can limit or develop the way we think. Consider the words 'special needs', widely used in education and care, often with perfectly sound intentions. In reality, it could be argued that these words imply that children with 'special needs' have different needs or requirements from other children. All children have the same needs, but some have additional needs at certain points in their lives.

The language that we use reflects and influences the way that disability and impairments are viewed by society, including people with a disability or impairment themselves. Over the years people with disabilities or impairments have been referred to using many different terms, usually bestowed on them by non-disabled professionals, such as 'the handicapped' or 'the disabled,' or even more offensive terms, such as 'spastics'. Much of the language used about people with a disability reflects the medical model of disability. This creates and reinforces stereotypical attitudes and labelling.

There are many different conditions or impairments that people can have and the correct name or term should always be used. Explaining these terms or names to children provides opportunities to teach basic information about their bodies, health and possible illnesses. This will also help to dispel some of the myths and fears around disability issues and influence children's attitudes in a positive way.

Many images come from the media, such as television, films and magazines. Many of these images are negative and sometimes emotive. We are often encouraged to feel sympathy and sometimes pity for people with additional needs, rather than focusing on their positive achievements.

Attitudes are slowing changing – the Athens Paralympics in 2004 brought many talented athletes who had additional needs to public attention. These athletes were able to achieve standards within their particular disciplines that the majority of the population could never meet.

Many charitable organisations were originally set up by parents and carers of disabled people, often with the aim of seeking a cure for a specific condition or treatment. To persuade the public to donate to these charities, images are often used that show disabled people as helpless or in need of support; they invoke pity rather than respect and undermine dignity and self-esteem, keeping alive the 'victim' image. While many charities do exemplary work, some of the fund-raising methods used are questionable.

Inclusion and home-based childcare

In an ideal world all settings, home-based or otherwise, would be inclusive. Children and adults would be encouraged to remove barriers and develop mutual understanding.

Finding suitable childcare can be daunting for the parents of children with a disability, but a new initiative, funded by the National Lottery, and shared between two charities – Scope and HemiHelp – aims to show that extending normal good practice is the main requirement. A total of 3,000 information packs have been distributed to early years childcare practitioners giving practical guidance on how better to support the inclusion of disabled children. Further information can be obtained from www.hemihelp.org.uk

Recognising a child's individuality is the basis of anti-discriminatory practice. How often have you heard someone refer to two twins as 'the twins'? All children are different, with different strengths, patterns of behaviour, appearances and attitudes. We must value and respect these differences, which could mean providing activities that encourage self-expression such as painting, dancing, or mime. It can also mean that we show interest and share in the activities and things that the children like to do.

The importance of treating the child as an individual, not labelled by the impairment or condition

Key Term

Individuality – unique and different aspects of a person that make them different from everyone else.

Case Study

Josh has limited mobility. He is a great fan of football but has difficulty kicking a ball and maintaining his balance. The registered childminder suggested that Josh uses his hands to pass the ball to the other children, in this way he can participate in the game.

What else could the registered childminder do to make sure that Josh is included?

Self expression is equally important for children

Labelling is a form of discrimination; for instance, we cannot say that all children with cerebral palsy have poor speech. Some children may have speech difficulties but many children with cerebral palsy can speak well. Labelling takes away individuality and therefore puts barriers in the way of a child reaching their full potential.

Case Study

A registered childminder has cared for two brothers after school and has now agreed to care for their younger sibling. When collecting the children one of the staff at the school says to the registered childminder, 'You will have your hands full with this one.'

Why is this labelling?

What should the registered childminder do?

In order to meet the individual needs of children who have a disability or impairment it is helpful to have some knowledge of the causes and medical implications of their specific condition. This knowledge will help you to maximise the child's full potential and make you more able to support the parents. However, you are not expected to be an expert on any disability, impairment or condition, just be informed.

Link to assessment

E8 Describe strategies for challenging prejudice and discrimination when working with children and families.

Hint

Think about what is meant by prejudice and discrimination.

Make a list of possible situations where prejudice and discrimination might happen.

For each item on your list, write alongside it why it is wrong and how you could challenge it.

B Analyse the role of the home-based childcarer in promoting children's rights.

This criterion is a development of **E2** and **E8** above.

Hint

Look at the study skills section at the end of the book to find out what the term 'analyse' means (page 289).

Also look at the link to assessment for **E2** (page 100) and what you have written to meet that criterion.

You will need to give a detailed section in your assignment which carefully considers your professional role and responsibilities. You may want to think about:

• how you respect and value the children and their families

• how you make sure that you are always aware of the rights of children

• why it is important that you are a positive role model and how you do this

• why it is important that you keep your knowledge and skills up to date (see Unit 1, page 91)

• why it is important that your practice is anti-discriminatory and how you do this.

How to provide play and learning activities for disabled children

Children with disabilities or impairments need adults who will facilitate play and learning activities, rather than direct them. However, it is important to remember that the needs of children with disabilities are the same as all children's needs.

Sometimes children with disabilities are given activities that do not challenge them, or do not allow them to freely express themselves – this is discriminatory. All children need play and

The needs of children

learning activities that are appropriate to their age, stage of development, and which also meet their individual needs. They need a variety of safe and stimulating experiences or activities from which they can learn and develop. In order to provide play experiences, opportunities and activities for children, you just need to know how to care for children, not children with specific disabilities.

Children with mobility difficulties may need wedges or foam slopes to support them, leaving their arms free so they can play. You may find that some toys will have to be adapted or stored in different ways to make them easily accessible to the children. For instance, sand and water trays may have to be positioned so that walking frames or wheelchairs will fit around them. You may find that you will need to have a door ramp so that children can easily access the garden and outside play opportunities. Do not assume that a child with a caliper cannot climb; they might take longer but may still be able to get to the top of the climbing frame. This assumption is discriminatory and the attitude will be a barrier to that child reaching their full potential.

Children with sensory impairments, such as hearing or visual impairments, may need specialised equipment such as large print books, stories on tape, headphones or hearing aids with adjustable volume controls. You may also need to consider how you speak to children with hearing impairments when giving suggestions

Resources can enable disabled children to engage in activities

or questioning them, making sure that you speak clearly and establish eye contact.

Children with coordination and/or fine motor skill difficulties may find the use of thick and wedge-shaped drawings and mark-making materials helpful. They may also benefit from books with thick pages which are easier to turn.

Children with learning difficulties may take longer than others to acquire a new skill so you will need to make sure that you have considered the time factor and are patient and supportive.

Case Study

Alex is a registered childminder who has been asked to mind nine-year-old Jess before and after school, and also during school holidays. Jess uses a walking frame. Alex's front and back doors have steps which means that Jess would not be able to access the garden, and could even have difficulty getting into the house. Alex approaches a local builder who makes a wooden ramp that fits over the steps and can be used at either door. Alex puts a non-slip mat over the ramp to make it safe. After the ramp has been fitted one of the other parents commented to Alex how helpful it was for getting in and out of the house with a buggy.

This is an example of how an adjustment to the environment can be of benefit to everyone, not just the child with a mobility difficulty.

You may find that it will not be necessary to adapt your equipment, but just to adapt your approach to the play activity. For example, a child who has difficulties controlling arm, hand and finger movements may struggle with a modelling activity. You could sit alongside the child and put your hand over theirs to guide their movements, praising their achievements frequently. Alternatively, do not plan to do a modelling activity – choose something else that this child could do.

Think about it

Look carefully at your working environment.

- Imagine that you are a child with some form of disability or impairment. What adjustments would benefit you?
- Are all parts of your childcare environment accessible to all children?
- Are the toys and play resources accessible to all of the children?
- Have you planned any activities recently that would not be accessible to all children, such as walking to the local park to play on the swings?

Keys to good practice

- Make sure that the activities you provide challenge and stimulate appropriate to the child's age and stage of development.
- If you have children with sensory impairments make sure that you have a consistent room layout.
- Position toys and equipment to encourage independent access, if necessary provide supports.
- Make sure that all parts of your childcare setting are accessible to all children.
- Make sure that all of your planned activities are accessible to all children.

All children need a range of play equipment. Toy libraries can be very useful places to extend your range and also get practical ideas for adapting or improving upon your existing equipment.

How to help children learn about disability

We know that children acquire some of their beliefs and attitudes from watching others.

Remember that you are a very powerful role model and can help children learn about disability. Children need accurate information about every aspect of their learning. This doesn't mean that you have to know everything, but you should know where you can access further information if it is required to help children understand.

Children will learn from watching and becoming aware of your attitudes and behaviour towards individuals with a disability. If you shout and speak very slowly to a person in a wheelchair, a child may learn that this is the way to speak to all people in wheelchairs. If you cross the road when a sight-impaired person with a guide dog approaches in the street, the child will think that it is acceptable to do this.

Learning through play is very effective and many childcare practitioners find that young children can learn about disabilities in this way. There are a few small-scale play materials and toys that include wheelchairs and crutches which may help younger children increase their understanding. Older children may ask more direct questions about specific conditions, impairments or disabilities. These questions should be answered factually and honestly.

The role of the childcare practitioner in working with the families of disabled children

Your relationship with any parent is very important, since they can tell you more about their child than anyone else and have the interests of the child at heart. When working with parents and families of disabled children you may find that they need more support from you and may want to share anxieties and concerns. Your role will be somewhat easier if you can develop an understanding of some of the difficulties and stresses that families can face.

The medical model of disability is usually the one that parents first meet upon diagnosis of their child's condition, which is likely to be in a medical situation. There is a danger that they see the disability as a problem with the child at the centre of the problem. Understandably, some families and parents begin to experience negative feelings.

- When first told of the condition some parents feel shock and anger that can lead to blame and guilt, either directed at themselves or at the medical practitioners present at the birth.
- Some parents can grieve and feel a sense of loss that their expectations have not been achieved.

- Some parents and families may feel shame and in some cases this can lead to the family feeling isolated and alone. In extreme cases this can lead to parents rejecting the child.

- Some families become very fearful of the future and whether or not they will be able to cope.

- Some parents can get very confused and feel bombarded by medical information, not getting the practical help and support needed.

- Some parents can feel very stressed by the demands of hospital appointments, medications, therapies and regimes that may be imposed. This can lead to difficulties finding time for their other children and even themselves.

You can help to support parents through these negative feelings by focusing upon the social model of disability.

You might be the only practitioner/professional that the family meets who does not focus on the medical model and takes a holistic approach to disability. You can help them to appreciate and enjoy the positive aspects of bringing up a child and to find pleasure in the development and achievements of that child, however small. You can make sure that you tell parents what the child has done whilst in your care and what they are learning to do. You may be able to help parents get access to local support groups.

Key Terms

Holistic – the belief that the whole being is more than the sum of the parts.

Holistic treatment focuses upon the whole person rather than just the symptoms of an illness or disability.

Holistic development focuses upon the development of the whole child, not just one aspect of the child's development.

You may also be able to support and help other children in the family. It is not unusual for siblings of a disabled child to feel left out, rejected or deprived of attention. Sometimes they do not want to bring friends home for fear that other children will not be able to cope with the disabled child, for example if the disabled child has to be fed or has uncontrolled movements or verbal outbursts. You can help to reassure them that they are still loved and offer them an emotionally safe and secure place where they can play with a friend.

You may be involved in specific learning programmes with children who are disabled, such as conductive education or portage, especially if you are caring for the child in their own home.

You should make sure that you are offered appropriate training and support to deliver the programme and should not become involved in techniques that have not been fully shown and explained to you, or with which you are not confident.

Key Terms

Conductive education – this technique comes from the Peto Institute in Hungary and aims to help children with motor/physical impairments. It can be very intensive and focuses upon a step-by-step approach, encouraging the child to gradually develop movement. Small movements are repeated frequently, sometimes to the point of exhaustion. The idea behind conductive education is that if the brain is forced to do something that it can't currently do, it will try to find a way to connect mind and muscle.

Portage breaks down skills that children need into small steps, each one of which is mastered before progressing to the next step. Portage workers come to the child's home, and use play and everyday activities to help children learn each step.

Children's development and well-being

Caring for children in home-based settings is not just about keeping them happy and safe, but is also about helping them to achieve their full potential. In order to do this it is important that you have a good understanding of children's development and the factors that can affect their development.

Development from birth to 16 years

All children are unique and will develop at different rates. However, they will all pass through the same sequence of development. As children get older the difference in the rates of development will become greater, which can make it difficult to make generalised statements about development at a certain chronological age.

Each child must pass through one stage of development before they can move on to the next; this progress is often measured through milestones. While the use of milestones can be very helpful it is important to remember that they are averages which have been recorded over many years, meaning that there will always be some individuals who are quicker or slower to reach them.

Think about it

Nature versus nurture

We are born with innate abilities and inherited characteristics from our parents and ancestors which will affect our development (nature). However, much of our development is affected by where we live, who we live with and the experiences that we have (nurture).

There is no exact way of knowing if what a child inherits from their parents has more of an effect on the way they develop than the influence of people and the environment. Educationalists and theorists can be found who will back either nature, nurture or a mixture of both as the primary force behind development, and are yet to reach firm conclusions.

What do you think has the greatest influence on how a child develops?

Think about it

Is development continuous or does it happen in stages?

It has been suggested that the development of those skills that are linked to maturation, physical growth, for example, could appear in stages, such as crawling before walking. Those skills that are not linked to maturation may not develop in stages. Using this argument, which of the following do you think might develop in stages or might be a continuous development?

Becoming sociable
Language
Showing affection
Being generous
Vision
Behaving inappropriately.

Each stage in a sequence of development can be clearly defined, for example a baby sits before crawling, and stands before walking. These are referred to as developmental milestones, or norms. Note that from now on in this book I refer to these as milestones, but norms is no less acceptable.

Development is often looked at or approached in separate areas in order to make accurate measurements and assessments, but it is important to remember that all aspects of a child's development are interrelated and affect each other. For example, a child with a language delay may find it difficult to communicate with their peers; this may affect their ability to make friends and develop social relationships, which in turn may make them feel frustrated and angry. The different areas of development are in many ways artificial divisions because children develop as whole human beings and not in separate categories.

Factors affecting development

There are many factors that can affect a child's growth and development. Some can be short-term, such as being temporarily hard of hearing after having a cold; others can be more long-lasting, such as food allergies, and some can even be permanent. It is almost impossible to list and consider all the factors that can affect a child's development. In most cases a factor that affects physical growth and development, for example, will affect other areas of a child's development and so it is difficult to separate them into 'developmental areas'.

Some experts who study child development divide the factors that can affect development into three areas.

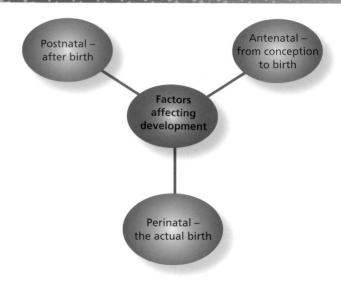

Factors affecting development

Antenatal

Condition of mother before birth

This factor includes such things as smoking, diet and alcohol intake whilst pregnant. Scientific studies have shown that the lifestyle of a pregnant woman affects the unborn baby. It has been

The condition of the mother before birth has an impact upon the child's development

proved that mothers who smoke and drink whilst pregnant generally give birth to smaller babies. Recent studies in America have shown that children with low birth weights tend to have lower intelligence scores than those children who are heavier at birth. However, low birth weight could mean that the baby is malnourished and that energy has to be spent on physical development rather than intellectual development in the early months. All children need energy to develop and those who are malnourished may not grow as well as others.

Perinatal

Prematurity

Premature babies are born early, and have not fully developed. Premature babies are usually born between 24 and 37 weeks of pregnancy, whereas a full-term baby is born between 38 and 40 weeks.

Premature babies have low birth weight, are small and can have developmental delays. Also, babies who have low birth weights are often more susceptible to infection, feeding difficulties and problems with breathing.

Birth difficulties

There can be many factors that will affect the birth of a baby. Significant medical developments in recent years have reduced the risk to both the baby and the mother, and in many cases increased care of the mother before birth can anticipate or avoid difficulties at birth. However, one of the most common birth difficulties is when the baby is deprived of oxygen during the birthing process. This is either called anoxia or hypoxia, depending upon the extent of the deprivation; anoxia relates to a total lack of oxygen and hypoxia to partial oxygen deprivation. Oxygen deprivation in any form can cause a wide range of problems, such as learning difficulties and cerebral palsy.

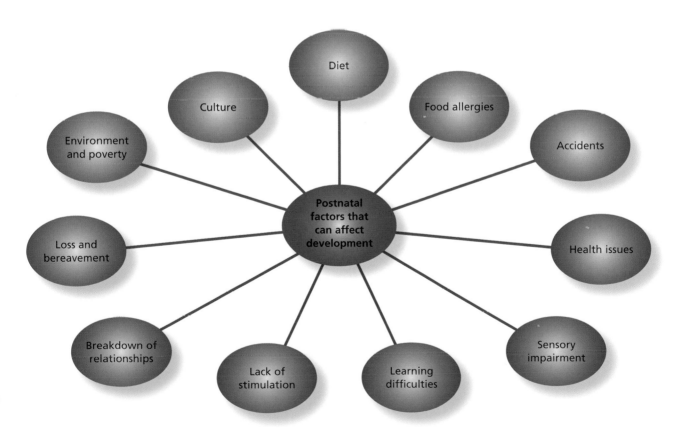

Postnatal factors that can affect development

Postnatal

Diet

Quality of diet is of crucial importance at all times, whether child or adult. Children who are undernourished – that is, those who do not get enough to eat, and those who do not have a balanced diet and are malnourished – can show signs of developmental delay. Food provides children with energy, which helps them to grow and develop.

It is very important that before you start to plan food and meals for the children in your care, you talk to the parents. There could be cultural, medical and religious reasons why children do not eat certain foods and you must respect the wishes of the parents. The chart on page 295 shows some of the customs and religious practices associated with food.

Diet will be considered in greater detail later on in this unit (see page 133).

Food allergies

Many children suffer from food allergies or intolerances, either all of their lives or only when young. Some food allergies can be potentially fatal, such as an intolerance to nuts and/or shellfish which can cause the body to go into anaphylactic shock. This means that breathing becomes difficult, and as the airways swell up it is often impossible to breathe. Children can die from anaphylactic shock.

Key Term

Allergy – sensitivity and/or an intolerant reaction to a particular food or substance.

Diabetes is another condition that can be potentially life-threatening. Most diabetic children have to avoid sugar in their diet, so it is very important that they have regular and well-balanced meals. If the sugar levels in the blood of diabetic children get too low a child can go into a diabetic coma or seizure, and will need glucose to raise the blood sugar levels. On the other hand, too much sugar in the blood can lead to excessive thirst, a need to pass urine frequently and weight loss.

Both asthma and eczema can be aggravated by some foods, especially dairy products. Some children are intolerant of gluten, which is found in cereal products. This intolerance is usually referred to as coeliac disease. Studies have shown that some hyperactive children and some children with behaviour problems are intolerant to a yellow food colouring called tartrazine. This additive can be found in many food products, such as the crunchy coating on chicken pieces, sweets, soft drinks and butter-type spreads. It cannot be emphasised enough that you must talk to the parents and find out if their child has a food allergy or intolerance before you start to care for them.

Accidents

Accidents can affect a child's growth and development, sometimes permanently. For instance, a child who has been involved in a serious accident that has affected the way that they move will suffer some form of developmental delay in that area. In such a case their social skills could also be affected as they may not be able to get out and about to meet other children. Their language skills will be affected as they could have limited opportunities to communicate with others and they could become frightened, clingy and unsure when previously they were confident.

In some cases developmental delay as a result of an accident is exactly that – a delay. Provided that the child has sensitive and understanding carers they may eventually reduce the delay or its impact upon their development.

Health issues

There are a huge range of health issues that can affect children's growth and development. They could range from infections such as childhood illnesses, colds and ear infections to a serious illness that may be life-threatening. You also need to think about the children's general health, diet and energy levels. A child who is always tired, for whatever reason, will not be able to concentrate, so their learning will be affected.

Impairment of the senses

Children who have a sensory impairment may show some delay in their intellectual or cognitive development. When very young they rely on their senses to give them information about the world and they build upon this information later on. Severe sensory impairments, such as lack of hearing or sight, are usually identified by the normal health checks. Sometimes, however, a child can suffer from a temporary sensory impairment, for example a bad cold can affect hearing for a while and this could temporarily delay their development, especially of language skills.

Learning difficulties

There are many reasons why a child may have learning difficulties which can affect all areas of growth and development. If you think that a child in your care has a learning difficulty, discuss the difficulty with the parents and suggest that they seek expert advice and help.

Lack of stimulation

In order for all children to develop and grow they need to be active and involved. Activity or stimulation appropriate to their stage of development is essential if children are to progress and learn. Lack of stimulation will mean that they do not progress.

Breakdown of relationships

Children's social and emotional development can be affected by the breakdown of relationships between their parents, or their friends. Children can become anxious, unsure and sometimes frightened that their parents will not come back for them. Confident, happy children can become withdrawn, tearful and lack trust in adults or other children. If their parents are in conflict the child could become drawn into the arguments. However, not all children are affected by relationship breakdowns and some cope well with little, if any, effect on their development, so do not always assume that children in such situations will have problems or difficulties. You need to talk to the parents and take your cues from the child.

Loss and bereavement

Loss and bereavement for children can be as traumatic as it is for adults. However, to a child, losing a favourite cuddly toy, moving house or losing a well-loved registered childminder can be just as traumatic as the death of a parent, brother or sister, or other close family relative. Sometimes children will try to hide their feelings about loss and death, especially if they think that it will upset other people. This can lead to children showing their emotions in other ways, such as aggression or withdrawal.

Think about it

In Romania, which was ruled by a Communist dictatorship for many years, a lot of orphaned and abandoned children were put into orphanages and more or less forgotten. In the early 1990s, following the downfall of the Communist government, aid agencies of the West discovered the appalling conditions in which these children were existing. Some of the staff in the orphanages believed that the children were mentally impaired from birth. In fact, many children had been completely normal at birth, but due to lack of stimulation and other factors, such as diet and quality of care, they had not been able to develop. There were documented cases of children of six and seven years with the behaviour and development of babies of six or seven months. Eventually, with much sensitive care, stimulation and attention, some of the children began to show signs of development in all areas, and so were not as intellectually impaired as had been thought by their former carers.

Mick is a registered childminder for Tom, aged five. Tom was collected each day by his grandfather, with whom he had a very close and loving relationship. Tom is confident, very sociable and friendly. Sadly, Tom's grandfather had a fatal heart attack. Tom is now collected much later in the day by his mother after work. She is also grieving for the loss of her father and often looks tired. Tom has become withdrawn and does not want to play with the other children after school. He has started running away and hiding when his mother comes to collect him, shouting that he wants his grandad. Naturally his mother finds this very upsetting and has asked Mick to help.

Mick goes to the local library and finds some books on loss and grief. He is also given the number of a voluntary organisation for help. Mick and Tom find a quiet time to read the books together. Mick encourages Tom to draw pictures of his grandfather and talk about how he is feeling. He answers Tom's questions honestly and simply, and tries to explain to Tom that his mother is also upset, but wants to talk about grandad too. Gradually Tom is able to show and share with his mother the pictures that he has drawn and Mick gives them the books to read together. Tom starts to watch the other children playing and gradually asks if he can join in with their games. He stops running away when his mother comes to collect him. It takes time, but by doing things together and with Mick's sensitive support, both Tom and his mother cope with their loss.

What other things could Mick do to support Tom and his mother?

Environment and poverty

Poverty can have a detrimental effect on all aspects of a child's growth, development and their rights. Poor housing can affect a child's health, and lack of money can affect the amount of food that is bought, which also affects the child's health.

The environment in which a child is cared for can also have very positive effects. A loving, secure environment will help a child develop good relationships and social skills. A stimulating environment will enable them to explore and investigate the world around them, developing good language and cognitive skills.

Culture

A child's cultural background must always be respected, even if the traditions of that culture are not yours. We live in a multicultural society, with many parenting styles, languages and religions. Children should be encouraged to learn about cultures other than their own in a positive way. They need to feel confident about themselves and be sure that they are valued. You should be a very positive role model in encouraging this aspect of a child's development.

Frameworks for understanding child care and development from birth to 16 years

Children's development can be grouped in a variety of ways, some of which are age related, for example the Birth to Three Matters Framework aims to cover all the developmental issues affecting children from birth to three years of age.

Key Term

Birth to Three Matters Framework – a framework to support those people working with and caring for babies and young children under three years old.

Children's development can be grouped into four areas.

1 **Physical development**, which can include:

- fine manipulative skills
- fine motor skills
- gross motor skills
- locomotive skills
- coordination skills
- balance.

2 **Intellectual or cognitive development**, which can include:

- how children learn
- sensory development
- memory skills
- attention and concentration
- perception.

3 **Social and emotional development**, which can include:

- relationships
- understanding about oneself
- behaviour
- expressing and understanding feelings.

4 **Language and communication**, which can include:

- learning to communicate in different ways
- oratory skills and literacy.

These developmental areas are sometimes referred to as **PILES**:

Physical
Intellectual or cognitive
Language and communication
Emotional
Social

They can also be called **SPICE**:

Social
Physical
Intellectual or cognitive
Communication or cultural
Emotional

Cultural development considers how cultures, society, customs and traditions affect and influence a child's development. Many cultures have different views on child rearing, behaviour and social rules. It is essential that every childcare practitioner creates an inclusive environment in which all children are welcome, their rights are respected and met, and opportunities for them to reach their full potential are provided.

The **Seven Cs** is another popular approach:

1 Confidence   5 Communication
2 Coordination   6 Concentration
3 Competence   7 Cooperation.
4 Creativity

The Birth to Three Matters Framework was produced in 2002 in order to help childcare practitioners observe, reflect and plan as a way of meeting the needs of children. In 2005, Scotland also produced an approach to supporting the development of young children called 'Birth to Three – supporting our youngest children'. There is also an interest in adopting the approach of Birth to Three from local authorities in Northern Ireland and Wales.

The Birth to Three Matters Framework is divided into four aspects:

- a strong child
- a skilful communicator
- a competent learner
- a healthy child.

Each of the four aspects is divided into four areas called components, shown in the table below.

Aspect	Component 1	Component 2	Component 3	Component 4
A strong child	Me, myself and I	Being acknowledged and affirmed	Developing self-assurance	A sense of belonging
A skilful communicator	Being together	Finding a voice	Listening and responding	Making meaning
A competent learner	Making connections	Being imaginative	Being creative	Representing
A healthy child	Emotional well-being	Growing and developing	Keeping safe	Healthy choices

One important feature of the Birth to Three Matters Framework is that the baby's development is considered in a holistic way.

Planning and providing care for mixed-age groups of children

Most home-based childcarers do not just care for one age group of children. In any one working day registered childminders may care for school-aged children before and after school, as well as babies and toddlers. Nannies will often take care of siblings across different age groups. Planning and providing care for mixed-age groups can be very stimulating, but at the same time it is important that the home-based childcarer has flexible routines and practices that can accommodate the different needs of the children.

It can be quite a juggling act to organise the rest time for a baby, collect one child from nursery or pre-school, organise mealtimes, take a different child to nursery, do a school pick-up and remember important information to share with the parents.

It is important to remember that all children develop at different rates and that their care needs will change as they develop, so whilst care should be consistent and of the best quality the home-based childcarer must also take into account the fact that needs can be met in an adaptable way.

Think about it

Children have cultural as well as developmental needs and you should ask yourself if your care routines and practices reflect a child's culture.

Caring for school-aged children

With the development of 'wrap-around' care and extended schools, more and more home-based childcarers, particularly registered childminders, will become involved in the care of school-aged children. Many children's centres are actively seeking the support of registered childminders in providing this care.

Providing care for mixed-age groups is a challenge

As with any age of child it is vital that the care you offer reflects their individual needs, for example school-aged children will be able to take responsibility for many aspects of their personal care with minimal supervision from the carer.

Childcare practitioners must also support the growing need for independence, especially in older children.

The importance of three-way communication between you, the children's parents and school

Your role in supporting school-aged children can be quite different from your role with pre-schoolers, but it is still very important that you establish effective lines of communication between the school, the child's parents and yourself. It is very helpful if the parents can explain to the school and child's teacher who you are and what your job is. This can be very helpful if issues of confidentiality arise. Parents should be encouraged to give the school written permission to share information with you.

Most schools rely on letters and bulletins to communicate with parents. It is not unheard of for school-aged children to forget to pass these on! Home-based childcarers need to make sure that this important information is passed on the parents either by the carer or the child themselves.

It is good practice for home-based childcarers to make themselves aware of the child's school routine and timetable. In doing this they can make sure that the parents are also aware and that children go to school with the appropriate kit, equipment and resources for each day.

It is also important that you are aware of what the child has or has not eaten whilst at school. This will have a direct impact on the care of the child before and after school. It may be easy for you to see what has been eaten when sorting out a lunch box, but if you have any concerns about what a child is eating you should check with the school staff. Any concerns should be shared with both the school and the parents.

Case Study

Jenna is a nanny caring for an eighteen-month-old boy and his two siblings aged six and nine. Both of the older children attend the same school. Jenna's employers write to each class teacher at the beginning of the school year to explain who Jenna is and to give their permission for her to be given information about the children. This has been very important as the six-year-old has some difficulties managing his behaviour. Because the teachers could speak directly to Jenna they were able to implement a strategy that could be continued after school. Jenna shared this information with the parents and the same strategy was followed at weekends and at times when Jenna did not have care of the children. Because effective lines of communication had been established between Jenna, the school and the parents, the child benefited greatly and was able to learn how to manage his behaviour.

How do you ensure effective three-way communication between school, parents, and yourself?

In what ways could this be improved?

Planning suitable activities for before and after school, and in school holidays

School-aged children are growing more independent and are influenced by many factors outside their home, and that of their carer. They still need care and attention from you and you will need to make sure that you provide appropriate things to do and play with.

Before school

Children have a busy time at school and need to be as well prepared as possible. Before school can be a busy time for everyone, with parents coming and going, children trying to get themselves organised and so on, therefore activities should be uncomplicated and will not tire or over-excite a child. Older children can take responsibility at this time of the day for their school kit and/or lunch boxes.

Make sure that you have organised and planned your time so that you and the children are not late for the start of the school day. Not only do accidents happen when people are rushed or agitated, but tempers fray and patience levels drop – hardly a positive start to the day.

After school

Some children may appear to lose ground slightly when they first start school, so it is important that you remember this when planning activities for after school. Some children find a full school day exhausting and when it is over they just want to be quiet, have a snack and recharge. Equally, some children come out of school excited by the day's activities and bursting to tell someone about them. This makes it important that you are on time when collecting a child from school. It is also important that you do not leave a child waiting around for you; not only could the well-being of the child be at risk, but they could lose confidence in you.

It is helpful for the child if you can make yourself aware of the curriculum that they are following in school (this will be discussed in more detail in Unit 5). If you have some knowledge of the subjects within the curriculum you will be in better position to help with homework. This is not to suggest that the activities and experiences you plan are linked into a specific curriculum, which is the role of a teacher in school, but you will be far better able to support the holistic development of school-aged children if you have some understanding of what they will be doing in school.

Children may occasionally be involved in after-school activities that involve them being picked up at a different time. Again, how you organise your time is very important. Remember, because school-aged children may not spend a lot of time with you after school, especially if you are a registered childminder, it does not mean that you do not have to plan activities for them.

During school holidays
Many local authorities and sports and leisure centres organise holiday play schemes during school holidays. If children are booked into these it is your responsibility to treat them the same way as you would if they were at school. However, some parents find such schemes quite costly and you may be caring for the children the whole day, rather than just before and after school. During school holidays you will have to think about play activities carefully as you may have different age groups to consider. Many activities that you do with younger children can easily be extended to meet the needs of older children, such as painting and art activities, modelling and dance.

The difficulties that may arise in combining the care of babies with looking after older children

One issue that many home-based childcarers can encounter is that they may not have a sufficient range of toys and equipment when caring for children of different ages. This can be especially applicable to registered childminders. Toy libraries are an invaluable source of extending toys and equipment to meet the needs of different age groups. Some registered childminders, especially those in networks, informally share toys and

Keys to good practice

Listed below are some suggested home-based activities for during school holidays. These are in no way exhaustive and you may decide that you want to do something else.

- Try a keep-fit session in a suitably open space or cleared room. This can involve all of the children whatever their age.

- Use a roll of wallpaper for children to draw or paint on. Older children could be encouraged to draw a story that develops along the roll of paper.

- Make dens with old sheets, curtains, boxes, then prepare a picnic to eat.

- Get together with other home-based childcarers and organise mini-sports events,

treasure hunts or picnics if the weather is good.

- Encourage children to get together with their friends and put on shows to entertain you and the younger children.

- Plan special days out to local parks, museums, places of interest. Take a camera and let children take pictures of things that interest them. These pictures can then be made into a scrap book or copied later.

Do not forget to let parents know of your plans and get their written permission to take the children out.

equipment among themselves. Note that if you borrow any toys or equipment it is your responsibility to check them to ensure that they are safe before they are used.

Local libraries also will give childcare professionals extra tickets so that they can borrow larger numbers of books.

Mealtimes are another thing that you need to plan, and even with thorough preparation it may be hard to meet everyone's needs. Older children may want to have responsibility for preparing their snacks and meals, but babies will need you to feed them and toddlers will also need support.

At all times the safety of the children is paramount and at no time should you leave any child unattended.

Another issue for home-based childcarers is matching the rest and sleep needs of babies and toddlers with the needs of older children. Ask yourself, is it fair that older children have to be quiet or are restricted in their activities because a baby is asleep, or does it help them to learn consideration for others?

Case Study

Alex is a nanny to a six-month-old baby girl, Daisy, a two-year-old boy, Charles, and Jack aged five. Alex has organised mealtimes, especially their evening meal with the baby safely harnessed in her baby seat, and an appropriate toy to hand. Charles sits at the table with Jack and Alex. Jack independently feeds himself and can use cutlery. Alex cuts Charles's food into manageable pieces and encourages him to use a fork and spoon. When the boys have finished their meal Alex picks the baby up and gives her a bottle. Alex eats later after the children are in bed. By organising the time in this way, the needs of both boys can be met and Daisy can share the social aspect of mealtimes.

Do you think that this is a good way to organise mealtimes?

Are the needs of all the children being met?

What would you do in a similar situation?

Are the needs of all the children being met?

You will also have to think about the way that you communicate with children of different ages, and may have to say the same things in different ways to meet the needs and understanding of different ages, which can take a lot of time and patience.

You may also have to think about how you manage children's behaviour when caring for different age groups. It can sometimes appear to a child that you are treating them differently and therefore unfairly because of their age. Careful, appropriate and sensitive communication with simple explanations should help overcome this potential problem.

Child health

The state of a child's health impacts on all aspects of their development, growth and learning. There is growing concern about childhood obesity, lack of exercise in children and the quality of their diet.

The Health Survey for England in 2001 produced some quite frightening statistics, for example in the past 10 years the level of obesity in six-year-olds has doubled and amongst 15-year-olds it has trebled. Home-based childcarers can have a very positive impact on a child's overall health, helping children to learn about their bodies and how to keep healthy.

The importance of working with parents to establish routines and continuity of all aspects of care

See also Unit 1, page 50.

Routines, whatever length or whatever the focus, should always be planned to meet individual needs. Care routines should be planned to give continuity of care, following the same pattern of events that has been established by the parents. This will help the children feel emotionally safe and secure whilst in your care.

It is important to discuss the planning of all routines with parents so that you make sure that the individual needs of both the child and the family can be met. Just as all children are different, so are parents, so it is important to discuss care routines with parents before you start to care for their children, to avoid any misunderstandings. Your daily routine should also be discussed with the parents so that they have some idea of what their child will be doing whilst in your care, and so they also know where you are at any given time if they need to contact you.

Routines are usually planned with one specific age group in mind, for example feeding a baby or toilet training. However, it is important to remember that all children are individuals, so trying to impose a routine that does not cater for individual differences will result in a less than satisfactory situation. Some parents may want their child to be fed following a structured method, whereas others may be happy for their baby to be fed on demand.

Routines can also focus just upon one aspect of care or development, such as sterilising bottles or the sequence of events that you and children have organised to get to a gymnastic club on time.

Food given at mealtimes can be an issue for some parents, not only might their child have allergies or specific dietary needs, but a parent may want their child to have only organic food, vegetarian meals, or meals that are appropriate to their culture or religion.

Some parents will want you to use disposable nappies, others may want you to use washable, reusable nappies, or may have a special way or place for changing nappies. In this case you should ask the parents to actually show you what they do.

Some parents may have established a routine for rest and sleep which they want you to follow, or a routine pattern of events to follow when coming in from school, such as the child having a wash, changing their clothes, having a snack, quiet time, homework, evening meal.

Making sure that you are working with the parents in establishing your care routines will make sure that the needs of the child are met and misunderstandings are avoided. This is especially important if a child has a medical condition, an allergy or a specific need relating to their religion or culture. Following the same routines as the parents will help you to settle the child into your care, especially if you are not caring for them in their own home.

Keys to good practice

There are many routines for babies and children that are important to their care and well-being, for example:

- care of skin, teeth and hair
- nappy changing, toileting
- feeding and mealtimes, including weaning
- cleaning/sterilising of feeding equipment
- prevention of infection
- sleep and rest, settling
- hand washing, bathing
- personal hygiene.

It is very important that you follow the best possible practice when planning your routines.

If you have any doubt about your practices, make sure that you find out how you can improve your routines. There are many sources of information available, such as leaflets at your health centre, articles in professional journals and textbooks on care, websites on the Internet and talking to health care professionals.

Think about it

What do you do if the care routines of the parents do not meet good professional practice?

Firstly, and of great importance, you will have to talk to the parents about why they want you to do things in a certain way or at a certain time. They may, for example, want to start toilet training before a child is ready, because another baby is expected and they do not want to have two children in nappies. Another request might be to stop a child having a daytime rest or sleep, so that the child will go to bed earlier at night.

These situations can be difficult to handle and whilst you have to consider parents' wishes, you must remember that the child's needs and well-being are paramount. Good communication and positive relationships with parents are critical in situations like this and should avoid misunderstandings.

How to promote the health and physical development of children in a home-based setting

In order to be able to promote health and physical development it is important to understand what we actually mean by these terms.

All aspects of a child's health and physical development can be met through appropriate activities and experiences; some will need forethought, structure and planning, such as diet and healthy eating; others will be carried out in spontaneous, unstructured ways, both indoors and outside. Most activities and experiences will cover a range of physical developmental areas, for example a four-year-old riding a tricycle is developing balance, coordination and gross motor skills; whereas a seven-year-old on a computer is developing hand–eye coordination and fine motor skills.

Find out!

Spend some time watching the children in your care, both individually and in groups, and both indoors and outside.

Can you identify which physical skills are being developed through their activities and experiences?

All children develop at different rates and sometimes it can be helpful to compare children's development to developmental milestones.

Key Term

Developmental milestones (or norms) are quantitative measurements that provide typical values and variations in height, weight and skill acquisition. These can also be referred to as norms.

However, whilst developmental milestones are valued because they give us some indication of what a child should be doing at a certain age, such as the fact that a baby can smile at six weeks, or a five-year-old has good control of a pencil, they do not take different rates of development into consideration and any factors that may affect a child's development such as illness or genetic influences.

As mentioned several times already, all children are unique, with individual differences and needs,

so in order to promote the health and physical development of the children in your care you must take this into consideration.

Keys to good practice

Before you plan any activities or experiences with the children you need to ask yourself the following questions.

1 Have I thought about this child's age? Is this appropriate or am I expecting too much? For example, is it realistic to expect a two-year-old to wash their hands without supervision?

2 Have I thought about this child's experience? For example, is it unrealistic to expect a fifteen-month-old child to drink from a cup when they have had only a bottle in the past?

3 Have I thought about this child's skills and abilities? For example, should I insist, for safety reasons, that a seven-year-old rides a bike with stabilisers when they clearly have good balance and coordination skills?

4 Have I thought about this child's specific needs, including gender, cultural and religious issues? For example, have I got sun cream to protect the child's skin when outside (with parental permission to apply it), have I made a picnic that takes allergies into account and religious dietary needs, can I provide privacy for a teenage girl when she needs to use the bathroom?

It is not possible to cover all stages of physical development from 0 to 16 years within the scope of this book. The chart below is provided only as an approximate guide. It is suggested that you research further into this aspect of children's development, looking in textbooks that have been written specifically on child development.

Approximate age	Main features
Newborn	Primitive reflexes should be present. Moves legs less often than arms. Sucks vigorously. Sleeps for about 21 out of 24 hours.
Six weeks	Can lift head. Will follow a moving object with eyes for a few seconds. Looks into space when awake. Limb movements still uncoordinated. Still spends most of time asleep or drowsing. *Six-week-old baby*
Three to five months	Waves arms in controlled manner. Kicks and pushes feet against a firm surface. Can roll from back to side. Can hold head steadily. Watches hands and fingers, clasps hands. When lying on stomach can lift head and pushes upwards with arms. Sleeps for about 16 hours a day.
Six to eight months	Can sit with support for long periods and for short periods without support. Can grasp using whole hand (palmar grasp). Takes every object to the mouth. Arms move purposefully. Can roll from back to stomach. Can pull themselves into a standing position if helped. Hands and eyes are coordinated. First tooth may appear. Practises making different sounds.
Nine to eleven months	Very active, rolls and wriggles, begins to crawl or shuffle. Can reach sitting position without help. Can pick up objects with first finger and thumb (pincer grasp). Top lateral incisors may appear. Sleeps for about 14 hours each day. *Nine-month-old baby*

Approximate age	Main features
Twelve to fourteen months	Can pull themselves into a standing position. May walk around furniture. May walk with adult support or independently. Can crawl or shuffle very quickly. Can hold a cup. Points and can put small objects into a container. Uses hands and eyes to explore objects rather than mouth.
Fifteen to seventeen months	Restless and active. Stands alone. Can walk unaided. Can kneel. Can go upstairs on hands and knees. Can build a tower of two blocks. Can make marks with crayons. Can feed themselves with finger foods, tries to use spoon.
Eighteen to twenty-one months	Walks fairly well, can push and pull toys when walking, can walk backwards. Can come down stairs with adult help. Squats and bends from waist to pick up objects. Canine teeth may erupt.
Two years	Can run, kick a ball from a standing position, climbs on furniture. Uses a spoon to feed themselves. Can zip and unzip larger zippers. Can draw circles and dots. Will build a tower of five or six blocks. Begins to use preferred hand. Begins to develop bowel and bladder control. *Two-year-old child*
Three years	Walks and runs with confidence, can walk on tiptoes, can throw and kick a ball. Jumps off low steps. Can pedal and steer a tricycle. Washes and dries hands with help. Can put on and take off some items of clothing independently. Turns pages in a book independently. Can use scissors. By the end of the third year usually has a full set of milk teeth.
Four years	Can walk on a line, hop on one foot. Bounces and catches a large ball. Runs changing direction. Buttons and unbuttons own clothing. Can cut out simple shapes.

Approximate age	Main features
Five years	Skips with a rope. Can form letters, writes own name. Dresses and undresses independently. Can complete a 20-piece jigsaw. Can hit a ball with a bat. Begins to lose milk teeth. *Five-year-old child*
Six to seven years	Active and energetic. Enjoys using large play apparatus. Moves to music with understanding. Can use a bicycle without stabilisers. Hops, skips and jumps with confidence. Kicks a ball with direction. Balances on a beam or wall. Handwriting is evenly spaced.
Eight to eleven years	Greater agility and control. All physical activities carried out with poise, coordination and precision. General health is usually good, appetite is good and food is enjoyed. Energy levels can suddenly drop so may need a short rest and food, but usually recovers quickly. Girls may be starting the process of adolescence.
Twelve years plus	Boys may begin the process of adolescence. Girls' periods have usually started and by 16 are, as a rule, regular. Boys usually grow much taller than girls and may become less coordinated at times. Boys usually stronger than girls. Diet and exercise very important.

The safety and equality issues involved in physical development

Risk and challenge are essential aspects of physical development. Any activity that a child does, whether indoors or outside, has an element of risk, even something as simple as playing with play dough. For example, a child might have an allergic reaction to the flour, or choke if a piece gets stuck in their throat.

It is important that you understand the risks involved in any activity and can balance these out against the benefits to the child and the safety of the child. This is often referred to as risk assessment. Risk assessment is an ongoing activity for all childcare practitioners. Registered childminders must meet minimum standards of care and the safety of their home will be assessed by Ofsted (see Unit 1).

NCMA has produced a risk assessment checklist specifically designed to be used by nannies in the home. A copy of this is reproduced in Unit 1 on page 4.

There is the danger that home-based childcarers may interpret risk assessment as not allowing the children to do anything that might compromise their safety. So think about:

- the dangers of riding a tricycle

- the dangers of climbing up a frame in the garden

- the dangers of using scissors.

Taking risks that provide opportunities to explore and experiment with skills is part of a child's natural development. You must balance risks against the rewards, then judge whether or not an activity is worth doing.

Well-organised and planned environments in which you have overall control will minimise risks whilst giving children freedom to develop, explore and try out new skills. You should give children opportunities to develop their physical skills with adult support but minimal intervention. It is important to think about the use of the space that is available to you when you plan activities to develop gross motor skills – have you got the room indoors for children to run, hop, skip and jump? If not then you will need to take children to a local park, the garden, or a sports centre. You will also need to think about the safety of the equipment that you or the parents provide (see Unit 1).

It is important that you discuss safety rules or boundaries with children so that they understand the possible risks.

Link to assessment

E5 Discuss how you promote children's safety.

Hint

Look again at Unit 1 at the section on establishing a safe and healthy environment on page 2.

Write about what you actually do to ensure that all children are safe and how you make sure that you are a positive role model. Think about the differing needs of children of different ages and how you can provide safe and appropriate resources and equipment. Think about your risk assessment procedures, how you develop and establish rules for safety with the children.

Some children may need additional encouragement to explore their physical skills. This could be because they have an illness, injury or medical condition that limits their movements and strength. You may also have to consider the needs of over-anxious parents who may have restricted their child's attempts at exploration.

Case Study

The family that Bea, a nanny, works for bought a set of outdoor play equipment for their two boys. Bea was concerned that the boys might be at risk if they jumped from the top section of the climbing frame, especially as there was only grass underneath. Bea discussed this problem with the parents, telling them that a proper safety surface was needed under the play equipment, and they agreed to organise this. Bea also discussed the safety and risks of play equipment with the boys, explaining why a proper safety surface was needed. They agreed that they would not jump from the top and talked about other things that they could safely do.

Case Study

Chris cares for three children in their home. The eldest child, a girl, Jade, is ten years old. When Chris meets her from school Jade tells Chris that she has been picked for the school football team and is clearly very excited. However, when Chris tells Jade's parents they are horrified that their daughter is going to be playing football at this level.

Why might the parents be feeling this way?

How can Chris consider the wishes of the parents while at the same time meeting the needs of Jade?

Children should have opportunities to develop physical skills at every stage of their development. As they grow and develop children might begin to show gender preferences, for example a boy might not want to dance if he feels it is too 'girly', and girls may not want to play football because they think it is a boys' game. It is very important that you are a positive role model and can discourage these stereotypes.

The principles of providing a healthy, balanced and appropriate diet

The quality of a child's diet is crucial at all times during their life. Childhood eating patterns and habits determine adult food tastes in later life and the body's metabolic rate. It is a well-established fact that overweight adults who were overweight as children find it very difficult to lose weight compared to those who where relatively thin as children.

Children who are undernourished, that is, those who do not get enough to eat, and those who do not have a balanced diet and are malnourished, can show many signs of developmental delay. Food provides children with energy, which helps them to grow and develop.

It is very important that you talk to the parents before you start to plan food and meals for the children in your care. There could be cultural, medical and religious reasons why children do not

Keys to good practice

There are eight basic guidelines for a healthy diet.

1   Eat a variety of foods.

2   Eat the right amount to maintain a healthy weight.

3   Eat plenty of food that is rich in fibre and starch.

4   Eat plenty of vegetables and fruit.

5   Reduce your intake of fatty foods.

6   Reduce the number of times that you consume food or drinks that are high in sugar.

7   Enjoy your food.

8   This final guideline does not apply to children – limit your intake of alcohol.

eat some foods and you must respect the wishes of the parents. The chart at the end of this book shows you some of the customs and religious practices associated with food (page 295).

In order for the body to grow and develop it requires nutrients, of which there are five types. These are shown in the table below.

Nutrient	Examples of food it is found in	Benefits and guidelines for intake
Fats	Dairy products Meat Fish Vegetable oils	Help to provide the body with energy, but only moderate amounts are required to maintain a healthy diet.
Proteins	Meat Fish Dairy products Soya Vegetables	Help the body to grow and helps with healing.
Vitamins	Most fresh food products Fruit Vegetables	Vitamins are essential to all types of growth and development, for example Vitamin C, found in fruit, is required for wound healing, and may prevent chronic heart disease and some forms of cancer.

Nutrient	Examples of food it is found in	Benefits and guidelines for intake
Carbohydrates	Bread Potatoes Bananas Vegetables	Provide energy. When adults want to lose weight they often cut out carbohydrates from their diet, which could explain why many dieters complain of feeling tired.
Mineral elements	Like vitamins, found in many foods. For example calcium is found in dairy products; iron is found in red meat and some green vegetables.	Calcium needed for healthy teeth. Lack of iron can lead to anaemia, where people lack energy and are pale.

Think about it

In Victorian England, many children had limited diets and developed a bone disease called rickets. It was found that vitamin D, which is present in dairy products and fish, helped the body to develop strong bones and teeth, so by giving children milk to drink doctors were able to eliminate rickets.

Listed below are the five main food groups, which, when eaten in the correct proportions, will provide the types of food required for a healthy diet.

1   Bread, other cereals and potatoes.

2   Fruit and vegetables – it is recommended that we eat five portions of fruit and vegetables each day.

3   Milk and dairy foods.

4   Meat, fish and organic alternatives, for example pulses.

5   Foods containing fat and/or sugar.

Recommended daily intake of foods from each of the main groups

There is much debate over the safety of some foods, such as beef products, genetically modified products and chemical additives. Many food products contain added salt or sugar, so it is always good practice to read the nutritional information on food labels as you shop.

You will clearly have your own opinion as to those matters and what you feed yourself and members of your own family, but you should discuss these issues with the parents of the children in your care and respect their views. Nannies may not do shopping for the children or the family, but it is still very important that you discuss with the parents what foods are given to the children.

You want the children in your care to develop and grow in a healthy way, understanding which foods are good for them and which are not. A good starting point is to think about your own eating habits. What sort of role model are you and what are your attitudes towards food? If you are always eating while you rush about, rather than sitting down to eat a meal in a calm and relaxed way, the children in your care will believe that this is an acceptable way to eat, which you know is not the case.

Think about it

In 2004 the celebrity chef Jamie Oliver began a campaign to improve the quality of school meals offered to children. This campaign met with opposition from children, staff and parents in its early stages, but gradually, and with the help of the media, he was able to change eating habits in schools for the better. In 2005 the government increased the amount of money available to provide healthier school meals and in September 2005 Ruth Kelly, the Minister of State for Education, announced limits on the levels of salt in school meals, and a new bill focusing on the quality of school meals went before parliament in November 2005.

Some experts in children's care believe that young children should be offered small meals and snacks throughout the day rather than just three large meals per day. Snacks can be just as good for children as normal meals, provided that what you give the children is good for them. Pieces of fresh fruit, raw vegetables and certain types of cracker are healthy snacks. Remember that you must always be aware of possible allergic reactions to certain foods, such as nuts, milk, gluten or sugar.

The importance of ensuring that children have opportunities for physical activity and rest appropriate to their stage of development

All children need time to rest and recover from physical activity, doing so through rest and sleep. Often, the level of physical activity will determine the amount of rest that is required. Rest does not have to be in a bed or asleep, and for older children in particular it can just be sitting down watching television, a DVD, listening to music or reading a book. When a child sleeps, growth hormones which are essential for development are released through the pituitary gland.

When we are deprived of sleep and/or rest our body functions are impaired. Lack of sleep affects energy, concentration levels, memory, and can cause mood swings. Sometimes an overtired child will appear listless, with their skin tone and condition being affected as well as their appetite. Extreme sleep deprivation can lead to brain damage.

When and how long a child needs to sleep or rest will depend on their age and individual needs. Babies and young children seem to follow their own inbuilt body clock by taking rest as and when they need it. It is very important that you discuss with parents how you can meet this need, especially if you are caring for other children. For example, some parents are quite happy for their young child to sleep in a buggy while you collect others from school, while some may insist that their child sleeps in a cot in a quiet room.

Newborn babies spend a lot of time asleep, sometimes up to 21 hours out of 24. By the time that they have reached three months or so they may have developed a sleep pattern; they may

Sleep and rest are vital for development

sleep through the night and have a morning and afternoon sleep, especially after being fed. As babies become more physically active they still need to sleep or nap during the day, although some babies may have reduced their need for sleep during the day by the time they are one year old. However, they may have periods of time when they are less active and are essentially resting.

Most five-year-olds need at least 12 hours of sleep each day. This does not necessarily mean that they will sleep for twelve hours in one go, but may nap during the day, especially after coming back from school. Some parents may discourage this type of napping because they may feel that their child will not be ready for bed in the evening. However, an overtired child can be just as difficult to settle as a child who has napped during the day.

Some children find it difficult to nap during the day so it is important that you build into your daily routine opportunities for a child to play in a relaxed and restful way, such as reading, drawing, watching television or listening to music.

Older children may become more tired as their school day changes, for instance when they move from primary to secondary school. They may have to adapt to a more formal curriculum, more teachers, and different pressures. While it is important to ensure that adolescents have opportunities to exercise they also need times for relaxation and rest as well as a regular sleep pattern at night.

Case Study

Branwen is 14 years old, and is preparing for GCSEs at school. On weekdays she gets home at around 5pm with her two siblings. The nanny usually suggests a snack to be eaten together before all of the children begin their homework. They eat their evening meal with their parents and/or nanny at around 7.30pm, after which Branwen continues with her coursework until bedtime (both parents are doctors and work shifts).

How can the nanny ensure that Branwen gets opportunities to rest and relax during the week, whilst at the same time meeting Branwen's need to complete her coursework and respect her need for independence?

How to recognise children's illnesses and how to deal with children who become ill whilst in your care

Children and babies who are unwell or sick have exactly the same needs as healthy children, as well as additional needs. It is important that you understand how to meet these additional needs. As part of the registration process for registered childminders, you will have had first-aid training. It is good practice for all nannies to undertake a specialised first-aid course. Both nannies and registered childminders must ensure that they keep this training up to date.

Working with parents

In all aspects of your childcare practices you are working in partnership with the parents, helping the children in your care to develop and grow in a healthy and safe environment. Together you want to ensure that the children are in reasonable health.

One way you can do this is to support the children's parents in the maintenance of regular health screening programmes and developmental checks for their children. Encourage them to keep the appointments and share the information with you. If you take the children to these appointments it is essential that you make sure any important information is passed on to the parents.

Children can often become unwell or sick with very little warning, and parents can leave their child with you in the morning but by lunchtime the child could be unwell. In most cases children and babies who are sick need to be with their main carer in their own home, if possible. Sometimes this can be a source of guilt and anxiety for parents and can sometimes cause conflict between the employers of parents, the parents and yourself.

One way that you can reduce any possible conflict is to make sure that in your contract of services you cover circumstances when children and babies are sick or unwell.

Registered childminders may want to remind parents that the terms and conditions of their registration do not allow them to care for children who have an infectious illness. You also have a responsibility to the other children in your care to make sure that you provide a safe and healthy environment. If you find out that a child in your care has developed an infectious disease, you must inform the parents of all the other children.

Keys to good practice

You may want to include the following points in your contract.

- You must be able to contact the parents at all times.

- If the parents are not able to collect their sick child from your home, or get home to support you, they must make alternative arrangements.

- You are not able to give permission for any treatment to be given to a child.

- You have the final decision to decide not to care for a child, if this means that the health of other children could be at risk, especially if you are a registered childminder.

Caring for children who are unwell

Your first-aid kit should include a children's thermometer. One of the first things you should do if a child is feeling or looking unwell is to take their temperature. It is also very important that you make contact with the parents as soon as possible.

There are several types of thermometer available:

- digital thermometers, which are easy to read

- fever strips, which change colour

- mercury thermometers, which can be difficult to read.

It is a matter of personal preference which one you use, but make sure than you can read it correctly.

Normal body temperature is 37°C, so a temperature above this should indicate the body is fighting an infection. A child with a high temperature has an increased risk of convulsions so you should help the child to get rid of the additional heat.

Signs and symptoms of minor ailments

It is not possible to cover all the signs and symptoms of each and every childhood ailment in a book like this. Whilst there are obvious general signs, such as raised body temperature, flushed appearance, rash, or sickness and diarrhoea, each child is unique and can display a wide range of signs and symptoms. There is always the danger that you could jump to the wrong conclusions about a child because they are showing certain symptoms. On the other hand, the opposite could be true, you could decide not to act because the child is not showing certain symptoms. The parents know their child best and you should use this knowledge, together with your own professional knowledge of the child, to decide what course of action you need to take.

This is where it is essential that you have an up-to-date first-aid qualification.

Remember

- Keep calm.
- Inform the parents.
- Deal with what you can actually see or know, not what you think you can see or think you know.
- If in doubt seek medical help.
- Keep your first-aid qualification up to date.

Find out!

Medical centres and doctors' surgeries are invaluable sources of information because many health authorities provide leaflets and booklets about the signs and symptoms of common childhood ailments, more serious diseases such as meningitis, and information about health screening programmes and immunisation programmes.

Next time you are in a medical centre or surgery have a look at what information is available.

Ways of helping children learn how to keep themselves safe and healthy

The most effective way of helping children learn how to keep themselves safe and healthy is by your own positive example.

Children need to learn independence, confidence, how to evaluate risks while considering their safety and the safety of those around them. While you will strive to maintain a safe and healthy environment for the children in your care, you must, as discussed earlier, provide opportunities for challenges and risk-taking. For example, children can make their own sandwiches, but they should be shown how to use knives correctly and be supervised.

Think about it

Children will learn good hygiene practices from you, so it is important that you set a good example.

- Do you cover your mouth when you cough and then wash your hands?
- Do you wash your hands after handling money?
- Do you dispose of leftover food in a safe and hygienic way?

How you answer the above questions might make you think about the messages that you are giving to the children in your care.

Safety and healthy practices are part of the Personal, Social and Health Education (PSHE) curriculum in schools. Teachers encourage the children to learn about how to prevent the spread of infections, personal hygiene, drug abuse and sex education.

How can you help older children to develop greater understanding of some of the topics covered in their PSHE classes?

How can you support a three-year-old to blow their nose on a tissue, then dispose of it correctly before washing their hands?

How children learn

Learning is an individual process for everyone. You may remember being in school, in a class with others of the same age and all being taught the same thing. Some of the class will learn what was being taught the first time, some will need to go away and think about it, others will have to ask questions and some may need to be taught the same thing again in a different way. A few will never really learn what was being taught. The way that the teacher will find out if any learning has taken place will be to test the class in some way. We all have different learning styles and preferences, and these will be discussed in more detail in Unit 5.

Learning does not just take place in schools, it can happen in any situation and at any age. Learning is not only about cognitive or intellectual growth and development. These areas are a fundamental part of learning, but not all of it. Physical development, controlling and coordinating movement is a form of learning. Knowing how to act and behave in certain places and situations is part of social development, but is also learning. Understanding how to talk and communicate with others is a form of learning.

Children's learning is often referred to as cognitive, or intellectual development. It includes:

- memory skills, both long and short term
- attention and concentration skills
- perception skills, about how children use the information around them
- sensory development of sight, hearing, touch, taste and smell, but these are also linked to physical development.

Whilst the table below gives a brief overview of cognitive development following Piaget's theory, it is important to recognise that there are other approaches and you should look in other books on child development to expand and develop your knowledge.

Stage	Approximate age	Main characteristics
Sensori-motor	Birth to two years	Development of object permanence. Begins to use language and symbols to express thought.
Pre-operational	Two to seven years	Uses symbols in play and thought. Egocentric. Cannot conserve.
Concrete operational	Seven to eleven years	Can conserve. Begin to solve mental problems using practical aides such as counters, objects, etc.
Formal operations	Eleven to fifteen years	Can think about situations that they have not experienced. Can play with ideas in their minds.

There are many theories and points of view on how children learn. In general they fall into three categories.

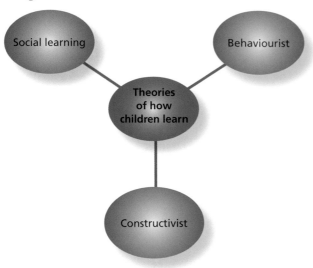

Theories of how children learn

1 **Behaviourist theories** suggest that children learn by making links between their actions and what happens next. This is also known as *association*. An example of this is a young child who learns that by pressing a certain button on a toy something will happen, such as a sound being heard, or something popping up. In the same way a child will learn when they get a good reaction for doing certain things, such as praise and smiles from the adult, and they will do it again. In contrast, this way of learning can also have negative associations, for example if a young child has had an unpleasant or hurtful experience with a doctor wearing a white coat, they might associate being upset and hurt with anyone who wears a white coat.

Advertisers and retailers use association to entice us to buy things. For example, the smell of freshly baked bread in a supermarket may make you think of something pleasant or feel hungry, so you go and buy bread.

For more on behaviourism, see the Find out! feature on page 143.

2 **Constructivist theories** take the idea that rather than children learning because of things happening to them, they learn from exploring, doing things for themselves and then building on those experiences. This is often referred to as learning from first-hand experiences. The theorist Jean Piaget (1896–1980) developed this theory. He suggested that children explore, play and collect information about the world around them. When presented with new experiences they use what they already know to build and develop new ideas and learn. This works in the following way.

• Assume that you always give a toddler in your care milk to drink in a yellow cup.

• The child learns that all yellow cups have milk in them. This happens every day so the idea is firmly established.

• One day you put water in the yellow cup, so the idea that all yellow cups have milk in them does not work.

• The child now learns that yellow cups can have both milk and water in them. Eventually the child will learn that there are many different drinks and many different colours and sizes of cups.

The main point of this theory is that the child has learnt new ideas for themselves through first-hand experience, and not as a result of something happening to them. If you are a driver, you learnt to drive by first-hand experience. You learnt how to reverse around a corner, for example by doing it yourself, not by watching someone else doing it.

Find out!

Find more about Jean Piaget and especially how his work has influenced the research of Martin Hughes, Margaret Donaldson and Chris Athey in understanding the ways in which children learn.

Find put more about the constructivist theories of Jerome Bruner (born 1915) and Lev Vygotsky (1896–1934), and the current research of V Das Gupta.

Ivan Pavlov (1849–1936) developed the theory of classical conditioning, in which an automatic response can be triggered by repeated exposure to a stimulus or stimuli.

Pavlov noticed that dogs produced saliva (a response) when food (a stimulus) was placed in front of them. After repeated trials he was able to make the dogs salivate upon hearing a bell being rung, which they associated with the food. It was an automatic, or conditioned, response that would happen whether or not food was put in front of the dogs.

They had learnt to associate the sound of the bell with food.

A teacher might clap their hands and say 'tidy up time' to get the children to respond. After a while the teacher will only have to clap their hands to make the children respond by tidying up.

Find out about B. F. Skinner's theory of reinforcement and ways that you can use this theory to help children develop their verbal language skills.

Find out about the research of David Premack and the use of rewards.

Food arrives when the bell has rung.

After some time the dog associates food with the bell ringing and salivates ready to eat. This is a conditioned response.

Pavlov's classical conditioning

3   **Social learning theories** build upon the ideas of association and behaviourist theories, but also consider that children learn from watching other people. This explains why children

copy and learn from adults. If you are playing alongside a child and start making a tower with a construction set, the child will often copy you and make a tower as well. Children will often copy adult mannerisms, such as the way they walk, or their gestures. Children also learn negative things from others, such as bad language, prejudiced attitudes and unacceptable behaviour. This makes you realise how important it is for children to have good role models.

In order to meet the developmental needs of the children in your care it is important that you have an understanding of how children learn. This way you will be able to plan and provide activities and experiences that are developmentally appropriate and which will meet individual needs.

The ways that children learn are still hotly debated amongst educationalists, psychologists and childcare practitioners, but it is generally accepted that in order for learning to take place the child needs the support of a sensitive adult.

The significance of children's sensory experiences

The development of the senses is an important part of how children learn. Piaget named the first stage of his theory of cognitive development the **sensori-motor stage** because children use their senses to provide information for the brain. Babies and young children explore and learn about their environment through their senses. Babies put objects in their mouths in order to explore shape, feel and texture as the mouth is very sensitive and can send messages to the brain about the object being examined. Many children and adults have to hold something in their hands in order 'to see' it properly, the sense of touch being an important way to send information to the brain.

Sensory information that is sent to the brain helps children to stay attentive and to concentrate. Multi-sensory activities, those in which children can use sight, smell, hearing and touch, can be very effective in helping children develop concentration skills and how to differentiate between experiences. A meal with others, for example, can be a valuable multi-sensory experience for all children.

Heuristic and treasure basket play provides excellent opportunities for sensory development. This type of play is designed to stimulate a baby's and young child's concentration and exploration. In addition, curiosity is stimulated and children develop an understanding of the properties of different materials as well as developing fine motor skills and hand–eye coordination.

Toddlers and older pre-school children can explore natural objects through heuristic play. You will need to provide a range of clean tins in various sizes, boxes, cartons, tubes, plastic bottles, chains, and other natural everyday objects that children can fit together, put inside each other, make different sounds and carry around.

Sand, water, clay and dough are also play materials that will promote sensory development. 'Gloop' – cornflour and water – has a unique texture and feel and encourages exploration.

Play with a treasure basket provides excellent opportunities for sensory development

Find out!

Look at the Birth to Three Matters Framework – A competent learner (green cards), in particular the component on making connections. Read what it suggests for heuristic play.

explorations with the senses. Through treasure basket play, for example, a baby can begin to predict, anticipate and control situations, all important beginnings of creativity.

As children become more mobile they express their creativity in more physical ways and verbal sounds. They dance, respond and move to music and rhythms, create 2-D and 3-D shapes and models, act, pretend and mime, and talk about and share their experiences and activities.

How children develop imagination and creativity

Imagination could be described as making mental images or pictures and is an important aspect of developing the ability to become a symbol user. We need to be able to use symbols in order to read and write.

Babies show imagination in the ways that they respond to people and the world around them. They imitate and copy facial expressions, movements and sounds, especially of their main carers. Playing imitative games such as 'round and round the garden' will help develop imagination.

From about eighteen months imaginative play seems to come almost naturally to toddlers and young children. They imitate adult actions, such as putting a teddy to bed, or talking on a telephone. Children recreate their recent learning to develop a sense of control, within which they can safely explore and express feelings, both negative and positive.

Older children can use role-play and acting to repeat events in their lives, express complex feelings and emotions, and to develop and understand relationships.

Creativity is an individual response, it brings into existence new ideas and new and different ways of doing things. Creativity is much more than just painting, dancing or responding to music, although these can be important aspects of creativity.

Creativity in babies begins through their relationships with people and non-verbal communications. It also begins through

Keys to good practice

In order for imagination and creativity to develop, babies and children need a supportive adult who can:

- provide a rich range of materials

- provide a range of experiences which stimulate and interest

- encourage them to explore, make decisions and choices

- provide personal space to develop their own ideas

- balance the need for exploration with the need to keep children safe

- communicate effectively, giving full attention and eye contact

- be sensitive to children's moods and interests.

Think about it

Look at the Birth to Three Matters Framework – A competent learner (green cards), in particular the component on being creative. Read the section on challenges and dilemmas and reflect on your response to children's paintings.

The importance of developing attention span and memory

Memory and attention are fundamental components of how children learn.

Think about it

Short-term memory

Short-term memory is used to process information quickly, and psychologists believe that it only lasts for about 15 seconds. Researchers believe that this can be extended through rehearsal, or repeating something several times. Young children are not capable of rehearsal which is why they often quickly forget instructions.

Long-term memory

Long-term memory allows us to process information that we may not need immediately and then retrieve it at a later date.

Babies remember sensory experiences such as hearing their mother's voice and know that she will feed or comfort them. They will also remember the smell and touch of their mother or main carer and will learn that this person will meet their needs. Later, babies will remember and repeat sounds that they have heard and so begin to develop verbal communication skills.

We can help a child to develop memory skills by sensitive questioning to encourage them to remember events, experiences and activities. Often asking a child how they felt will help them to recall something because emotions will trigger a memory. Asking open-ended questions such as 'What happened next?' will help children learn to sequence and order events.

Attention and concentration are skills that the brain uses to focus on specific information and so filter out distractions such as noise and smells. This does not mean that we can only direct our attention to one single activity, for example we need to multitask when changing a nappy because the baby can concentrate on the adults facial expressions, verbal interchanges and enjoy the sensation of freedom.

If a child cannot concentrate for periods of time they will not be able to store information long enough to process it and will therefore not learn how to interpret their sensory experiences in order to learn new skills and knowledge.

Think about it

Attention Deficit Hyperactivity Disorder (ADHD)

Children with ADHD find it difficult to concentrate and can be disruptive or impulsive. It affects between three and five per cent of children. Some medical childcare practitioners and families believe that ADHD is linked to the use of chemicals and additives in food and so put children on special diets. The drug Ritalin can be given to children with ADHD, but it is a depressive, and although widely used in America, its long-term effects have not been monitored.

How children develop the understanding of mathematical and scientific concepts

Through their senses babies and children are learning mathematical and scientific concepts from the moment of birth. For example, they feel hot or cold and so begin to develop an understanding of temperature.

The development of scientific and mathematical concepts is an essential part of how a child makes sense of the world in which they live. Children will develop these concepts more effectively when they are with childcare practitioners who support them by positive encouragement and praise, and help them learn from exploration and making mistakes. Children need a wide range of practical experiences, activities and opportunities to help them develop their skills. They need to do things for themselves, and learning through first-hand experiences is one of the most effective ways that children learn.

The charts below show some of the key mathematical and scientific concepts that children learn during the early years.

Case Study

Javid, aged 8 years, is struggling to build a complicated robot figure, but is concentrating and is not distressed. His home-based childcarer asks him if he wants help, Javid shakes his head and continues to work out for himself how the pieces connect. It takes him longer on his own but when it is completed he is excited and rewarded by lots of praise and smiles by the childcarer.

Mathematical concept	Suggested activities
Pattern	Sewing cards, threading beads, jigsaw puzzles.
Colour	Sorting items into colours, painting and colour mixing.
Space	Jigsaw puzzles, moving freely around a large space with several other children.
Speed	Riding tricycles and bicycles, walking, running, talking with children about how slow or fast they are moving.
Time	Use egg timers to indicate the passage of time for younger children, routines, setting timers, talking about daily events, e.g. bedtime, lunchtime.
Shape	Contruction sets, modelling with recycled materials.
Volume and capacity	Water and sand play, language associated with, e.g. empty, full.
Length and height	Language associated with, e.g. tall, small, long, short. Construction sets, measuring with non-specific units such as hand spans.
Number	Counting, setting a table for a meal, songs, rhymes and stories, recognition of telephone numbers, car registration numbers.
Mass	Cooking, handling objects, talking about size and weight, stories, books and rhymes, e.g. Goldilocks and the three bears.
Temperature	Talking about the weather, different clothing, cooking, mealtimes.
Opposites	Stories, rhymes and songs, talking about and finding opposites, e.g. big/little items, under/over or on top of.
Symbolic representation	Understanding that letters and numbers have meaning can be developed through reading books together and talking about the signs and symbols around us.

All these concepts can be developed through play activities and routine daily events in a home setting. For example, setting the table for four people could include counting, sorting, patterns and mathematical language such as more, less, same, above, next to.

Scientific concepts	Suggested activities
Prediction	Ask open-ended questions, e.g. 'What do you think will happen if we mix blue and yellow paint?', 'What do you think will happen if we put this water in the freezer?'
Observation	Provide children with magnifying glasses so that they can look at things in detail. Talk about everyday events, things around them and the weather, e.g. 'Have you noticed how the spider web in the garden is covered with raindrops?', 'Have you watched the patterns of the rain running down the windows?'
Exploration	Provide children with toys that they can take apart and put back together to see how they work, provide a range of materials which stimulate the senses, e.g. wet and dry sand, shaving foam, treasure baskets
Problem solving	Ask open-ended questions, set up activities that encourage the children to work things out for themselves, e.g. construction and modelling sets, computer games.
Critical thinking	Ask open-ended questions that will encourage a child to think about their play in different ways, e.g. 'What would happen if you…'
Decision making	Lead on from problem solving and critical thinking, do not do everything for the child, let them make their own decisions, and mistakes; one way that children learn is through trial and error.
Discussion	Talk, talk and more talk, involve yourself in what the children are doing, do not dominate but use sensitive questioning to stimulate and extend the play.

Again, all of these concepts can be developed through play and routine events and activities.

Think about it

Think about a cooking activity that you do with children in your care. Look at the list of scientific concepts.

How many of these concepts can be developed through your cooking activity?

Social and emotional development

What is social development?

Social development is about learning how to be with other people, how to build relationships, make friends and understand who you are. It is also about knowing how to look after yourself, such as using a toilet independently or getting dressed. These skills are often referred to as self-help skills and generally involve aspects of physical development. Children who have difficulty with language and communication tend to have problems developing relationships with others.

What is emotional development?

Emotional development is about how children learn to deal with and express their feelings. It is also about how children learn to bond with their carers, or make strong relationships with important adults. This area of development also includes the development of self-confidence, self-control, self-image and self-esteem.

It is quite difficult to separate emotional development from social development as aspects of one affect the other. Sometimes

A toddler can sometimes be quite obstinate!

problems with emotional development can be far-reaching and have a long-lasting effect; unfortunately, in some people, lasting into adulthood.

The chart below gives an overview of emotional and social development. It is important that you research these aspects of a child's development to develop your knowledge and understanding.

Approximate age	Main features
Newborn	Seems most content when in close contact with mother or main carer. Needs to develop a strong bond or attachment.
Six weeks	Seems to sense presence of mother/main carer. Responds to human voice. Watches primary carer's face. Can swing rapidly from pleasure to unhappiness.
Three to five months	Smiles and shows pleasure. Enjoys being held and cuddled. Still has rapid mood swings.
Six to eight months	May show anxiety towards strangers. Eager and interested in everything that is going on around them. Laughs, chuckles and vocalises when with mother or familiar people, generally friendly. Shows anger when a plaything is removed but is easily distracted.
Nine to eleven months	Can distinguish between familiar people and strangers. Will show annoyance and anger through body movements. Begins to play peek-a-boo games. Begins to wait for attention.

Approximate age	Main features
Twelve to fourteen months	Affectionate towards family members and primary carers. Plays simple games. Growing independence can lead to rage when thwarted. Mood swings less violent. Shows little fear and much curiosity.
Fifteen to seventeen months	Emotionally more unstable than at one year. Can show jealousy. Swings from being independent to dependent on an adult. Has more sense of being an individual.
Eighteen to twenty-one months	Can be obstinate and unwilling to follow adult suggestions. Very curious, but short attention span. Mood swings.
Two years	Shows self-will and may have tantrums, nightmares and irrational fears. Tries to be independent. Has strong emotions. Copies adult actions and activities. Parallel play and begins to engage in pretend play.
Three years	Becomes more cooperative, adopts attitude and moods of adults. Wants adult approval. Asks lots of questions. Shows concern for others. Begins to share playthings.
Four years	Confident, shows purpose and persistence. Shows control over emotions. Has adopted standards of behaviour of parents and family members. Develops friendships with peers.
Five years	Self-confident. Shows desire to do well and will persevere at a new task. Still seeks adult approval. Shows good control of emotions. Cooperative play with both boys and girls, usually has a best friend. Enjoys stories of strong people.
Six to seven years	Emotions can be more unstable than at five, can be moody. Independent and may be solitary for short periods. Father's or male authority not usually questioned. Teacher's standards often accepted over mother's standards.
Eight to eleven	Emotionally independent of adults. Need to be accepted by peers. Usually good control of emotions. Intolerant of weak adults. Enjoys team games. Towards the end of this period sexes begin to socialise separately.
Twelve plus	A time of great change as moving from childhood to adulthood. Can be a time of pressure to gain qualifications, fit in with peers, experiment, take risks and face challenges. Still needs meaningful praise and to know that they are valued.

The importance of the development of self-image and self-esteem

Self-esteem is how we see ourselves. It has three basic features.

- **Worth and significance** – children need to feel accepted, loved and respected by those around them. It is difficult to feel good about yourself if you know that you are not loved or have been rejected by others.

- **Competence** – children need to feel competent and capable. This will encourage them to learn new skills and feel motivated. Obviously, competence is limited by a child's age, size and stage of growth and development, but it may also be affected by unrealistic expectations of what a child can achieve. Repeated failure can lead to frustration and dissatisfaction. Consequently, a child will develop negative views of their own competences and have low self-esteem.

- **Control** – the level of an individual's self-esteem may be directly affected by the amount of control they feel that they have got over a situation or their environment. Even young children can gain control over their environment, for example when a baby cries the parent or childcarer comes to find out why. Children quickly learn that when they behave or act in a certain way, their actions can produce a change in their environment.

Sometimes the term 'confidence' is used instead of self-esteem. Having high self-esteem allows a child to reach their full potential. If a child is not confident, they may think that they are not capable of doing something and will be reluctant to try new things. It is not uncommon for children with low self-esteem to behave in ways that are considered unacceptable because they do not want to be put into situations where they might fail.

Children with high self-esteem will feel positive about themselves and will be more likely to explore and experiment. They will seek help to enable them to succeed in specific activities and can often make friends more easily.

Children's interactions and relationships with others

The formation and quality of relationships in a child's early life can have a direct impact on how they socialise and build relationships in later life. The term 'attachment' is often used to describe how young children make relationships, especially with an adult.

Key Term

Attachment is a unique emotional bond between a child and an adult.

Keys to good practice

We can help children to develop self-esteem by following certain rules.

- Provide a positive atmosphere where children feel that they can explore and experiment without the fear of failure or being criticised.

- Make children feel special and valued by those around them, ensuring that all children are included.

- Have realistic expectations of what a child can do at their age, stage of development, level of competence, and also be aware of situations that might damage a child's confidence.

- Offer praise and verbal encouragement, but not just when children achieve. You can offer praise when a child smiles, looks happy or is cooperative.

Attachment theory

John Bowlby (1907–1990) was one of the first researchers to study relationships between young babies, children, and their mothers or primary carers. Bowlby stated that babies need to form one main attachment that would be 'special' and of more importance than any other. He believed that prolonged separation during the first four years from this special person would result in long-term psychological damage.

This theory has been very influential in social care policy, childcare practices and research.

Find out more about Bowlby's theory of attachment.

Some parents are concerned that their baby or young child might make a stronger emotional bond with their childminder or nanny. However, recent research has shown that babies and children can make strong emotional bonds with several individuals.

The Birth to Three Matters Framework and Birth to Three Framework, 'Supporting our youngest children' both place a great deal of emphasis on the quality of relationships between young children and their carers. For example, the component 'A strong child' from 'Being acknowledged and affirmed' gives many positive pointers to ways that childcare practitioners can help babies and children develop positive relationships.

As well as developing attachments, children need to learn how to make friends with their peers. The older a child becomes, the more important their friends are to them; to the extent that by the time a child is 12 or 13 years old their friends can be more important than their family members.

Children under three are social beings but are not usually cooperative in their play and interactions with others. They are aware of and respond to other children and by the age of two will play alongside another child, rather than with them. By the time a child is three years old they will begin to play more cooperatively and can perhaps share.

The school years are times when children develop friendships, often of the same sex. Girls generally have fewer close friends than boys. By the time a child is in their teens, friendships can be of either sex and sometimes can be a source of problems for the young person, especially if the values of their friendship groups are at odds with what they believe, for example with regard to issues around drugs, alcohol and sex.

Friendships are very important to children

Balancing children's growing needs for independence with the need to keep children safe

See also Unit 1, page 22.

All children regardless of their age need opportunities to develop their independence. The independence needs of babies can be met by encouraging them to push their legs through trousers, their arms through tops, or offering a choice of playthings such as a treasure basket. Young children can be offered real choices to help them develop independence, such as asking them whether they want milk or water to drink with their snack and by encouraging them to help with daily routine events such as clearing away toys, setting a table for snacks.

As a child's cognitive and physical skills develop they will naturally want to be more independent. Older children will want to take responsibility for their play and as such will need to assess risks, solve problems, undertake challenges and perhaps develop rules of games. You can encourage them to do this by asking appropriate questions about how they plan to make their play safe and whether they have considered risks. It is also very important that you can recognise when you have to become involved and when you are able to 'take a back seat'.

The most common causes of challenging behaviour in children

There are many things that may influence a child's behaviour and all children react and behave in their own unique way.

In many ways there are no common causes of challenging behaviour, as all children are different. However, it is possible to group some of possible causes into the four groups shown in the spider chart below.

Whilst the features on the spider chart are common causes it is important that you also think about the following points.

- Social learning theory as discussed earlier in this unit and the importance of positive role models.

- The way a child feels about themselves can affect the way that they behave, and, as mentioned earlier, poor self-image can result in challenging behaviour.

- Peer group pressure can be a common cause of challenging behaviour, especially if children find themselves in conflict with their need to belong to a group and respecting the wishes of their parents or childcarer.

- It is important to consider if some challenging behaviour in children may be linked to abuse (see also Units 1 and 3).

- Bullying can have a significant effect on a child's behaviour and the child may not be willing or able to talk about it. They may therefore become withdrawn, uncommunicative, angry, upset or aggressive.

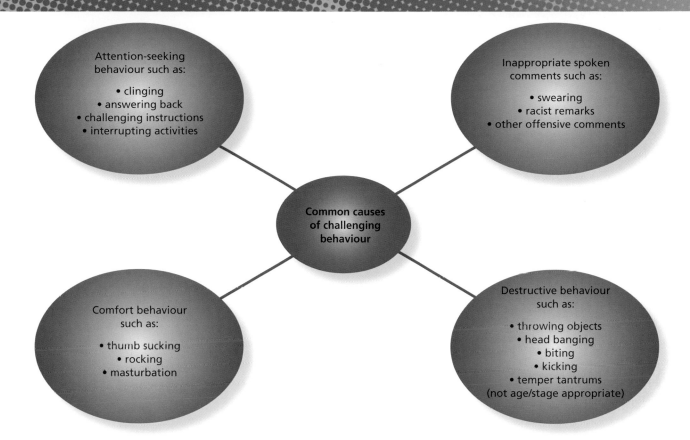

Common causes of challenging behaviour

- Behaviour can be a problem when it is developmentally inappropriate, for example a two-year-old having temper tantrums is developmentally appropriate, at five years old you have to ask yourself if it is.

- A child's behaviour may change if they are feeling unwell. Sometimes a child may regress in their behaviour, for example a child who has been potty trained may start to have 'accidents' if they are not feeling well. They may also become more clingy or aggressive. Some children can also become withdrawn and unwilling to communicate or play, preferring to be left alone.

Think about it

Think about the influence of the media on children's behaviour.

It can be quite difficult to explain to a keen footballer why it is not acceptable to make offensive gestures and use inappropriate language to the referee.

Think about it

Behaviourist theory explains why some children show challenging behaviour. Children receive attention from adults or other children when they behave in certain ways. Negative attention is better than no attention at all, and in effect reinforces the behaviour that you are actually trying to stop. For example, a child is playing cooperatively, but this does not attract your attention so the child hits another child; you tell the first child off, therefore they have your attention.

E7 Discuss one factor that affects children's behaviour.

Hint

Think about one thing that can affect a child's behaviour and write about what behavioural changes you might observe.

patronising. Also, some rewards that you may consider appropriate may not be seen in the same way by the parents, sweets and chocolate for example.

Think about ways in which you can simply explain to children why they are being rewarded. Telling a child that you are rewarding them because they have played together well will boost the self-esteem of that child.

Children's behaviour can be managed in positive ways following the ABC approach. Consider the antecedents, the actual behaviour and then the consequences in turn.

How you can take a positive approach to managing children's behaviour

- One of the most effective ways of promoting positive behaviour is to reinforce the behaviour that you want to encourage by praising children. For example, you praise the child and give them your attention when they are sharing, sitting at the table at mealtimes or listening to instructions about what is going to happen next. The more that you praise, the more that the children keep on showing positive behaviour.

- Another way is to reward the child when they are showing or managing positive behaviour. In that way they will learn to associate the reward with the positive behaviour. However, you must think carefully about the rewards that you use. Some younger children may respond well to stickers but older children may find them

A – antecedents
In other words, what happened just before the behaviour? You may have to consider factors relating to the family, not just the child, such as relationship breakdowns.

B – behaviour
Ask yourself the following questions.

- What actually happened?

- Where?

- Who was involved?

- How long does it last?

- Does it happen at certain times of the day?

- Does it happen with certain people?

C – consequences
What happened afterwards, what is the pay-off?

Case Study

Five-year-old Meg has become very defiant and will not comply with simple requests made by her childminder, such as tidying away toys. The childminder, Viv, has spoken to the parents and they have decided to try to use a sticker chart with Meg when she does as asked. The parents have agreed that the chart will be used at home as well as at Viv's house, and when it is full Meg will get a treat, such as a special trip.

Viv asks Meg to come to the table to have her snack, Meg refuses, so Viv does not give her a sticker; however, when Meg starts to pick up toys in the playroom Viv praises her and gives her a sticker.

Do you think this is a positive way of managing Meg's behaviour?

What else could you do?

When deciding how to manage challenging behaviour there are numerous things that you can do following the ABC approach.

- Think about changing the antecedents – preventing what triggered the behaviour from happening.

- Think about changing the background factors – meet the child's needs.

- Think about changing the consequences – do not let the pay-off be positive; for example if one child hits another child, give your attention to the child who has been hurt, so that the child who hits does not get your attention.

> Kath, a registered childminder, says 'I found out about the ABC process from a behaviour course I went on. It made a lot of sense and made me focus on the child, rather than the effect that the behaviour was having on me. I was able to think about different ways to work with one child and together we successfully developed a strategy to deal with their angry outbursts.'

Think about it

Many home-based childcarers use 'time-out' as an effective strategy to help manage challenging behaviour, with children being removed from adult attention and contact for one minute for every year of their age; for example, a three-year-old would have 'time-out' for three minutes.

However, you must remember that this strategy should be used only sparingly, and if you 'time-out' for bad behaviour you should also 'time-in' for good behaviour.

Sometimes children will behave in challenging ways to attract attention. You need to recognise this need for attention and meet the child's need.

Give lots of attention at times when the child is quiet, cooperative, smiles at you or other children, listens to you, etc. Increase positive comments, especially at times when the child is not used to receiving them, and change your response to the challenging behaviour.

The importance of working in partnership with parents

See also Units 1 and 4.

As stated earlier, parents are the first educators of their children, so if children are to reach their full potential in all aspects of their development it is essential that the home-based childcarer works in partnership with parents.

Many parents become stressed, distressed or even angry when they realise that their child's behaviour is challenging and causing concern. However, if they are working in an effective partnership with their child's carer these negative feelings can be less powerful as they will feel better supported.

Case Study

Toby, aged four, has become defiant and will not do what his registered childminder, Angie, asks of him. He has also become rude and angry towards the other children. Angie has cared for Toby since he was nine months old; his older sister also comes to Angie's house after school, so she knows their mother very well. Angie telephones Toby's mother one evening after work and they talk about him. Toby's mother tearfully tells Angie that their father has left and Toby is very upset. If Angie had not established a good relationship with this mother she may not have been able to understand Toby's behaviour.

What would you do to help Toby manage his anger?

How would you manage Toby's defiant behaviour?

When there is an effective partnership, children's behaviour is more likely to be managed in a consistent way. Partnerships take time and effort from both sides. It is not especially beneficial to the partnership if you report to the parents only negative aspects of what the child has done, because sometimes when a child is showing very challenging behaviour it can be difficult to be positive. While you must always be truthful in your dealings with parents, even the most challenging child will have done something appropriate, such as eating all of their lunch, or putting their coat in the right place.

If you have established good and effective relationships with the parents it will be easier for all concerned to discuss a child's challenging behaviour if you suspect that the antecedents of that behaviour might be related to something that is going on in the family.

How to develop and promote positive relationships with children

Children are social beings from birth and need to establish positive relationships with adults and each other from a very early age. The main key to developing relationships with children is the way that you meet their needs. All children are unique so their needs must be met in individual ways. Simply treating all children in the same way is not inclusive practice because you are not meeting individual needs.

The way that you settle a child in your care is of paramount importance to establishing a positive relationship (see Unit 1, page 65). It is at this time that you can get to know each other, build bonds and begin to get comfortable in each other's company.

Appropriate physical contact, such as holding or a cuddle, can make a child feel wanted and secure, but you should never insist a child kisses or cuddles you if they do not want to do so. Older children rely more on verbal approval and interactions, although they still may want physical contact. A smile or a thumbs-up gesture can speak volumes and reassure a less confident child that you are aware of them and that you value them. Reassurance and adult approval should not be conditional; children should be reminded that they are valued at all times, not just when they are doing something that pleases an adult or when they are achieving. Lack of reassurance can result in a loss of the child's self-confidence and lead to a damaged relationship.

Sometimes when children are displaying challenging behaviour it can be difficult to detach the child from the behaviour, for example a child who hits could be told that he is a very naughty boy. This is focusing on the child rather than what they have done. It is better to say to the child that hitting hurts and that they should not do it. This tells the child that what they have *done* is wrong and not, as in the first example, that *they* are wrong. This approach does not damage your relationship with the child because you have responded to their actions rather then the child as a whole. You know that they can play cooperatively because you have seen them doing so, so tell them and praise them for doing it.

Language and communication

This aspect of a child's development is not just about talking. It is about all of the ways in which a child can communicate, from the different cries of a baby, such as I am hungry, wet, bored, to having a conversation with someone or sending a text message.

The importance of oracy and literacy development

People use language in many different ways. We use it to express feelings and make our needs known, to find out more information through questioning others or reading, we describe events and situations to others and use language to get reassurance and confirmation.

Key Terms

Oracy – what is said and how it is said.

Literacy – how we use words, either in writing or reading.

Many theorists believe that there are very close links between language and cognitive development. There are also close links with physical development, because children need to be able to control the muscles of the face, throat and tongue in order to make sounds. Children also need to be able to communicate in order to establish and develop social relationships because a lack of social relationships can affect emotional development.

How children develop communication and language skills

There is a clear sequence in which children learn to communicate with others. However, it is important to remember that whilst all children will at some point develop language, the speed and rate in which they do so will be different for each child.

Find out!

Find out about the following theories of language development.

Lev Vygotsky (1896–1934)
Jerome S Bruner (1915–)
Noam Chomsky (1928–)

Find out about the current research of Judy Dunn and A Karmiloff-Smith.

The issues involved in adults' communication with children

Adults play a key part in the development of communication and language. It is through hearing language and seeing gestures and imitation that babies and young children are

Children need to communicate with others

Stage	Age (approximately)	Features	Comments
Pre-linguistic stage			
Cooing	Six weeks	Cooing sounds show pleasure. Babies also cry to communicate needs.	These early sounds are quite different from later sounds as the muscles of the mouth are still developing.
Babbling	6–12 months	Blends of consonants and vowels to make strings of sounds, later with intonation which copies the pattern of adult speech.	Babbling makes up about 50% of non-crying sounds. By the end of this stage babies can usually recognise 15–20 words.
Linguistic stage			
First words	12 months	Babies will repeat words that have most meaning to them.	Words may be unclear at first and can be mixed into babbling.
Holophrases	12–18 months	One word can be used to express more than one meaning.	Tone of voice and the context of a situation is used to supplement holophrases. Most children now have 10–15 words.
Two words	18–24 months	Two words put together to communicate meaning, e.g. 'me down'.	Sometimes known as telegraphic speech.
Language explosion	24–36 months	A rapid increase in vocabulary, plus greater use of sentences.	Children begin to use plurals and negatives, but can make errors, e.g. 'I doned it'.
	3–4 years	Longer sentences and imitation of adult speech; speech can be understood by non-family members or close carers.	Use language in a more complete way, but can still make grammatical errors.
Fluency	4 years onwards	Language is refined and a child understands that language can be written symbolically.	Have mastered basic grammar rules and are usually fluent.

encouraged to learn. In the early days adults talk to babies in simple repetitive ways; this is called 'Motherese' or 'Baby Talk Register'. At these times it is essential that good eye contact is maintained with the baby and that praise and recognition is given whenever the baby attempts to communicate.

Whatever the age of the child it is important that they feel they are being understood and listened to. It is important that we give children time to answer or use language and do not try to 'speak' for them; however we can correct grammatical errors and mispronunciations by modelling, repeating the child's words, but doing it correctly;

if, for example, a child says, 'I've doned it,' the adult could reply, 'I am really pleased that you have done it'.

Adults need to provide opportunities to extend and stimulate a child's language and communication through the use of questions, especially open-ended ones, repetition, naming objects, and playing listening games appropriate to the child's age and stage of development. It is also important that we remember to listen carefully and with interest to what the children are saying.

We can communicate very effectively with children by using body language, for example facial expressions and gestures. Sometimes a shy child may feel embarrassed if verbally praised in front of others, but will respond well to a thumbs-up sign and a big smile.

The activities and experiences that we provide should give plenty of opportunities for children to communicate, listen and express their feelings and views.

Case Study

Chris, a registered childminder, is very interested in dance and mime and plans many opportunities for the children in her care to share her interest. She finds that dance helps the children to express their feelings, and sometimes the older children plan dance and mime routines together to tell a story or recall a past experience.

Think about the communication opportunities in some of the activities that you provide, such as cooking or going for a walk.

Many children speak more than one language. A child who speaks two languages is usually referred to as bilingual, whereas a child who speaks more than two languages is referred to as multilingual. Studies have shown that unless a child is competent in their home language they will find it difficult to move forwards in others. It is therefore very important that any adult caring for a child respect the child's culture and home environment. It is sometimes easier for a multilingual child to associate one language with a particular person, for example mother speaks to the child in Welsh, the childminder speaks to the child in English. The speed at which a child can learn another language depends on the level and quality of adult support, which can be linked directly to the quality of the emotional attachment that the child has with the adult. Look back at the work of Bowlby and his theory of attachment.

Using books and stories with children

Although babies and very young children cannot read they are usually interested in books. The shared act of reading books together encourages bonding and attachments, emotional security and closeness. Babies are usually offered picture books that reflect their environment, containing pictures of toys and things that they may see around them, such as a cup and a spoon. You should try to offer a variety of different books, such as pop-up books, and things that move or make a noise. Try to encourage the baby or young child to turn the pages as you read together. This will help their fine motor and coordination skills as well as introducing the idea of how books work.

It will become quite clear to you that the baby or young child will have a favourite book which you will have to read over and over again.

Case Study

Daisy's favourite book is *The Hungry Caterpillar* and she seems to know it by heart. Her nanny sometimes reads this book five or six times a day. Jude, the nanny, says that sometimes she deliberately makes a mistake, getting the number of cupcakes wrong, for example. Jude says, 'Daisy gets quite cross with me, shakes her head and calls me silly Judey, then giggles with glee because she knows I have made a mistake. We have lots of fun with this story.'

Can you think of a book that you have read over and over again with a child?

Why did the child like the book?

Shared reading with older children can be a very satisfying experience for you and the child. Avoid multitasking when children are reading to you. Listening with interest and attention is very important. It will make the child feel valued and appreciated, and help to develop stronger emotional bonds between you.

Children of different ages can share the same book with you and can become involved at the level that is appropriate to them. There is a very a good sequence on the video that accompanies the Birth to Three Matters Framework, 'A skilful communicator'. It shows a registered childminder reading with a baby and a small girl. All three are involved and enjoying the story.

Reading together can be a very pleasurable activity

Keys to good practice

We all like books that are attractive, that catch our eye for whatever reason and therefore our interest.

When you are choosing books for children think about:

- inappropriate language or images, including those that portray stereotypical images

- providing a range of books: factual, fictional, poetry books, activity books, hardbacks, paperbacks, different sizes, comedy/funny books and joke books, for instance

- using props like finger puppets that you or the children can make to enliven a story

- providing new as well as favourite stories

- making books yourself and with the children, using photographs (with parents' written permission) and drawings

- using your local library to increase the range and number of books that can be used with children. This can be especially useful if you are helping and supporting older children with homework.

The role of home-based childcare practitioners in providing play and experiences of the real world, to help children develop and learn

Play is all about encouraging the children that you care for to develop and learn in every way possible. It is not necessary to have expensive toys and play equipment to encourage development. There are many things around the home, routine things that you do, and experiences in the real world that will help children of all ages develop. You must remember that whatever you give the children to play with must be safe and not be likely to harm them in any way.

One of the main skills of any childcare practitioner is to know when to support and intervene in activities and when to stand back. In any situation the activities that you provide should offer a balance of structured experiences that you or other adults have greater control over, as well as less structured experiences that the children can control. In general terms, adult intervention in any activity, whether unstructured or structured, must take place when the well-being and health and safety of the child, or any other person, is at risk.

Activities that you provide will always be more appealing and successful if you build upon children's interests. This will also help them to make connections between what they already know and have done and new experiences being presented to them.

Activities in the wider world will depend very much on where you live; nevertheless they can be extensive. Wherever and whenever you decide to go, you must have the written permission of the parents before you take the children out of the home environment. It is also good practice to take with you emergency contact details for the children in case of accidents or emergencies

Many local authorities provide play schemes for children and young people during school holiday times. Discuss these with the parents if they wish their children to take part, because they can have both advantages and disadvantages.

Some advantages of such schemes are:

- children can have opportunities to mix with children of a similar age
- they can visit places of interest further away from home
- they can have access to a wider range of activities and experiences.

Some disadvantages are:

- these schemes can prove costly for a family if more than one child is involved, especially over a long holiday
- some shy children may find them overwhelming.

The childcare practitioner in the home-based setting

Childcare in a home-based setting has unique and distinct characteristics. You may have decided upon this career because of the flexibility it offers, or the fact that you can match your workload to the demands of your own family. Nannies may have opportunities for travel that they would not otherwise have. There are of course many other reasons why you have chosen this career. Whatever your reason, it is essential that you have a professional approach to your work at all times and can look objectively at your strengths and weaknesses.

This unit is assessed by one assignment that can be presented in a variety of formats. It will be marked by your tutor and then externally moderated by CACHE.

This unit will teach you about:

- the reflective practitioner
- assertiveness and valuing yourself
- marketing your childcare service
- policy writing
- inter-agency working and other professionals
- child protection
- continuing professional development.

The reflective practitioner

Working with children is a challenging, demanding and rewarding career. It is a skilled job that requires a love of children and a good understanding of the issues that can affect their lives. You need to be able to change and adapt to the many demands on you, often at very short notice! Being reflective means that you make time to think about your work and how you change or improve what you do.

Understanding what is meant by being 'a reflective practitioner'

The term 'reflective practitioner' is quite new to the childcare profession and can be quite daunting to some people.

Key Term

Reflective practice – thinking about and critically analysing your practice, actions and work with the intention of changing and improving what you do.

Keys to good practice

If you are reflective you:

- are contemplative, thoughtful and consider carefully what you do and why you are doing it

- are analytical about all aspects of your work; you have a logical approach to what you do and can be critical of yourself and how you do things

- ask yourself specific questions about your work such as those shown below.

  o Where can I find out more about…?

  o Why didn't this activity work?

  o How can I make this better?

  o Who could help me do this?

  o What might happen if I did this?

Being reflective is a learning process as it helps you to increase your understanding and learning skills. It will mean that you can recognise your strengths, yet at the same time understand and accept that you have weaknesses, or things that you could do better. Being reflective should result in you offering a better service to the children that you care for and to their families.

In order to think about what we do and why we do it, we need time. Time is often in short supply for many home-based childcarers, but if you are to take this aspect of your work seriously, you will need to find time to think about and evaluate what you are doing and why.

Case Study

Caroline is working towards achieving a quality assurance award with her local authority. She is very busy and is finding it very difficult to find time to reflect and evaluate what she is doing, let alone write things down. Her mentor suggests that she keeps a pad of post-it notes and a pen in her pocket and makes a quick, brief note under the headings What, How, Why whenever something occurs. For example:

What – play dough
How – children didn't play with it for very
      long
Why – maybe they are bored with it

As each post-it note is used, Caroline sticks it on the fridge door. At the end of the working day she collects them together and reads what she has scribbled down. After a couple days of doing this Caroline realised that she was not offering the children many new activities and was sticking to the same few ones she had used for a long time. She was able to recognise this as a weakness and realise that she could do something about it.

How can you find time to be reflective?

Try the post-it note method, or do you have another way of analysing what you do?

Reflection on practice

You need to think about all aspects of your work and should not assume that because you think something is working well, it actually is. For example, a registered childminder may think that they have a good way of managing risks because there are very few incidents or accidents. In actual fact, the childminder does not allow the children to engage in risky play or challenge themselves physically, therefore minimising the risk, but not actually meeting the needs of the children.

If you have always done something in one particular way, that does not mean it is necessarily the best or most effective way in which to do things. There is an old saying 'familiarity breeds contempt', in other words there is the danger of becoming complacent about your work, something that must be avoided at all costs. Every professional needs to think about their skills and keep up to date with the latest research.

You need to think about the way you manage children's behaviour and how you respond to the children. Managing children's behaviour is an emotive issue and is subject to constant debate. It is recognised now that we need to think about how we respond to the behaviour and make sure that we do not see any one child as a problem. Ask yourself if your current practice reflects this approach and if not, what can you do about it?

You should be reflective about what experiences and activities you provide for the children. Are you like Caroline in the case study above, providing good activities but only ones that you are confident with and that are 'tried and tested'? Or are you innovative, constantly looking for new, different or original ideas? Do you talk to other home-based childcarers about what they are doing and share ideas? Do you encourage the children to plan their own activities or do you prefer to 'keep control' of what is happening?

You also need to look at the resources and equipment that you have and are using.

Resources should interest and stimulate children as well as supporting the activity; there should also be sufficient resources appropriate to the activity.

As well as reflecting on what you provide for the children you should reflect on how you relate to and work with parents. As has already been said several times, a successful working partnership with parents will make a considerable difference to the quality of care that you give to the children. Think about the way that you communicate with parents, is it a two-way process with shared views and information? How do you react to parents when they leave in the morning and return in the evening, what impression do you give to parents? Are you harassed, rushed and stressed or do you present a calm professional image?

Another way of reflecting on your practice is to do a SWOT analysis for yourself. **SWOT** stands for:

Strengths
Weaknesses or areas for development
Opportunities
Threats

You can do this as a list or as a chart; whichever way will give you the information that you need. The benefits of doing a SWOT analysis enable you to focus on:

- the things that you do well

- those areas that you could improve upon

- those things in your life that could be regarded as professional opportunities, such as new courses or training events

- those things that could jeopardise your business.

Below is an example of a SWOT analysis done by a registered childminder. They decided to set it out as a chart and added a column for action points. Another column could have been added to give some indication as to when they hoped to implement the action points, but they have included a timescale in the action points.

Strengths	Action
1 No vacancies	Do not get complacent, start a waiting list as soon as possible.
2 Good Ofsted report	Try to get outstanding next time. Think about the recommendation now.
3 Good relationships with parents	Think about having an open day for all parents to meet each other, maybe in the summer.
4 All children are happy and enjoy being with me	Make sure that I meet all individual needs all of the time.
Weaknesses	**Action**
1 Ofsted recommendation to update behaviour policy	Talk to network coordinator about policy at the next network meeting.
2 Ofsted recommendation to update child protection policy	Talk to network coordinator about policy at the next network meeting.
3 Have not got a range of age groups, no babies	Difficult as have not got any vacancies, but could think about advertising at the health centre and talking to health visitors (see also Opportunities point 3).
Opportunities	**Action**
1 New training manual arrived last week	Book on some courses, especially about writing policies.
2 Been asked to mentor a new childminder	Contact childminder and set up a meeting as soon as possible.
3 Been asked to link with a young expectant mum	Contact her and arrange for her to come over within the next month as her baby is due in three months.
Threats	**Action**
1 New children's centre opening in the spring	Talk to network coordinator about this and what she is planning to do. Or Get in touch with centre manager as soon as possible to make sure that childminders have a voice and are included in the centre.
2 New childminders being recruited all the time	Make sure that I keep on top of my marketing, keep up to date and get involved with network activities.

Think about it

Do a SWOT analysis for yourself and identify your strengths, weakness, opportunities and threats. These points can be in relation to the children, their families, other professionals and your own practice. Think carefully about your action points and ways that you can reflect and develop your practice.

Evidence base for benefits of home-based care and learning

Some parents prefer registered childminders or nannies to care for their children in a home setting, and there are a variety of reasons for this.

- They feel that children will benefit from being either at home or in a setting similar to their own, believing that this will help the children to feel more secure.

- A registered childminder's home and working environment has been inspected by Ofsted or CSIW (in Wales), and parents can be sure that their child will be cared for in a safe and suitable environment.

- Often the registered childminder will be near the child's own home, or in the case of a nanny in the child's home, therefore cutting down the travel times for parents.

- Children will benefit from more individual attention, their needs will be better met when there are fewer children than compared to a daycare nursery. In addition, smaller numbers means that routines can be flexible and more adaptable. This is not always possible in settings with larger numbers of children.

- There are more opportunities for becoming familiar with the local environment in which the child lives through everyday activities such as shopping trips, school pick-ups, frequent visits to parks and leisure centres.

- Nannies and registered childminders can care for children outside of office hours, which can be a great benefit for parents who work shifts or irregular hours.

- Parents can develop more effective partnerships and relationships with one person. Sometimes in a daycare nursery, although they may operate a 'keyperson' system, the parents may not always talk to the same person about their child. Home-based childcare can be much more personal.

- Childminders and nannies can offer out-of-school care for children over the age of eight. This oftens mean that siblings can be cared for together.

- It is not unusual for registered childminders and nannies to care for children from when they were very young to 16 years old. This level of continuity of care cannot be matched by any other part of the sector.

Case Study

Chandani has just employed a nanny to care for nine-month-old twins, Jamie and Joe, when she returns to work. When asked why she has chosen this option, Chandani said that she felt her established routines with the twins would be followed and that they would be happier at home than in a daycare nursery. She then added that an unexpected benefit of employing a nanny was that it was actually cheaper than the local daycare nursery!

E1 Identify the benefits of home-based childcare.

Hint

You will need to think of the benefits of home-based care for:

- the child
- the family
- yourself.

E9 Show an understanding of anti-discriminatory/anti-bias practice in relation to your home-based childcare service.

Hint

Evidence for this criterion can also be found in **E2** and **E5** as well as in your answer for **E1** above. However, this criterion should be reflected throughout your assignment.

A Evaluate the role of the reflective practitioner.

Hint

Look at the study skills section at the back of the book (page 289) to find out what the term 'evaluate' means.

This criterion is a development of **E6** and is about all aspects of reflective practice. You will need to consider how reflective practice helps you to deliver a high-quality home-based childcare service, taking into account support, development and change. This may include you looking at the value of being self-aware and regularly reflecting on your strengths and areas for development. You will need to think about your targets or action points for change, how you will implement these and over how long a period of time. You must consider both negative and positive aspects of being reflective and self-aware.

Think about it

Some parents do have concerns about leaving their child with only one person and may think that with the staff in a daycare nursery there is safety in numbers. This view could be attributed to the negative press that some home-based childcarers have had due to illegal practices. It is not unknown for parents to install webcams and CCTV in their homes to monitor the activities of the nanny and the child. Whilst there is sympathy for this view, all home-based childcarers are to a certain extent exposed to accusations.

It is up to you to present a professional image to the parents, being open to their questions and concerns and responding positively to both parents and children. A reflective practitioner would have thought about these issues before they arose and should have considered a strategy for dealing with such situations.

Assertiveness and valuing yourself

Part of being a professional home-based childcarer is to be assertive when required. This does not mean that you should be aggressive, always want your own way, or are always right. Assertiveness is about being confident in what you do, having clear professional standards and sticking to them.

The significance of valuing and protecting yourself

Everyone has something that they can do well and something that someone else will admire, either in your personality, physical attributes or skills. Recognising your strengths is part of your self-image, self-esteem and valuing yourself. This does not mean that you should develop an unrealistically inflated view of your skills, but should value the things that are important to you and the children and families that you work with.

Being a reflective practitioner is also about valuing yourself. Recognising your good points and strengths is part of valuing yourself, as is knowing that you are providing the best possible care for the children that you can.

As mentioned in Unit 1, there are many ways that you can protect yourself from false allegations. It is not only accusations of abuse that you face. You may be accused of stealing, for example if you are working in the child's home. Parents may be in dispute with you over the payment of fees. You must always make sure that all your business dealings are professional, open and honest. If you have nothing to hide, you should have nothing to fear.

There have been cases of childminders and other childcare professionals being accused of abuse. This can be a most distressing time and experience for all concerned. If this happens to you, you must remain calm and professional. Keep records of all conversations that you have regarding the accusation, and keep copies of all the letters that you write. It would be sensible to seek legal advice because once an accusation is made there is a legal requirement that it be investigated. Some organisations, NCMA for example, offer legal help and advice to members, or you can seek independent advice from the Citizens' Advice Bureau.

The importance of seeking support when you need it

There are times when we all need support in our working lives, and recognising this fact is an important step along the way. In many places there are local informal groups of home-based childminders that meet in children's centres, community centres and each other's homes. These groups can be invaluable sources of support as well as friendship for both the adults and children. However, it is essential that you maintain confidentiality at all times and do not place yourself or the child in an uncompromising position. In other words, do not gossip.

Registered childminders can join a network and will find this an invaluable source of support. Not only will the network coordinator organise events for people to get together, but the network will offer training opportunities and access to other professionals.

Registered childminders who are working in a community childminding network may be asked to care for children who are already on the 'at risk register' or subject to a protection order. In such cases there will be a range of other professionals that you could turn to for support, as in the diagram below.

Professionals involved in a community childminding network

If you work on your own, you may wish to contact your local early years adviser before anyone else. If they are not able to offer you the type of support that you require, then they should be able to suggest other professionals who will support you. Organisations such as the NSPCC and Kidscape will often lend a 'listening ear'. The contacts for these organisations are at the end of this book.

The need to balance the demands of the job with family life

The life/work balance is sometimes difficult to achieve in any profession, but can be even more so for those individuals who work from home. Your work is always there, even if the children are not. You may find that you spend much your free time working: sorting out toys, cleaning equipment, keeping records and accounts up to date, and attending training events, amongst other things!

It is important that you think about what arrangements you will need to make if you or another family member are unwell, or suddenly taken sick. You have a legal responsibility to the children in your care to make sure that if you have to leave them with someone else, that individual is known to Ofsted and to the parents. Many home-based childcarers include this information in their welcome packs or at the initial meeting.

What do you do if you have made plans to go out for the evening and the parents are late back? Sometimes parents can be delayed at work or in traffic and you must make allowances, especially if they have let you know. However, if this scenario is a regular event, you should discuss it with the parents. Professionally and calmly explain to them the impact that this has on your personal life and come to some agreement.

The everyday running of your business can affect your home life in many ways, such as where you store confidential information. This can be quite a contentious issue as your partner's garage, or your bedroom, may not be the most appropriate place.

Everyone needs to have time for themselves, and spending all of your free time involved in activities that are associated with work will not necessarily make you a better childcarer. In some cases the reverse is actually true. You can become so involved in childcare issues that you close your mind to everything else going on around you, which can make you boring to others.

How much free time you spend away from the demands of your working life is very much up to the individual, and nobody can say that another person should spend a specific amount of time away from work.

Link to assessment

E6 Describe ways to balance the individual needs of the home-based childcarer with the demands of the role.

Hint

Think about what you would do in the following situations.

When children are collected late or the parents return home after your working hours are supposed to have ended.

If you are unwell or another family member has an emergency and needs you.

Where you store confidential records so that they are unobtrusive.

How you organise your working life to make sure that you have time for yourself.

Case Study

Karly is an experienced nanny and has had several jobs living with families over the years. She found that at one point her work was all she had in her life. She had moved away from the area where she had gone to college and lost contact with many of her friends. Although Karly loved her work she recognised that on her days off she had to do things that didn't involve the family or the children. It took her quite a while to establish contact with her friends from college again, but she now meets them regularly to socialise.

Why do you think Karly needed to see her friends?

What is your work/life balance like?

What can you do about it?

The meaning of assertiveness

Assertive people know their own mind, but are not closed to other people's views and opinions. They have a good self-image and value and respect themselves. Assertive people know what strengths they have and have recognised areas that they could develop or improve on. People who are assertive have usually addressed work/life balance issues and are comfortable with what they have got.

Use of assertiveness techniques

Assertive techniques are aimed at meeting the needs of both parties, without either one feeling that they have 'lost'. They recognise the needs and rights of the individual and enable the home-based childcarer to cope with difficult and challenging situations.

Personal rights and responsibilities

We all have personal rights and responsibilities. Sometimes these become clouded by emotional issues, for example when we are stressed it is more likely that we will become submissive or aggressive. Assertive people are able to control these basic emotions and try to negotiate and solve problems in order to meet their personal rights and responsibilities as well as those of others.

Responding to requests

Sometimes we can interpret requests as demands, which may make us defensive and therefore not responsive to the request, however reasonable.

An assertive person would consider any request in the following ways:

- attempt to understand the circumstances of the other person by getting all of the relevant facts
- stay calm and professional and control personal emotions
- think carefully before speaking, using the right words and gestures.

Dealing with criticism and conflict

Some people take criticism very personally so the situation can become emotional and stressful. In the same way conflicts, or disagreements, can also be hurtful to all concerned. An assertive person will try very hard to keep their emotions in check in such situations and will not allow an argument to develop.

Case Study

One parent has asked Mandy, a registered childminder, to mind her two children for an extra two hours each weekday as the parent has to work late for the next month. This means that the children will not leave Mandy's until 8pm. Mandy is unhappy about this request because of the impact that this will have on her own children and family life, but cannot really afford to lose the income.

What would an assertive person do in this situation?

What would your response to this situation be?

Keys to good practice

Being assertive involves more than just knowing your own strengths and weaknesses, as the following points illustrate.

- Ask open-ended questions to find out why the criticisms have been made, for example 'Please can you give me more information?'

- Remember that you are working within a professional framework if you are registered childminders who have joined NCMA. You will be meeting the National Standards and the standards outlined in NCMA's Quality Standards. If the criticism is about the quality of your service you will need to make sure that you have maintained these standards.

- Keep speech calm and delivered at a normal rate, sometimes when we are feeling defensive we tend to speak more quickly than usual and may raise our voice level – do not try to 'shout someone down'.

- Maintain eye contact with the other person, but do not become intimidating, use positive body language.

- An assertive person is always ready to apologise, admit that they have made a mistake and show that they do not bear grudges, whilst making every effort to rectify their mistakes.

Case Study

Debbie was very upset to receive an angry phone call from a parent one evening saying that her baby had a dirty nappy when she picked her up and now she had a very sore bottom. The parent implied that Debbie had not cared properly for the baby and should not have sent her home with a soiled nappy. Debbie asked the parent to come a bit earlier in the morning so that they could talk properly and so Debbie could show her the chart that she kept on nappy changes. The next morning Debbie showed the mum that she had changed the baby's nappy only five minutes before she was collected and that when she handed the baby over she was clean and dry. The mum reluctantly agreed that maybe the baby had soiled her nappy in the car when they were stuck in traffic on the way home.

Debbie followed good practice in that she made a note of every time she had changed the baby's nappy. She didn't get into a conflict situation on the telephone because she suggested that the parent talk to her the next morning, so she was assertive but not challenging.

What would you do if a parent criticised your standards of care?

Challenging

It is important that you do not view challenging behaviour as threatening, and should be prepared to challenge all prejudicial and discriminatory remarks regardless of who makes them. You should never ignore what was said or done,

mumble an incoherent reply or avoid eye contact. Assertive people would check that they had heard or seen the challenging behaviour or circumstances correctly before acting. Remember that assertive people stay calm and deal with the situation.

Communication is a two-way process

Listening

Listening is a basic communication skill. It is not a passive activity; to be a good listener requires time, effort and concentration.

You should be aware that listening is a two-way skill involving a giver (speaker) and a receiver (listener).

There are pitfalls that you can 'fall into' if you are not aware. Researchers at the University of Leeds came up with a list of barriers to good listening, which are outlined below. All of these can be turned around into positive points of good practice.

- **'On-off' listening.** This is a bad habit which comes from the fact that most people think about four times as fast as the average person speaks. This means that the person who is listening has about a quarter of a minute of spare thinking time for each listening minute. Sometimes we use this 'extra' time to think about personal details, concerns, troubles or interests, instead of actually listening.

Keys to good practice

Give the person who is speaking your undivided attention.

- Ask questions to either show that you have listened, want more information or to clarify something that you may not have heard correctly.

- Summarise what has been said. This makes you listen carefully, lets the person who was speaking know that you have understood what they were saying and reduces the possibility of misunderstandings.

- Let the speaker know that you are listening carefully. Maintain eye contact, use appropriate gestures and body language, such as nods of the head, perhaps also saying 'mmm' or 'yes'.

- **'Red-flag' listening**. Some people react negatively to certain words. When we become upset or irritated we stop listening. Think about your own 'red flag' words.

- **'Open ears, closed mind' listening**. Sometimes we make decisions that the person who is speaking, or what they are talking about, is boring, or does not make sense, so we stop listening.

- **'Glassy-eyed' listening**. Sometimes when we look intently at someone we can appear to be listening although our minds might be on other things. It is usually quite easy to see when someone is doing this.

- **'Too-deep-for-me' listening**. When we are listening to something that we think is too difficult or complex for us, we switch off.

- **'Matter-over-mind' listening**. We do not feel comfortable when our views and opinions are challenged. When someone does this we can stand firm as to our own opinions and in effect stop listening to the other person's point of view.

Listening attentively can be difficult!

- Being 'subject-centred' instead of 'speaker-centred'. Sometimes we concentrate on the problem and not the person.

- 'Fact' listening. Sometimes when we listen we go over facts in our minds to make sure that we do not forget them. While we are doing this, the speaker has moved on to something new and we have missed it.

- 'Pencil' listening. This is the classic note-taker's problem, when you try to put everything that is being said down on paper. The speaker speaks faster than we can write so we miss something. It is also difficult to maintain eye contact in this situation.

- 'Hubbub' listening. Sometimes there are so many distractions when we try to listen that we cannot concentrate fully.

Affirmation

Affirmation means that you confirm or verify the actions or speech of others, in a non-judgemental but professional way. Assertive people do not blindly agree with everyone else's point of view regardless of what their personal values and views are. Assertive people are usually good at building social and professional relationships and understanding the differences between the two. They do not make assumptions or label people, but respect differences and value other people, as well as negotiate and solve problems.

Marketing and managing your childcare service

In an ideal world you would never have to market your childcare services, and would never be unemployed or have vacancies. However, we do not live in an ideal world so marketing and managing your childcare service is essential.

Key Term

Marketing – advertising, promoting and selling your business/childcare service.

Key Term

Managing – the organisation, supervision, administration and running of your business/childcare service

See also Unit 1, page 87.

Delivering a quality childcare service

A quality childcare service, whether it is delivered in your home or the children's home, does not just happen. It has to be worked at all the time. You need to make sure that people remember you for the quality of care that you give to the children.

Think about it

It is not 'big headed' or pretentious to tell others publicly about your quality service. If you have good news, share it. Contact your local newspaper, radio station, childminding/nanny network or group and tell people. Some childminders produce a newsletter for the families they work with and nannies that work with more than one family could do the same.

Many home-based childcarers develop a welcome pack that includes the aims and values of their service (see Unit, 1 page 52). This shows the parents that you have really thought about what you are trying to achieve. Aims and values do not have to be complicated or full of technical jargon, very often the simpler the better.

Katie says 'I thought long and hard about what I wanted to offer. I decided that I wanted the children to be happy and well cared for in a safe environment. This became my aim for my business.'

Being reliable and committed

A quality service is characterised by the commitment and reliability of the people delivering the service. Caring for children in any situation cannot be regarded as a stopgap career choice.

A reliable person is:

- dependable
- consistent
- trustworthy
- steadfast
- dedicated.

Do you recognise yourself in the above list?

Do you do what you say you will do?

Are you always on time, or do you often run five or ten minutes late? This may not be a problem for you, but can be very distressing for a child going to school who always arrives after the register has been taken.

Can other people be confident in your skills and abilities?

A committed person is:

- dedicated
- loyal
- faithful
- enthusiastic.

Again, do you recognise yourself in this list?

Are you enthusiastic about what you do and do the children and other people know it?

Are you dedicated to the care and well-being of all children in your care? This does not mean that you have to be fanatical or obsessive, just realistic about what you can do to the best of your ability.

Being well organised and businesslike

The key to being well organised and businesslike is planning.

Remember the 5Ps:

Prior

Planning

Prevents

Poor

Performance

Think about how you plan your day and the working week – do you go about this in the best possible way? You should be reflective in all aspects of your work.

Being well organised is very individual; you may think that you are organised but someone else might find your working practices chaotic! However you decide to organise your business you must remember that children's records should be kept in a secure place and that you must maintain confidentiality at all times.

NCMA produces many documents, such as contracts, account books and permission forms, to name only a few, that will help you to run your business/practice in a professional way. Many banks have small business advisers that can offer you support and help, especially with issues such as tax and insurance. For nannies and parents employing them, there are independent companies that can offer a tax management and advice service.

Some childminding networks have promotional clothing, such as sweatshirts, fleeces and polo tops. These not only advertise your business but promote a professional and businesslike manner to other people.

Case Study

Sherrie is a member of her local childminding network. When working or at work-related events, such as training courses and network meetings she always wears smart blue or white polo shirts with the network logo embroidered on the front. 'These are my work clothes', she says, 'I feel more professional dressed like this and other people know what I do.'

How do you dress for work?

Does it matter, do appearances matter?

Many childminding networks organise open days to advertise the services of home-based childcarers. These can take place in many different venues, like drop-in centres, children's centres, health centres, leisure centres and local authority offices. These events provide opportunities for parents to find out about home-based childcare, costs, times, vacancies and availability of practitioners, whilst maintaining the confidentiality of individual home-based childcarers.

Continuing to keep up to date and develop new knowledge and skills

Being professional involves continuing to learn, develop and extend your skills and knowledge whilst keeping up to date with current trends and thinking. Childcare is a go-ahead, dynamic profession. It requires people to be lively, self-motivated and is an exciting choice of career. There is always something new and different to learn and read about, and there are literally dozens of courses and training events that you can attend. It is so easy to say to yourself, 'Well, I've done my pre-registration course, I've got two children of my own, so I do not need to do anything more.' This attitude does little to raise the professional status of home-based childcare and nothing for the person who thinks in this way.

Running the financial side of your childcare service

There is no set way to run your finances – it is very much a matter of personal preference. However, if you do not approach this aspect of your work in a well-organised manner you may start making costly mistakes.

Keeping financial records

See also Unit 1, page 85.

Some people set up their accounts on a personal computer, which can be very helpful, provided you are a confident computer user. There are many straightforward computer programs available that require you to put in only the headings, such as fees, cost of materials and so on. The computer program will then neatly set the items out for you and each time you add an item, the total will be

Think about it

1 Some years ago it was common practice to cover up a burn or scald. Today we know that the skin and tissue under the burn or scald can go on being damaged for some time after the heat source has gone. Burns and scalds are now treated by putting the injured part under cold running water for several minutes. In such a case, if you do not keep up with your first-aid qualifications and research you could do more harm than good.

2 Children with a disability were often referred to as handicapped and people felt sorry for them. Today, children with a disability are encouraged to lead full and active lives, and society is starting to see the child first, not the disability. If you are not aware of how attitudes have changed over recent years you could not offer a non-discriminatory service in which every child is respected as an individual.

These are two examples of the ways in which care for children has changed in recent years. Unless home-based childcarers keep up to date they will not be offering a professional service.

adjusted. However, there are many people who do not want to use computers and prefer to keep handwritten accounts. Many high-street stores sell accounts books that are already printed with columns to help people produce logical accounts. The NCMA also has accounts books that you can buy from them; these are produced in a format that is acceptable to HM Revenue and Customs as record of trading.

Using the services of an accountant can be helpful and can take the pressure off you. However, whilst an efficient way of organising your finances, accountancy services can be expensive.

It is good practice to bank money regularly and not keep large amounts of cash on your premises. Many registered childminders ask parents to set up direct debit payments to cover fees so that they have to pay cash only for extras such as trips during the school holidays. Nannies should encourage their employers to pay their fees directly into a bank account, deducting tax and insurance from the gross pay. This means that the nanny is an employee of the family and as such is entitled to employment benefits such as holiday and sick pay. A self-employed person, whilst having full responsibility for their own tax and insurance, is not eligible for holiday or sick pay.

Maintaining effective contracts and reviewing your rates

See also Unit 1, page 83.

A contract setting out the terms and conditions of the care of a child that is signed by you and the parents is not the end of the matter. A contract should be reviewed at least once every six months and it is essential that every time there is a change, regardless of how minor, the contract must be reviewed. For example, if the hours that you are going to care for a child are extended for a short period, such as two weeks, to cover special circumstances, you must review the contract. This is one way of protecting yourself.

Many registered childminders find that their local authority or Children's Information Service will do a review of childcare charges annually and will pass the data on to the childminders. This is very useful and can save the childminder a lot of time. However, it is important to remember that your rates are dictated by market forces in your locality. If you want to charge more than the going rate then you have to be able to offer something different for which there is a demand.

Case Study

Belle and her partner are vegans and grow all of their own food following organic practices. Both are registered childminders and charge a higher rate per hour than other childminders in the area. They justify this by offering an 'organic and vegan' childminding service.

Ameera has become trained to give massage and therapy to children with cystic fibrosis. As a nanny she specialises in caring for children with this condition and her income reflects her specific capabilities.

What could you offer that is different from other home-based childcarers and could have a direct impact on your rates and income?

Claiming benefits

The rules and regulations affecting benefits claims are getting increasingly complex. If you or a member of your family had been claiming benefits, such as income support, before you began your childminding business, your earnings could affect the benefits. It is very important that you inform the local benefits office about your childminding business. NCMA can offer you guidance on this aspect of your business.

Key Term

Contract – a written agreement which sets out the terms and conditions relating to the specific care of a child.

Claiming milk refunds

Many childminders are not aware that they are able to get milk refunds. At the present time you are entitled to claim the cost of one-third of a pint of milk for each day that every child under five years old is in your care. For the purposes of the claim, the child must be in your care for over two hours for it to count as one day. For babies you can claim the cost of one-third of a pint of formula milk made up as instructed on the packaging. This entitlement can add up to quite a substantial amount of money over a year, so you should make your claims regularly. You will need to keep receipts to prove that you have bought the milk and also keep accurate records of the attendance of the children. This is definitely a case of 'use it or lose it'. Your local Early Years Development and Childcare Partnership (EYDCP) should be able to tell you how to get the claim forms.

There is a possibility of fruit refunds as a future initiative designed to encourage healthy eating amongst children and young children. You will need to watch out for announcements in the press and media for further details.

Tax credits

Child Tax Credit is available to families who have at least one child. Around 90 per cent of families are eligible, all those with a household income under £58,000. Higher amounts are paid to families who have lower earnings, a baby under one year, or a disabled child.

Most parents are able to get help with the cost of childcare. Also, employers who provide their staff with childcare vouchers will be able to offer the first £50 of vouchers each week free of tax and National Insurance contributions. Both of these extra benefits are available to parents as long as the childcarer they use is registered or approved (see Unit 1 for details of the nanny approval scheme, page 80).

Working Tax Credit supports working people with low incomes and is available to self-employed people as well as those who are employed. Working Tax Credit has a childcare element to help parents on low incomes meet the costs of childcare. Eligible parents who want to claim the childcare element must be using registered childcare, such as a registered childminder, an approved nanny or an approved over-7s childminder. Childminders cannot currently claim the childcare element of the Working Tax Credit when caring for their own children.

From November 2005, Working Tax Credits will be paid directly into a claimant's bank, building society or Post Office account, rather than as credit coming with wages or salaries.

Since April 2005, home-based childcarers, in England only, who care solely for children aged eight or over can become approved in the same way as nannies, thus enabling more families to claim the childcare element of the Working Tax Credit and employer-supported vouchers.

When claiming income-related benefits, such as Housing Benefit, Council Tax Benefit or Income Support, registered childminders have a special concession that is not available to other people. It is called the 'two-thirds disregard'. This means that two-thirds of your total income from childminding is disregarded when your entitlement to these benefits is calculated. Your business expenses, such as food, stationery, heating and lighting costs, are not taken into account. For other benefits and tax credits the amount that you receive will be based on your net income. Your net income is your total or gross income less your actual business expenses.

Income support is usually available only to people who work for less than 16 hours each week, but a special rule allows some registered childminders to claim it even if they are working full-time.

Find out!

For more information on benefits and tax credits visit www.dwp.gov.uk or for NCMA members more information can be found in the NCMA Members' Handbook.

Expenses

You need to remember that you can subtract any reasonable expenses directly linked to your childminding business from your total (or gross) income. Deducting your expenses in this way means that your income to be taxed will be lower, so you pay less tax and will be more eligible for tax credits.

Your expenses will include any costs that you would not have incurred if you had not been caring for children. These can include:

• playthings

• safety equipment

• insurance

• outings

• travel costs such as fares, vehicle mileage

• food

• stationery

• training course fees

• professional membership costs, such as NCMA subscriptions

• subscriptions to professional journals.

Special rules for registered childminders also mean that you can claim a part of your heating and lighting costs, water rates and council tax. You can also claim part of your rent if you live and work in rented property.

Ten per cent of your total childminding income can also be deducted to cover wear and tear on your home and belongings.

'Keeping on top of the financial side of my business is very important,' says Tricia, a registered childminder. 'I am a member of NCMA and I find that they have very useful publications that help me work out what my taxable income actually is. My local HMRC Enquiry Centre is also very helpful.'

Investing in your childcare service

No business, whatever its size, will look after itself. Large organisations such as retail stores aim to make a profit for shareholders, but at the same time put money back into the business to purchase stock, train staff, upgrade premises and so forth. A home-based childcare business is no different. If you are seriously going to make your service successful you will need to invest time, effort and money.

You will need to spend time talking to parents, your Children's Information Service, childcare support workers and other childcarers to find out what families would like from their ideal childcarer. It will cost you time, effort and money to invest in your professional development and update your skills and knowledge. You will need to spend money on renewing and extending your equipment, resources and maybe in some cases your premises.

Marketing your childcare service

All businesses should be continually marketing their services; even if you are fully employed and have no vacancies it still pays to make sure that your business and childcare services get the best publicity they can.

Working with local information and other services

It is very important that you regularly update your details with your local Children's Information Service (CIS). Make sure that you complete any forms sent to you by CIS and try to answer every question. If your details change, such as a vacancy arises, or you get an additional qualification, let CIS know as soon as possible. Under the Data Protection Act any information that you give to CIS will be held by them and supplied to the public; it will also be placed upon the Internet if you give your consent for them to do so. Consent usually involves a signature on the contact and vacancy details form. If you do not give such permission the information will be used only for statistical information, but you will not receive any free publicity.

Registered childminders should consider joining a childminding network. Not only will you have support of the network coordinator when you have vacancies to fill, but you may also get the chance to become quality assured or accredited and offer early years education – another positive marketing point.

All home-based childcarers should make every effort to get involved in their local children's centre. This may well provide opportunities to extend your services in different directions such as offering respite care, wrap-around care, and out-of-hours or holiday care.

Marketing materials and advertising

All businesses have their unique benefits and selling points. It is good practice to put together a list of your key selling points.

The home
Registered childminders might want to think about the following points within the home.

- Is it safe and secure as shown by your Ofsted report?
- Is it part of a local community and near to local amenities?
- Is it a non-smoking environment?
- Has it been checked by local fire safety officers?
- Does it have good transport links?
- Do you have lots of parking spaces?

Put together a list of your key selling points

- Does it have close proximity to schools – ones you can pick up from or drop off at?

- Can you offer overnight stays?

- Have you got a dedicated play area and a safe garden?

Skills, qualifications and experience

All home-based childcarers can use their skills, qualifications and experience as selling points. Think about including the following points in any advertisements.

- Your first-aid qualification.

- Your initial training, pre-registration or approval.

- Your membership of a professional organisation, such as NCMA.

- Other qualifications you have or are working towards, such as the Diploma in Home-based Childcare, an NVQ, baby massage, British Sign Language, Makaton.

- Other training courses you have attended, such as caring for a newborn baby, Birth to Three Matters Framework, working with children who have a specific medical conditions such as diabetes and cystic fibrosis.

- Belonging to a childminding network and being quality assured.

- Speaking more than one language (this can include sign language).

- Your personal health checks.

- An enhanced Criminal Record Bureau (CRB) check.

- Experience with particular forms of childcare, such as a disabled child, triplets, premature babies.

- Previous childcare experience, such as working in a daycare nursery, after-school club or holiday play scheme.

Unique features of service

All home-based childcarers can think about the unique features of their service.

- Can you be flexible enough to meet the shift work patterns of parents, working at weekends or overnight?

- Do you have back-up in case you are sick or unable to work?

- Do you have references that are up to date?

- Can you drive and so take children to different after-school activities? Do you have a clean driving licence?

- Are you offering to cook all meals and meet specific dietary needs or requirements, such as diabetes, vegetarian, organic?

- Are you prepared to do children's laundry, clean and tidy their rooms?

- Can you provide evidence that you offer a wide range of stimulating, creative and enjoyable experiences and opportunities for development and learning?

Other selling points

There are also other selling points that you may want to think about.

- If you are eligible for tax credit claims.

- If as a nanny you have public liability insurance (all registered childminders must have this).

- If you have a vehicle that is insured for business use.

- If you have house insurance for damage.

- If other members of your family have CRB checks.

The above lists are suggested points only and are by no means complete. They are intended to help you recognise your unique selling points – you may be able to add a lot more.

Advertising your service

Now you have a list of your selling points what next? How do you advertise yourself? If you are happy about your full address being published you could consider advertising in:

- free ads newspapers

- local evening or weekly papers

- parish newsletters, school fair programmes, organisations newsletters

- on the Internet: set up your own website or join a group of like-minded people and set one up together

- your local radio station.

Business cards/leaflets

You can also organise some business cards and/or leaflets either by doing them yourself on a computer or getting a local print shop to do them. Give these out to:

- your local CIS
- parents that you already know
- your home-based childcare group coordinator or members
- friends
- neighbours
- midwives
- health visitors
- social workers
- staff at schools and pre-school groups
- crèche managers
- staff running parenting classes such as Sure Start employees
- staff running exercise classes for pregnant women and new mothers.

Other ways to advertise

Other things that you can do include:

- putting a sign in your garden or window if you are a registered childminder

- joining an agency; there are many reputable nanny agencies
- putting a poster in your car
- putting a business card or leaflet in local shops, libraries, colleges, schools, leisure and health centres
- putting your CV/details on a Internet job site and searching relevant websites for vacancies.

How much marketing you do is a matter of individual choice, but it is important to remember that you need to present a professional image at all times.

Link to assessment

E2 Describe how to market a home-based childcare service.

Hint

Re-read the section above as well as pages earlier in this section. Write about all the different marketing techniques that you could use, what information you need to include and how open days and other such events can help market your service.

Case Study

Candice is a registered childminder with several vacancies which she does not seem able to fill. She wrote out brief details of her service on the back of an envelope and paid 50 pence to advertise at her local newsagents for one week. She has had one enquiry from parents who wanted a drop-off and pick-up from school each day plus holiday care, but were only prepared to pay £2 per hour, when the going rate in the area was £3.10.

Candice's support worker suggested that the advert did not give the best impression, it was a bit rough and ready. Candice's elder son developed an attractive smaller flier on his computer which she used to replace the envelope at the newsagents. She also put it in the health centre, on the local school parents' noticeboard and contacted the local CIS.

Candice had several enquiries following this advertising, and although she didn't fill all of her vacancies she was able to provide a service for several families.

Think about how you advertise?

Is it effective, does it work?

Can you advertise better with higher-quality materials?

Does your local CIS have your details?

Policy writing

See also Unit 1, page 86

A policy can be a course of action that you intend to take, or a set of good practice guidelines that you follow in certain circumstances. They are not set in stone, but should be constantly updated and reviewed in line with statutory changes, new developments and changes in your service. A policy is a working document, not just a piece of paper to be filed away and brought out to show parents or an inspector. It can be a procedure that you follow in your work. You need to understand why you should have such procedures or guidelines and how they can help you develop and reflect upon your practice.

Find out!

Your policies do not have to be original; you may wish to adopt policies from other organisations such as NCMA, your early years team or network. However, it is good practice to read them through carefully and adapt or modify as needed.

Find out if you can use and adapt other organisations' policies for your service. If you do use a policy from another agency or organisation make sure that you have their agreement to do this.

Statutory requirements in relation to policies in home-based settings

Although Ofsted and CSIW do not specifically require home-based childcarers to have written policies, it is good practice to consider:

- child protection
- behaviour management
- confidentiality
- lost child
- nappy changing and other care routines.

If a registered childminder becomes part of a network they will be asked to develop more policies; these are listed in Unit 1 on page 86.

The Data Protection Act 1998 is designed to prevent personal and confidential information from being passed on without a person's permission. Therefore all home-based childcarers should have a policy, written or not, on how they ensure confidentiality.

Keys to good practice

As a registered or approved home-based childcarer you have a statutory duty to comply with the Children Act 1989 and the Children Act 2004. It is good practice to make sure that you fully understand your responsibilities and develop a policy to share with parents which clearly shows your understanding of these important Acts.

How to write a policy

How you write your policies is very much a matter of personal preference; there is no set way, but there are important things that you should consider.

- What is the policy about?
- Does it have a clear opening statement? For example, 'As a registered childminder I have a duty to protect all the children in my care at all times.'
- Does your policy go on to say *what* you will do, *how* you will do it and *when* (if appropriate) you will implement your policy actions?
- Does it say when you will review your policy?

The following is an example of a behaviour management policy from a working registered childminder. Names have been changed to maintain confidentiality.

Annie Jones – Registered Childminder
Ofsted number: 10203040

Behaviour management policy

I have very few 'rules' in my childcare setting, but I do expect all children that I care for in my home to learn to accept them and their parents to support me in implementing my policy.

I will discuss the boundaries for behaviour with all of the children. If the children know and understand why we have boundaries they will be more secure.

When setting boundaries I will be firm and fair and will take into account the age and stage of development and the needs of each individual child.

I will praise the children when they behave well and will be a positive role model for them at all times.

I will never use any form of physical punishment.

I will never humiliate, restrain or isolate a child.

The boundaries are:

we will all care for each other

we will not do anything that might hurt another person, or is dangerous or offensive.

I will record all incidences of unwanted behaviour and will discuss any concerns about your child with you.

I will review this policy when a new child comes into my care and/or if asked to do so by parents or legislation.

If you would like to talk to me about this behaviour management policy please speak to me when you bring or collect your child, or telephone me in the evening on 01234 567890.

A. Jones

April 2006

Compare this policy with the example in Unit 1, page 86.

Think about what policies it would be good for you to have in your home-based childcare setting.

Make a list of them.

Are your policies written down, just a brief statement in your welcome pack, or set out as a professional file for parents?

When did you last look at your policies?

How can you make sure that parents read your policies and support you in implementing them?

What do you need to do to be a reflective practitioner when it comes to your policies?

Sharing policies with parents and others

A policy is a working document that should be shared, discussed, monitored and reviewed by all concerned, including children. It is good practice for older children to develop policies, for example behaviour management, or safety and independence when outside.

Just because you give parents a file of your policies or procedures you cannot necessarily assume that they will read them. We are all guilty of this sometimes, for example have you really read the instruction book for your washing machine from page one to the end, and can you remember what you read? To go one step further, have you read the introduction to this book? If not then go back and read the introduction – it contains valuable information that could help you get the most from your studies.

Parents can provide you with valuable feedback on your service because children may tell them what they have been doing. This feedback can influence and inform your practice.

In the same way children can tell you important information about your service. If you take time to listen to them they may tell you about the things that they like and the things that they dislike. This will provide opportunities to talk about issues; for example a child might think that you have not been fair when managing behaviour. Discussing children's individual needs will help older children become more aware.

You may be asked to share your policies, procedures and/or guidelines with other professionals. If you join a childminding network your coordinator will ask to see your policies. Ofsted or CSIW may ask to see some, especially behaviour management and child protection. If you are caring for a child with specific needs or difficulties it may be appropriate for other health or education professionals to share your policies. It might also be helpful to share some policies with other settings, such as a school, especially if you have a behaviour management strategy for a child that is effective.

Monitoring, evaluating and reviewing your policies

NCMA recommends that all policies and procedures are reviewed and evaluated at least once each year. Many home-based childcarers will monitor and evaluate their policies more frequently if they change their working hours or if it becomes clear that something is not working well, such as when a new child starts.

Monitoring, evaluating and reviewing your policies is much more than just reading them through or printing another copy off from the computer and putting a different date at the bottom! It involves:

- gathering information, both informally and formally, about your service

- listening to the views of everyone involved with your service

- taking into account new developments and changes to legislation

- being realistic and reflective about your service and being able to take positive criticism as well as praise.

Case Study

Mel works as a nanny with three children under six years. She developed a behaviour management policy with the parents when she started working with the family two years ago. However, she has not reconsidered the policy since and the circumstances have changed, for example the two older children are now at school full-time.

Why does Mel need to review this policy?

Who should be involved?

Link to assessment

E3 Identify two policies that a home-based childcarer may use in a home-based setting.

Hint

Look at the list of suggested policies in Unit 1 (page 86).

You will need to name and briefly write about two policies that are appropriate to your work.

D Describe how to implement one childcare policy in your home-based childcare setting.

Hint

Choose one of the policies that you named to meet the criterion **E3**. Write about how you use this policy and what the benefits are to you, the children and their families.

Inter-agency working and other professionals

With the development of Children's Centres across the country more home-based childcarers will be involved with other professionals. This is an exciting new development and will present home-based carers with opportunities to develop their skills, knowledge and careers.

It is also important that you understand the roles and responsibilities of other professionals. This will also include knowing their correct job titles and their legal responsibilities to children and their families.

The importance of treating your childcare role as a profession, and presenting yourself as a professional carer

Home-based care is a profession which requires expertise and specific skills and knowledge. It is an unfortunate reality than many sectors of society do not regard childcare as a 'real job'; people will actually say, 'I'm just a childminder.' This negative attitude by members of the profession is destructive and undermines the excellent work that professional organisations such as NCMA are doing to raise the status of home-based childcare in particular.

There are many positive things that you can do to raise your professional status and the image of home-based childcare.

• Wear promotional clothing, like your network polo shirt, when working. This will not only advertise your business but will present a professional image, providing of course that it is presentable, not stained or dirty!

• Attend events and arrange stands at local schools or shopping centres to promote your professional image.

• Through your network or local group, nominate a person to attend local authority meetings, take part in early years forums and respond to consultations so that the voice of home-based carers is heard.

Wearing promotional clothing when working will present a professional image

Working with other professionals

Throughout your professional work it is inevitable that you will come into contact with people who care for or educate children. Below is a list of some of the professionals that you may work with, although this list is by no means complete and you can probably add several more:

- teachers
- pre-school or playgroup staff
- playworkers
- nursery staff
- other home-based childcarers
- doctors, including GPs and those specialising in specific illnesses, ailments and disorders
- health visitors
- dentists
- Ofsted or CSIW staff
- nurses
- therapists, including speech therapists and physiotherapists

- education welfare staff
- early years teams
- network coordinators and staff
- social workers.

It is important to remember that you and the other professionals are working in the best interests of the child and their family. You will both have different but specific knowledge about the child and this gives you a sound starting point on which to build your relationship.

As a result of the Children Act 2004, the outcomes, or objectives, for children have been clearly defined. These are:

- be healthy
- stay safe
- enjoy and achieve
- make a positive contribution
- achieve economic well-being.

These outcomes involve many professionals and agencies with clear roles and responsibilities. In addition, many terms have been generated, some of which are explained in the table below.

Term	Meaning
Annual Performance Assessment (APA)	A yearly assessment of a council's specific contributions to improving outcomes for children and young people, carried out by the Commission for Social Care Inspection (CSCI) and the Office for Standards in Education (Ofsted).
Children and Young People's Plan	Single overarching multi-agency plan covering the activities required to improve outcomes for children and young people.
Children's Centres	A range of services for children and families, including information, advice and guidance, early years provision, health services, family support and parental outreach and employment advice.
Children's Trust	A high-level partnership arrangement of agencies involved in children and young people's services.
Commissioning	Developing an overall picture of children's and young people's needs in an area, and developing provision through public, private, voluntary and community providers to respond to those needs.

Term	Meaning
Common Assessment Framework (CAF)	A new, standardised approach to assessing children's and young people's needs, designed to help practitioners communicate and work together more effectively.
Extended schools	A range of services and activities that go beyond the school day, involving schools and other partners to help meet the needs of children, their families and the wider community.
Information Sharing and Assessment (ISA)	The process through which agencies can appropriately share information to better meet the needs of children and young people with whom they are working.
Joint Area Review (JAR)	A review or inspection of all services for children and young people in a local authority area, carried out by two or more inspectorates or commissions, to evaluate the way local services, taken together, contribute to the well-being of children and young people.
Local Area Agreements (LAA)	Agreements made between central and local government in an area, aimed at achieving local solutions that meet local needs, whilst also contributing to national priorities.
Local Safeguarding Children Board (LSCB)	Has replaced the Area Child Protection Committee (ACPC) and is a statutory body responsible for overseeing the safeguarding of children and young people in a local area.
Multi-Agency Teams (MATs)	Co-located teams of practitioners from different agencies, working together to support children and young people in the area, but managed by their parent organisation.
National Service Framework (NSF)	National standards for children's health and social care.

Sharing information and liaising in the interests of the child

When information is to be shared with other professionals it is essential that you have the written permission of the parents to do this, even for what might seem to be the most insignificant thing. For example, if a parent tells you that their child didn't sleep well last night you may need to tell the nursery staff as well, because tiredness might affect that child's behaviour.

The only exception to getting parental permission, is to share information that might be a child protection issue, if talking to the parents about your concerns could possibly result in the child being harmed.

The factors which make for successful relationships with other professionals

There are several things that you can do to make sure that any relationship you develop with other professionals is successful and effective.

Keys to good practice

- Be professional yourself. Present your work with the children in a businesslike way.

- Appear confident, assertive, but not aggressive.

- Remember that the people with whom you are dealing will not know the children or know the children as well as you in certain aspects of their development. You will have very valuable information to share.

- Do not try to give the impression that you know more than you do. Be honest and say if you do not know something or are not sure.

- Be willing to seek advice and extra information yourself from other childcare practitioners or support groups if necessary.

- If you are attending a meeting about a child in which you could be asked to contribute, it is a good idea to make notes beforehand.

- Take time to think about what you are going to say, how you will say it, and use your notes to make sure that you do not leave out any important information.

- Remember to maintain issues of confidentiality at all times.

- Avoid using jargon – it can lead to misunderstanding. Most professions have a specialist vocabulary that is perfectly acceptable to use with people of the same profession. However, it is best avoided because it may not be fully understood by people from outside the profession.

- Another form of jargon can be the use of initial letters for complete words, such as ELGs for Early Learning Goals and NCMA for the National Childminding Association. Say what you want to say in clear, plain language.

- Similarly, if someone you are with uses jargon and you do not know what they mean, ask. It is far better to ask a sensible question to gain information, than to pretend that you understand when you do not.

Link to assessment

E4 Describe how the home-based childcarer can work with other professionals.

Hint

Think about all of the professionals that you may work with.

Write about ways that you can:

- understand their roles and responsibilities

- communicate effectively with them

- what you need to record and/or report

- issues of confidentiality.

B Analyse the importance of working with other professionals in the interests of the child.

Hint

This is linked to your answer for criterion **E4** above, but requires detailed information about:

- legal requirements for the country in which you live and work

- ensuring the safety of children

- helping children to meet their full potential

- ways to meet individual needs

- ways to ensure consistency of care

- children's rights

- confidentiality and exchanges of information

- liaison with parents

- expertise of other professionals.

Child protection

It is a distressing fact that the number of children on child protection registers is increasing year on year despite efforts by government and local authorities to reduce the risk of abuse. The most common reason for children being placed on the register is neglect, followed by physical abuse. A sound understanding of child protection issues is essential for every childcare practitioner, and as such should be reviewed and updated regularly.

Key Term

Child protection – defending the basic right of a child to be protected from abuse.

Review of previous learning and experience

Unit 1 looked at the signs and symptoms of abuse and your role if you suspect that a child is in need of protection. It is strongly recommended that you re-read Unit 1. Make sure that you understand the signs and symptoms and your role.

It is good practice to attend any training events or courses that your local early years team organise about protecting children. Attending a course in the early days of your career will not necessarily mean that you do not need to attend another one on the same subject at a later date.

The social context of abuse including reasons for abusive behaviour

Key Term

Abuse – when a child is suffering or may suffer considerable harm from physical abuse, emotional abuse, sexual abuse, neglect or bullying.

The green paper *Every Child Matters* and the resulting Children Act 2004 came about as a result of the death of Victoria Climbié who was killed by her carers. The independent inquiry which followed this death highlighted the continuing failings of the child protection system. The inquiry found that the system had become increasingly complex and distant from the work of the majority of health, childcare and education practitioners. *Every Child Matters* made significant proposals:

- to place Sure Start centres in the 205 most deprived neighbourhoods

- extending out-of-school activities

- developing full-service extended schools

- increased investment in child and adolescent mental health services

- reforms to the youth justice system

- tackling homelessness

- improvements to speech and language therapy services

- more effective information sharing between agencies

- a common assessment framework for children's services

- every case to a have a lead professional

- on-the-spot service delivery through multi-disciplinary teams based within children's centres and schools.

These proposals will have an important bearing on the structure of children's services and the roles of practitioners within these services.

Find out!

Find out how your local area is responding to the Children Act 2004?

Where is or where will your nearest Children's Centre be?

Why are children abused or bullied? This is a difficult and emotive question to answer fully because the reasons can be complex and perhaps not really fully understood. Abuse can be an isolated incident in a child's life, although some forms of abuse can last for years. Abuse and bullying can take place anywhere, for example bullying by text messaging is increasing and the bully can be miles away. Abuse and bullying can be carried out by anyone, but is in most cases instigated by someone that the child knows.

- There is a stronger likelihood of a parent abusing their child if there are difficulties in their attachments (see Unit 2, page 152).

- The risk of abuse increases if the parent has been separated from their child, as in premature births or severe neonatal/maternal illness, for example.

- Postnatal depression can sometimes affect how a mother responds to her child and can sometimes lead to abuse.

- Lack of parenting skills can mean that some parents are unable to respond to their child. Sometimes such parents have been abused themselves at some point in their lives and are in a 'vicious circle', in that they know no different.

- Disabled children can be vulnerable to abuse because they may not respond to their parents or bond with other children.

- Stress can be a major factor in abusive situations and problems like poverty and relationship breakdowns can be highly significant.

Bullying and harassment can happen to all individuals, but research shows that older children are generally more at risk. This form of abuse can last for a long time. It can be carried out by one individual or by groups and can take many forms; read the section on bullying in Unit 1 again (page 76) to refresh your knowledge.

Strategies to enable children to protect themselves from abuse and bullying

Children have a right to feel safe, protected and to have people that they can tell if they do not feel safe. To be able to protect themselves from abuse

Bullying can be carried out by both individuals and groups

and bullying, children need to feel good about themselves, they need to have a high level of self-esteem and a positive self-image. Children who are abused or bullied often have low self-esteem or a negative self-image.

Children need:

- lots of praise and encouragement to raise their self-esteem
- opportunities to encourage independence
- opportunities to develop assertiveness
- opportunities to make choices
- opportunities to express their feelings and wishes
- opportunities to succeed without fear of failure or 'getting something wrong'
- activities and experiences that are appropriate to their needs and age and stage of development

- positive role models who encourage tolerance, respect and cooperation between children
- to be respected and valued as individuals
- a good understanding of their own bodies using correct anatomical language through age-appropriate activities
- a trusted adult who they can talk to.

It is important to work in partnership with parents; there are many things that parents can do to raise their child's self-esteem and self-image. For example, parents can be encouraged to:

- become involved and extend activities that you have provided, such as sharing a favourite story together
- stay informed of what their children are doing and with whom
- talk to you about their children.

However, you must respect the child's right to be protected if you suspect that the parents may be involved in some way in the abuse of their child. You must report your suspicions to your Local Safeguarding Children Board (LSCB, formerly the Area Child Protection Committee or ACPC) or the NSPCC immediately.

Issues in relation to home-based childcare and child protection

Some home-based childcarers find it very difficult to report parents who they suspect of abuse. They feel that they are betraying the trust and relationship that they have with the parents, but this is not the case. You have a duty of care and a legal responsibility to report all suspicions.

If you were working in an organisation with several employees there is a process where you can air your concerns about bad practice, usually referred to as 'whistle blowing'. The Public Interest Disclosure Act 1998 protects staff from victimisation provided they make their claim in good faith. But home-based carers do not have such protection and are therefore vulnerable to accusations. It is essential that you make sure you have a support mechanism in place for yourself, as discussed earlier in this unit.

In general terms, there is a possibility of abuse when a child shows a number of signs or any one sign significantly. It should also be remembered that a child can be the victim of more than one form of abuse, such as neglect and sexual abuse.

Children who are possible victims of abuse can be very vulnerable and your dealings with them should be sensitive at all times. You must take your cues from the child and make sure that you do not upset them any further.

The issues involved in working with children who have been abused

Read the section on abuse in Unit 1 (page 72) again if you have not already done so. Abuse and bullying can have long-term effects on the victims. One of the biggest impacts is on self-esteem and self-image. The victims grow up thinking that they have no value or worth and in turn may become abusers themselves.

Confidentiality is essential in all aspects of child protection and this cannot be stressed strongly enough. A careless or thoughtless word can put a child at greater risk. It is essential that you keep records of signs or symptoms or things that a child may have told you by way of evidence. This information must be kept confidential, stored in a secure place and disclosed only on a need-to-know basis to the relevant professionals.

Case Study

In Unit 1, page 78, there is a case study about Kerrie and her experience of child protection. Kerrie kept written records of the evidence of signs of abuse, for example the child showing sexual behaviour in their play. She kept these records in a locked filing cabinet in the study, a room that the minded children did not have access to. Kerrie was asked by a member of the LSCB about the content of her records, but did not have to hand them over.

If you were in such a situation, do you have a secure place to keep records where you can be certain they will remain confidential?

The importance of developing clear communication and shared expectations in working with the child's family, social worker or other professionals

Once you have contacted either the LSCB or NSPCC they are required to investigate. This will involve talking to you, the child and their family. A case conference is then set up to decide what will happen next in the best interests of the child. After the case conference an action plan is agreed.

The case conference aims to gather as much information as possible about the child. Parents are often invited to case conferences and can bring legal representation of they wish. There will also be social workers, medical professionals, such as the child's GP, and maybe the child's teacher and carer.

If you are invited to attend a case conference you must make sure that any information you give is accurate, factual and can be backed up with evidence. All of this information is completely confidential; to breach this confidentiality is a very serious offence.

The importance of understanding the boundaries of your role

Once you have reported a case of possible abuse to the LSCB or NSPCC your responsibilities, as far as protecting the child is concerned, are to a certain extent taken out of your hands. However, in reality do your responsibilities ever stop? You still have the responsibility to care for the child to the best of your ability, and must prevent further abuse by:

- empowering the child
- listening to the child
- creating opportunities for children to talk about how they are feeling
- continuing to be aware of possible signs and symptoms.

The importance of seeking support for yourself

See also Unit 1, page 78.

There are times when we all need support and it is not a sign of weakness when we recognise that we need help. In fact it is a sign of professionalism. You will need opportunities to talk about your own feelings, which can be very powerful. Whilst it is vital that you maintain confidentiality, there will be other adults, such as a network coordinator, nanny agency staff, church or religious leader, who may be able to help you. If you would prefer to speak to someone less personal, you can get support from the NSPCC or other agencies and charities dealing with child abuse. Contact details for these places are at the back of this book.

Think about it

Keeping secrets – is this a good idea? Children are sometimes told that if they do not keep a secret they will be punished, but this cannot be right. Children should be told that they can break secrets, especially if the secret is a bad one. However, isn't it better not to have any secrets? Tell children that you are hoping to have or give someone a surprise, but if they want to tell they can.

Read what Bea said earlier in the last Think about it box about keeping secrets.

Link to assessment

E5 Identify two ways the home-based childcarer can help children protect themselves from bullying or abuse.

Hint

Re-read the section in Unit 1 (page 75) as well as the above sections. Write about two different ways children can be helped, such as discussions, opportunities to develop self-esteem, helping children to understand their rights, activities to empower children.

Continuing professional development

No childcare practitioner can ever say that there is nothing else to learn. We live in a rapidly changing world and we all need to keep our knowledge and skills up to date.

The importance of continuing to undertake training to update and refresh skills and knowledge

See also Unit 1, page 91.

People no longer stay in the same job all of their lives and it is quite feasible for an individual to have different careers at different times in their lives. However, it is important that you are proficient enough to undertake the demands of your chosen career at any time and to do this you must continue to undertake training to refresh your existing skills, learn new ones and develop your knowledge. This is also part of being a reflective practitioner, which was discussed earlier in this unit.

The approaches to caring and educating children are constantly developing to ensure that children have the best possible experiences at all times. It is essential that you keep up to date, and there are several ways in which you can do this without going on courses or training. For example, you can read professional journals. You do not necessarily have to subscribe to these as some can be quite expensive and many local libraries will have them. Surf the Internet for relevant websites, which can often give you a much broader perspective because you can access sites from other countries. Home-based childcare can be quite isolating and it can take great effort to get out and meet other like-minded professionals. But this is important because it will help you to find out about what other people are doing, suggest ways that you can change your practice and also get feedback from other like-minded people about what you are doing.

Planning, recording and reflecting on your professional development needs

Some home-based carers make a personal development plan which helps them to clearly identify their strengths, weaknesses and areas for development. This must not be set in stone but should act as a flexible working plan that can be changed and modified at any time.

Making a plan that records and reflects on your professional development puts you in control of what you are doing, it empowers you and means that any timescales you set are more likely to be realistic.

A plan can be devised in several ways, but there are six key steps that you need to think about.

1 Your skills, strengths and weaknesses. Try to rate each one, for example between 1 and 5, with 5 being high.

2 After you have completed step 1 you should be able to identify areas for development – your lowest weaknesses scores.

3 Now decide on a plan to do something about the areas for development. Include what you need to do, when you need to do it, how long it will take, what will it cost, who might be affected, for example it might affect your partner if you decide to take a Saturday training course when you normally go out shopping together.

> ## Think about it
>
> Put together a short plan for your own professional development.
>
> Identify one important strength and one important weakness.
>
> Why have you chosen that particular weakness?
>
> Decide what you can realistically do about your weakness.

4   Talk about your plan with family, friends or other professionals if appropriate.

5   Put your plan into action, in other words do it!

6   Review your plan, be reflective, is it working and if not why not, what do you need to do?

Quality assurance schemes including Quality First for individual practitioners and Children Come First childminding networks

Launched in 2003, Quality First is NCMA's nationally recognised quality assurance scheme for individual registered childminders. Individuals with NCMA Quality First have:

- shown that they have a commitment to NCMA's 10 Quality Standards

- actively reflected on their practices and found ways of improving the service that they offer

- received support and guidance from a mentor

- been checked by an NCMA assessor who has observed how they communicate with and relate to the children in their care

- produced a portfolio to show how they achieve best practice.

There is also a quality assurance scheme for childminding networks – NCMA Children Come First; this is the only nationally recognised scheme of its type. It differs from the individual scheme in that a group of registered childminders work together with guidance and support from a network coordinator to provide a quality service for their local community.

Investors in Children is a government scheme which endorses childcare quality assurance schemes. It aims to help childcare providers choose a good quality assurance scheme and also helps parents identify good quality childcare. Over two-thirds of networks have chosen to become quality assured. Becoming an NCMA Children Come First network means that both the network and its members can easily show that they are offering a high quality of care.

The qualifications framework including NVQs and Foundation degrees

There are qualification frameworks for all professions established by the Department for Education and Skills (DfES). These frameworks will list any course that leads to a nationally recognised qualification and identify at what level it is at, for example Level 2 or Level 3.

For a qualification to be nationally recognised it has to be presented by an awarding body, such as Edexcel, City and Guilds or CACHE. These awarding bodies are responsible for the syllabus and assessment of their courses. Upon successful completion of the assessment the awarding body issues a certificate. Sometimes an awarding body will work in partnership with a professional organisation to develop a course, for example the NCMA or Pre-school Learning Alliance. It is important that before enrolling on any course you check that the qualification is on the framework. All the awarding bodies have websites and helplines that you can contact to check if you are in any doubt. This qualification, the Diploma in Home-based Childcare (DHC), is listed on the qualifications framework as a recognised qualification at Level 3.

National Vocational Qualifications (NVQs) are made up of nationally set standards that are accredited by the Qualifications and Curriculum Authority (QCA). For home-based childcarers the

Think about it

In Hertfordshire a joint initiative between NCMA and Young in Herts has enabled 76 per cent of primary schools and nurseries to offer extended services through registered childminders, providing parents with affordable childcare all year round, through the Hertfordshire School Childminding Network.

relevant standards are the National Occupational Standards in Children's Care, Learning and Development. These cover the care and development of children from birth to 16 years. NVQs can be achieved from Foundation Level to Level 5. The Diploma in Home-based Childcare is a Level 3 qualification and has been designed to offer training in many of the practical skills and competencies set out in the National Occupational Standards. Once the DHC has been achieved you could work towards the NVQ Level 3.

The Foundation Degree is a Level 4 qualification in its own right. It is also seen by the government as making a significant contribution to lifelong learning. Early Years Foundation Degrees aim to integrate study and work in order to develop practice. This is often done through work-based modules, projects, and assessments based on reflective practice-based applications of theoretical perspectives. They can be delivered in a variety of ways, for example through your local higher education institute, university or from the Open University, and are usually part-time over two years.

Sources of help, guidance and funding in relation to continuing professional development

There are many ways of finding out about local opportunities in your area.

Various funds are allocated to training and many qualifications can be subsidised or in some areas

are free, especially if you are under 25 years of age. If you are already in receipt of benefits it is a good idea to talk to your local Jobcentre staff to find out if any training can be paid for. You can also talk to the organiser of any course or training that you plan to do to find out if they can access any funding for you or know of any other sources of help.

It is also worth asking if you can pay for training in instalments, such as each module of a foundation degree, rather than paying for it all at once.

Find out!

- Talk to your local college student services department about courses and training that is available.
- Visit your local careers service office.
- Contact the Early Years Team in the workforce team of your local authority.
- Contact professional organisations such as NCMA or the Pre-school Learning Alliance.
- Look in professional journals, such as *Who Minds?, Practical Professional Child Care, Nursery World*.
- Look in local newspapers.
- Look at relevant websites, for example those of the DfES or QCA.

Working in partnership with parents in the home-based setting

Parents are the first educators of their children and it is imperative that anyone working with young people makes every effort to establish effective partnerships with parents. Children are more likely to reach their full potential if good lines of communication and sound partnerships with their parents have been established.

This unit is assessed by one assignment which can be presented in a variety of formats. It will be marked by your tutor and then externally moderated by CACHE.

This unit will teach you about:

- the childcare practitioner and the community
- families and cultures
- promoting positive relationships with parents or other primary carers
- confidentiality, data protection and the law
- contracts and complaints
- communication with the child's primary carer.

The childcare practitioner and the community

Childcare, parenting and government policy

Recent government childcare policies have supported working parents with schemes like the Working Families' Tax Credit, which is intended to help with the costs of childcare (see Units 1 and 3).

The government has also made significant steps towards eradicating child poverty with the establishment of Sure Start programmes across England, Scotland, Northern Ireland and Wales. Sure Start services include health, social care and education programmes and are intended to respond to local needs within any one community. One way that this service can be delivered is through children's centres and the government is aiming for every community to have a children's centre, offering integrated services for under-fives and their families. Government plans are for 3,500 children's centres by 2010.

Key Term

Sure Start – a government programme attempting to provide young children and their families with better life opportunities.

In addition to children's centres the government announced plans in June 2005 for schools offering wrap-around care, including parenting support, swift and easy referral to a wide range of specialist services and a variety of activities ranging from homework clubs to sport, music tuition, dance and drama.

Key Term

Wrap-around care – care for children before and after school, and during school holidays, but not necessarily provided by the same person or organisation. For example, a registered childminder may provide care before school and during some of the school holidays, whereas an after-school club could provide care after school. Similarly, a holiday play scheme could provide care during part of the school holidays.

The government does not intend that all primary schools offer extended services on their own sites. Schools can work with other schools and childcare providers, including home-based childcarers. Secondary schools are different and the government hopes that they will be open all year round from 8am to 6pm, offering a wide range of activities and services for young people.

Find out!

The childminding network at a children's centre in Gloucestershire works in close partnership with the centre's daycare facility. Childminders provide parents with childcare when the daycare facility is closed, such as evenings and weekends. Childminders can attend training opportunities at the centre, where with parental consent they can leave the minded children in a central crèche. They also have access to all of the centre resources such as the soft playroom.

Find out about your local children's centre.

What services are available to home-based childcarers?

One primary school in the north west of England is offering parents opportunities to develop their literacy and numeracy skills as part of the extended school provision. This programme is funded in part by the local authority and the Learning Skills Council. Parents can either work with their children there or without them, the aim being that some parents will feel more confident helping their children with homework whilst increasing their own skills.

Find out about the extended school provision in your area.

As a home-based childcarer how could you support this programme?

In November 2005 the government announced plans for a curriculum aimed at children under three that would focus on communication, language, literacy, numeracy and social skills. While they may have opponents, it cannot be denied that these plans will raise public debate about what skills young children need to have and how these skills can be encouraged and developed. Home-based childcarers are included in these plans as well as daycare nurseries and other childcare settings. The media interest in

Think about it

The charity Parentline produced a report in November 2005 that praised the work of Sure Start and children's centres, but raised the issue that much of their work is directed at disadvantaged areas of society, so more affluent parents could miss out on vital services. The charity is urging all parents to contact them when they experience family problems. Parentline can be contacted at www.parentlineplus.org.uk

this latest initiative will raise parents' awareness of what activities and experiences their children should be offered when being cared for by other people.

Factors that influence parents in choosing childcare

Finding the right childcare is perhaps one of the most difficult aspects of getting back to work for a parent. Parents have to find something suitable for their child and their income that is in their local area. Although the Children's Information Service provides excellent information for parents they do not necessarily evaluate the pros and cons of each type of childcare, so parents must decide which type of childcare best suits their needs.

There are many different forms of childcare, both registered and unregistered. At the present time, nannies, mother's helps and au pairs are usually unregistered, even if they are found through an agency and have qualifications in childcare. Informal, unregistered childcare, such as through family members or friends, can be successful but is actually illegal. Once the care is delivered in the family member's or friend's home and the parents offer payment, those individuals are technically home-based childminders and should be registered. Daycare nurseries, after-school and breakfast clubs, like childminders, are registered and have to meet the National Standards.

The factors that need to be taken into account by parents when considering childcare very much depend on their children and their working situation, in other words their individual needs.

Parents need to consider the following factors.

- **The age of the child**. Some parents may feel that a young baby would benefit from one-to-one care being given by a nanny or registered childminder; whereas some may feel that their toddler would benefit from being in the company of more children, especially if they are an only child. School-aged children might be tired at the end of the day and parents may feel that a home environment will be more conducive to relaxing and completing homework in a quiet atmosphere.

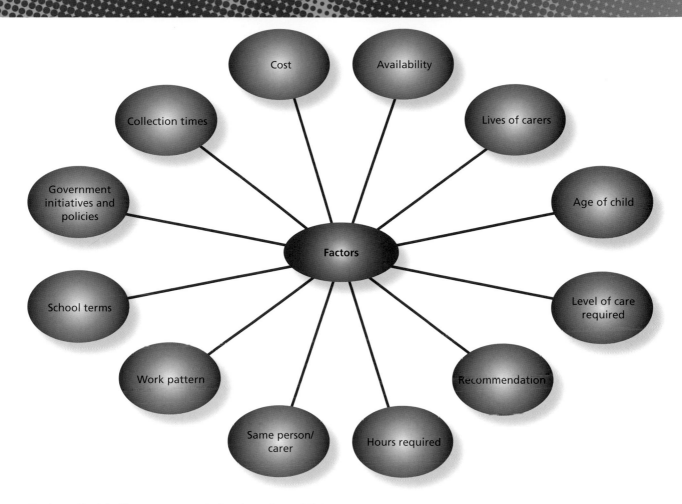

Factors that influence parents in choosing childcare

- **The level of care required**. Parents may feel that their child requires a lot of care. The needs of the child can be better met by a nanny or registered childminder, rather than in a setting where there are more children.

- **Whether or not the child prefers to be amongst other children**. While children are naturally social beings, some children thrive in the company of others but also like being in small groups for short periods of time. In such cases a combination of a nanny or registered childminder plus a pre-school group or nursery for a morning or afternoon might be a good option.

- **Recommendations from other parents**. Many registered childminders rely upon recommendations from other parents to fill their vacancies. This can be very effective as good news will travel fast!

- It is important that the **same person cares for the child all of the time**. Although most daycare nurseries use a key person system there will inevitably be times, due to staff rotas, holidays, sickness and shift patterns, when the key person may not be available. Unless there is an emergency such as illness, this situation is unlikely to happen with a nanny or registered childminder.

Key Term

Key person – a named member of staff who has responsibility for a small group of children. The key person will try to welcome the child each time they arrive at the setting, talk to the parents, complete observations and assessments and provide continuity of care as far as is possible.

Many daycare settings have installed CCTV and webcams that enable parents to observe the care levels of their child at any time of day. Some parents feel that there is safety in numbers in that the more people around at any one time, then the less the likelihood is of abuse happening. For some parents the idea of entrusting their child to one person causes them concern. It is up to registered childminders and approved nannies to do everything that they can to dispel these concerns and present a caring and professional service.

but this may not match the parents' work patterns. Again, nannies and registered childminders can usually offer the flexibility that some parents need.

Chris says, 'The two children I care for are at school during the day, so I have arranged with another family to care for their baby as well. This arrangement meets the needs of both families and the children.'

- **If the child has any special requirements**, such as a special diet or disability. Specific care requirements can be met well in daycare settings, although adverse media coverage of tragic incidences involving poor care and management can make parents feel concerned about their child's needs being met.

- **What hours they need childcare**. Not everyone works nine to five – more and more employers are now encouraging their staff to work flexi-time. Registered childminders and nannies can meet these work patterns more easily than daycare settings.

- If they have **regular work hours or changing shift patterns**. Most extended schools and daycare settings do not operate at night. A nanny can be very flexible, assuming that hours of work have been agreed in the contract. In the same way many registered childminders are extending the details of their registration to include weekends and overnight care.

- **If they need childcare through the school holidays, before and after school**. Some parents find that this type of care can be difficult to organise because it is not continuous. Many daycare settings and extended schools offer care before and after school, as well as during the school holidays,

- **If they have to take and collect their child at the same time each day**. These times of the day are very important for the children, parents and childcarer. Most childcare settings have fixed opening and closing times that will suit many parents.

- **If they need extra help with housework**. Sometimes a nanny will agree as part of their contract to help with light domestic work. They may also agree, for example, to do the children's laundry, clean the kitchen and the children's rooms.

- **What they can afford to pay**. Cost of childcare, even with government initiatives, can be a major consideration for some families. However, registered childminding should not be regarded as a cheaper option to day nurseries. The type of childcare offered can be quite different in each setting and it can be misleading to try to make comparisons.

- **Availability in the local area**. If there are no childcare places near a family's home, school or work locality, they will have to look elsewhere. Registered childminders need to consider the local availability as part of their marketing plans (see Unit 3, page 176).

- **If they have space for a live-in carer**. A live-in childcarer will need their own space and privacy. In an ideal world they should have a separate room and bathroom, and this can be a serious consideration for many families. Ask yourself if you would feel valued and professional if you had the family spare room and every time someone came to stay you had to sleep on the floor in the children's bedroom.

- **The ethos and policies of a setting are important**. For example, a setting may have an ethos which focuses on environmental and conservation matters, and these may be very important for parents. In the same way the ethos may endorse and promote one particular religion or faith. A setting may also place high value on academic achievement.

- **Recent government policies** have made a significant difference to the options for childcare that are available for parents. For example, Working Families' Tax Credit has helped people to meet some of the costs of childcare. For some parents this has meant that they can afford continuity of care.

- The issue of maternity and paternity leave for new parents has been widely discussed by employers and parents. Maternity leave has become a right for new mothers and many take full advantage of the benefit for up to nine months, or in some cases twelve months. Both maternity and paternity leave are dynamic issues and are still being debated within government departments and agencies.

Case Study

Bethany and her partner both work, but up to a year ago could not afford to pay a childminder to care for their three sons every day. This meant that one day each week the children's aunt looked after them and on the other day a neighbour had the children; both adults were unregistered and unpaid. Now the boys go to the same registered childminder five days each week with part of the cost being paid through the Working Families' Tax Credit system.

Can you think of at least three benefits to this family as a result of government policy? See if you can get more.

Link to assessment

E1 Discuss two factors that influence a parent's choice of childcare.

Hint 1

To find out more about how to 'discuss' an issue in your assessment, see page 289 of the study skills section.

Hint 2

Make a list of all forms of childcare and then think of the advantages and disadvantages of each (see Unit 3, page 168).

B Analyse the benefits of home-based childcare.

Hint

Look in the study skills section to find out what the term 'analyse' means.

This criterion may require you to look again at Unit 3, page 168, on the benefits of home-based childcare and also at the factors that influence parental decisions about childcare in this unit (page 202). Write about:

- parental needs and their preferences

- government initiatives

- the type of provision offered, including the environment, resources, and care given

- social issues such as paid parental leave

- recent research and development to support home-based care.

History of childminding, nannies and home-based childcare

The need for childcare is not uniquely modern. Throughout history there has been a need for some form of childcare, perhaps because the birth mother had died in childbirth or if a family had too many children for them to be cared for adequately by one person. In certain sectors of society it was not unusual for a baby to be cared for by a wet nurse, who was employed by the family to feed and care for an infant in either the child's own home or the wet nurse's home, so that the mother could continue her role in society. England has a long history of boarding schools and it was not unusual for small children to be sent to these establishments, but the main focus of these was on education, not necessarily care. Conditions in some boarding schools were very harsh, bullying was commonplace and in some instances it was a case of the survival of the fittest.

The use of nannies employed by families has historically been an option to those with high incomes. Often these nannies would stay with a family for many years, caring for generations of children. These nannies were often unmarried women from good families who had fallen on hard times, but were generally known to the parents.

In Victorian England many women had to work for economic reasons, for example to maintain the workforce in cotton mills and other factories. At this time, large families were not uncommon and childcare was a serious issue for many.

In the 1850s there were basically three main types of childcare.

1   Family relatives, usually elderly or those adults unfit for work.

2   Young girls, often between seven and 10 years of age, although increased pressure on these children to attend school made this a less favourable option.

3   Daycare nurseries – often expensive and not nationwide. These daycare nurseries were sometimes established by philanthropic mill and factory owners or by churches and charitable organisations. They would usually be open from 6.30am to 7pm, but the standard of care was often poor and many closed due to lack of staff and running costs.

Children waiting for food scraps with a carer

At the time many women simply could not afford to make childcare arrangements and it was not unheard of for mothers to administer narcotics to their children as they left for work with the intention that the children remained quiet and 'safe' in their homes during the working day. In some cases employers allowed mothers to bring their children into the factories and many children became unpaid workers in this way, often in highly dangerous situations.

Informal childcare arrangements in the home have always taken place, and still continue to happen despite legislation. Even today nannies do not need to have any qualifications, training or childcare credentials to gain employment, although this situation is changing with the establishment of the approved childcarer scheme. It is still possible for a young foreign student to be employed as an au pair by a family to care for the children and undertake some domestic work in return for free board, lodging and opportunities to learn English. These young people are not subjected to any checks, do not need to have any childcare qualifications and are often recruited through agencies who may or may not check references.

In the early 1970s local authorities recognised that many children were being cared for by unregistered childminders. In 1974 responsibility for the registration of childminders passed from local authority health departments and health visitors to the new social services departments. This move created new posts for childminder registration officers. At the same time a research study in Manchester and Huddersfield showed that large numbers of children were being cared for in very poor conditions, with childminders, who were often poorly educated, receiving very little remuneration for their work and little or no support from local authorities. It is really as a result of this study that the stigma of low childcare standards in childminding became the public face of childminders. However, the author of this study recognised the valuable work that many childminders were doing and worked hard to raise their public profile through a series of conferences for childminders and local authorities.

In 1977 the National Childminding Association, NCMA, was founded by a small group of registered childminders with the aim to improve the general standard of care offered and to promote improved support services. By 2004 NCMA had grown to the extent that it employed over 400 staff and had 50,000 members, provides a membership magazine, training, legal support and is a powerful voice in policy-making decisions by government. NCMA has representation in England and Wales. In addition to the establishment of childminding networks, many of which are quality assured, it has raised the public profile of the profession. In 2005, nannies were able to join NCMA and can become approved through the government's voluntary Childcare Approval Scheme.

Foster care has for centuries relied on the kindness of strangers. In 1536 the Poor Law allowed children to be apprenticed to tradespeople; and these apprentices were often fostered by the tradesperson's family. This tradition continued for several hundred years. The use of wet nurses, as previously mentioned, was a form of fostering and in some cases these infants never returned to their families, remaining with the wet nurse as domestic workers. Long-term fostering became more common from the 19th century as some adults went to live in the colonies and left their children in the home country to be educated and cared for. The Children Act 1948 provided for temporary fostering, especially in emergency situations. In the 1970s specialist fostering schemes were established to provide respite and emergency care. Today foster parents provide care for children in their own homes, sometimes offering short-term temporary care in crisis situations. Foster carers receive training for their role and several qualifications and training courses have been developed to meet the needs of foster carers.

In 1999, the NCMA working in partnership with the Council for Awards in Children's Care and Education (CACHE), developed the CACHE Level 3 Certificate in Childminding Practice, the first Level 3 qualification for childminders. In January 2006 this was replaced by the Level 3 Diploma in

Home-based Childcare, which is appropriate for anyone working with children in a home-based setting.

Families and cultures

Different family structures and traditions

The attitudes and values of societies are continually changing and with these changes our views on the family change. For example, the number of 'traditional' families of married parents and children has decreased over the years, the number of births outside of marriage has increased, and the number of children born into a family has decreased. In essence, no early years practitioners should make assumptions and judgements about the type of family in which a child is living.

Parenting styles

Parents do not really choose their parenting styles. Most parents are influenced by the way in which their own parents raised them. Parenting styles are also affected by the pressure of daily living. Remember that parenting styles can be very different and there is no single correct style.

Most parents want the best for their children and love and care for them. How they do this varies from family to family, and as a result there are many different parenting styles as well as different family structures. Family structure can affect the parenting style, as can cultural variations. Regardless of the parenting style, you must respect the way that parents choose to bring up their children. If you realise that there is likely to be serious conflict between what you expect of the child and what their parents want, you must discuss this very carefully with the parents. It may be that you will be able to reach an acceptable and professional compromise, but it may be that it would be less stressful for all concerned if the parents found alternative care arrangements for their children.

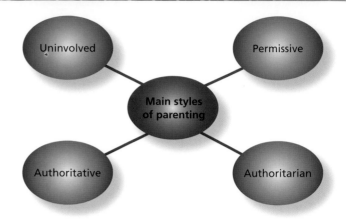

Main styles of parenting

There are generally considered to be three main styles of parenting.

1 Permissive
Permissive parents allow their children lots of personal choice and responsibilities. They do not always attempt to control or manage the behaviour of their children.

2 Authoritarian
Authoritarian parents are likely to be the opposite of permissive parents. They attempt to manage, limit and control the behaviour of their children, and may spend time setting down ground rules. Such parents often have high expectations of their children.

3 Authoritative
Most parents are authoritative. They try to manage and control their children's behaviour. They spend time listening to their children as well as explaining the reasons for certain rules or limits. It is believed that children generally gain most from this style of parenting, because they know and understand the limits and boundaries that are set and so feel secure.

Some cultures favour a more authoritarian style of parenting, with children not expected to question parental views or reasons for limiting behaviour. However, children growing up in an authoritative environment usually benefit due to the consistent approach.

There is also a fourth parenting style of **uninvolved parenting** in which some parents reject their children. This can be due to their own stresses and problems. These parents are uncontrolling, over-permissive and aloof. Children in this type of family can be hostile and rebellious as adolescents and involved in antisocial behaviour.

Family structures

There are a variety of family structures and units. The traditional view is of a family composed of two people of the opposite sex being married with children. This is no longer realistic and many childcare practitioners are not married to the person with whom they live, or they can be divorced or single parents. The family structure is not important as long as the children are loved, treated with consistency and have good physical care.

You need to make sure that you do not have any stereotypical views regarding a particular type of family. What is important for you as a home-based childcarer is that you and the parents agree on how you will care for the child, that the child is loved, that their needs are met through consistent care and that you show respect for the family's way of life.

A range of family structures are shown in the table below.

Family structure	Main features
The extended family	The traditional form of family for centuries in the UK, still common in many parts of the world. Parents, children and relatives live close together, in some cases in the same house. Family members often provide childcare.
Gay/lesbian families	These families can be made up of children being adopted or living with one natural parent who has a partner of the same sex.
Single or one-parent families	One parent lives on their own with the children as a result of divorce, relationship breakdown, death or personal choice.
Mixed ethnic background	Could include families where one parent has a different religion/belief or culture from the other.
Reconstituted families	Made up of one natural parent and one step-parent.
The nuclear family	Sometimes shown as the 'average' family because both parents are living with the children.
Nomadic family	Often associated with travellers and gypsies. Even though the family may not stay in one place for very long the children are often surrounded by other family members.
Adoptive family	Some children may not be aware that they are adopted and therefore can be part of an extended or nuclear family.
Foster family	Children are placed with foster parents for varying lengths of time, often for child protection concerns.
Communal families	Several unrelated families live together and act as an extended family for the children.

E2 Describe two different family structures.

Hint

Think about the families that you have worked with. Without breaching confidentiality, identify which structure they match and list what the key features of each structure are. You will also need to write about how each of the two different family structures that you have chosen are made up, what the key features are and how they function.

C Explain the importance of respecting and valuing different family structures.

Hint

Look at the study skills section on page 290 to find what the term 'explain' means.

This is a development of **E2** and you should write about the benefits to the child, their parents and yourself. This can include ways that you update and increase your own knowledge and awareness of different family structures, and how this can affect a child's development, learning and their overall potential. You may also want to consider the importance of relationships and anti-bias/anti-discriminatory practices.

The importance of understanding and respecting variations in family values and practices in childrearing and child care

The UK is a multicultural society and, whilst Christianity is regarded as the traditional religion and English the predominant language, there are large numbers of children who are bilingual or multilingual and brought up in other religions or with no religion. There are cultural differences between the types of family unit and structures in which children can be brought up. For example,

children from families who are Jehovah's Witnesses will not celebrate birthdays, Christmas or Easter, and one in ten Indian, Bangladeshi or Pakistani families are extended. Cultural differences can affect interactions because many gestures and the use of eye contact do not have universal meaning; as such they can be open to misinterpretation. Childrearing can be affected by cultural variations, although there can be striking similarities.

Think about it

In the late 1980s, studies undertaken by Beatrice Whiting and Carolyn Edwards compared the variations of parenting in such diverse societies as urban America, rural Kenya and Liberia. The studies showed that there were many similarities, despite the vast differences in economic, social and political conditions. With infants and toddlers, the universal emphasis was on providing routine care along with attention and support. By the time the child reached four years of age, most parents shifted their focus to controlling, correcting or managing inappropriate behaviour. Finally, when children reached the age for formal schooling, parents became concerned with training their children in the skills and social behaviours valued by the group. The study concluded that parents around the world resemble each other in numerous ways because of the universal needs of children as they grow and develop.

It is important to remember that some children may live in two different households, moving from one to another during school holidays and weekends. Many children can cope with this, but some may not. It is also important to remember that a change within any family unit or structure, such as moving away from family members, a death within the family, the birth of a sibling, or moving to another country, can be quite disruptive for children and family.

Childcare practitioners should make every effort to find out about and respect the customs of other cultures. What is important is that children in any family are fed, clothed, sheltered, loved and have the opportunity to learn and develop in a protective and caring environment.

Promoting positive relationships with parents and the importance of valuing the child's primary carer

Parents are the first educators of their children and if these children are to reach their full potential it is essential that the relationships between the practitioner and the parents are of the best possible quality. Continuity of care for children is essential. Information needs to be regularly exchanged, it is a two-way process with parents and practitioners seeking each other's opinions, agreeing upon plans and strategies and checking progress.

Find out!

There is much research into partnerships with parents. Look on the Internet, in professional magazines and relevant texts to extend your knowledge about parental partnerships.

How parenting skills are learned and the importance of acknowledging and respecting differences

It is sometimes said that parenting is the one job we can get without training or an interview, yet it is the most important job in the world. Antenatal classes can discuss what happens after birth, but many parents feel that they are not equipped with the knowledge that bringing up a young child

involves. Children's centres and extended school services are developing programmes to help parents build up their parenting skills, but there is often still a lot that needs to be learnt on the job.

Claire and her partner Tony said, 'We had loads of information about the birth and what to expect, but once Daisy was born and we were at home together there were times when we didn't feel very confident at all. Our health visitor offered quite a lot of help but she wasn't around in the middle of the night when we couldn't stop Daisy crying. One of Tony's colleagues used a registered childminder to care for her children and she suggested that we gave her a call. The childminder was really helpful and we now go to the same toddler group as her.'

One of the strongest influences on our own parenting skills is the way in which we were parented as a child. This also includes the social background of the family in which we grew up.

Think about it

If you are a parent think of the things that you do solely because that was the way you were parented as a child.

Or do you do the opposite simply because there were experiences in your childhood that you do not want your children to go through?

We can also learn parenting skills from our cultural background, which may be linked to religious faith and values or traditions and attitudes. Most parents draw on their own memories of being a child to help them deal with their own children, and tend to develop their skills and knowledge as the number of children in their family unit increases. There will be times when parents do not get it quite right, but what is important is that we learn from our mistakes.

The issues involved in supporting the child's parents in their role

It is vitally important to be non-judgemental and not to give parents messages that you disapprove in some way of what they are doing. However, you must remember that supporting parents can sometimes be emotionally demanding and you can put yourself under a lot of pressure. It is never a good idea to let yourself get personally involved with other people's problems.

Understanding that there is no single 'correct' way to bring up children

Everyone who works with children must recognise that parents are the most important people in a child's life, and all practitioners should constantly reaffirm this view to both parents and children.

Values and practices in parenting vary from one culture or social group to another and also from family to family. There is no single correct way to bring up children. Parents choose the methods and practices which are appropriate to their culture, traditions, beliefs and their own upbringing.

> Kasey says, 'I am a nanny and the way that the parents want to bring up their children is very different from the way that I was brought up. However, we have discussed their philosophy a lot and I can understand where they are coming from. If I have any doubts about how to deal with things I talk to them. It is really important to me that I have the same consistent approach as the parents, because we all want what is best for the children.'

Sometimes a parent's views about what they want for their children might be different from your own, so you need to talk about the differences.

You need to make clear to parents that you do your best to care for children as the parents want, but if you are a jobshare nanny or a childminder you may care for children from several different families. In such cases it will be necessary to compromise and negotiate.

Keys to good practice

- Find out how parents would like to be addressed – never assume that children have the same family name as their parents.

- Just because a parent's views are different from yours, they are not necessarily wrong. You should respect all views and wishes of parents.

- Comment positively to parents about what their child has done and reinforce the view that parents are central to the child's life.

- Be patient, using tact and understanding when you believe that parents feel guilty about leaving their children with you.

- You must not make the parents feel unskilled or lacking in information. Tell the parents what their child has been doing, and if appropriate share your plans for activities.

- Think about establishing a home/setting diary if you are not caring for the child in their home, encourage the parent to write in it, for example about what the child has done after they left you and how they have slept.

- You must take care not to appear an 'expert' in all subjects. If an inexperienced parent asks your advice and you do not know the answer, be honest and say so, but try and find out the answer.

- The needs of the child are paramount.

E3 Describe how the practitioner may promote positive relationships with parents.

Hint

Look back at Unit 1 on the importance of working in partnership with parents (see page 50).

Write about:

- how you form and maintain relationships with parents to make sure that the needs of the children can be met
- how you are aware of different lifestyles and parenting methods
- how you can communicate effectively with parents in all forms.

Case Study

Cassie, a nanny for Jenny and Ryan, prepares vegetarian meals for the children in accordance with the parents' wishes. Ryan sometimes goes to his friend's house after school where he is offered non-vegetarian treats by his friend's parents. Ryan's parents have asked Cassie to deal with the friend's parents and to make sure that Ryan sticks to a vegetarian diet.

How should Cassie handle this situation?

What could she say to Ryan and his friend's family?

Understanding that all parents find their role difficult at times

It is important to reassure parents that they are not the only ones facing problems and that most parents face difficulties from time to time. We all experience crises and stress at times in our lives and some cope better than others.

Parents find their role difficult at times

Understanding that the child's parents can have negative as well as positive feelings about their children

For some parents their parenting role can seem like a constant battle. They seem never to be able to manage or cope with their child's behaviour and appear to get little pleasure from interacting with their children. Their skills do not develop and their knowledge remains limited. They may struggle to provide the care, security and boundaries that their children need.

Some parents have unrealistic expectations of how and at what rate their child will develop, for example an inexperienced parent might expect their 12-month-old child to be potty trained. When the child cannot meet these unrealistic expectations parents can feel negative towards their children.

Some parents may not understand that their child has rights and may feel that by giving the child's needs priority, this in some way detracts from their own needs. They find it difficult to take on the responsibility of putting their child first which can lead to resentment of the child.

Case Study

Maggie is a mature first-time mother with a highly paid job. She is confident and professional. However, since the birth of her son she feels lacking in confidence and the parenting skills that she believes she needs, describing herself as 'de-skilled'. Maggie employed Sasha as a full-time nanny from when the baby was born, but is still finding it difficult because she does not trust her own parenting instincts.

How can Sasha support Maggie to raise her confidence levels?

How can Sasha help Maggie to become more skilled?

The stresses that parents may be under and how those stresses may affect their ability to exercise their parenting skills

The families that you work with may experience a variety of stresses that will put a strain on the parents. Community childminders working in a network may have children placed with them specifically because of the stresses and difficulties their family is going through. Such practitioners will need to give some thought not only to how such stress affects the children, but also the effect on the parents and their need for support.

There are many stresses that parents may be under, but remember that some parents will cope, others may not, and that everyone responds and reacts differently to pressure. However, in general terms such stresses can be:

- being a single parent
- poverty
- living away from other family members
- caring for and having responsibility for several children
- a baby who does not sleep
- ill health in the family
- parent's own mental and physical health
- caring for a disabled or elderly family member
- having literacy or communication difficulties
- being a very young or inexperienced parent
- financial difficulties
- relationship difficulties
- employment problems
- racial harassment or abuse
- domestic abuse
- drug or alcohol problems
- a family member in prison

- poor or overcrowded housing conditions if in an extended family
- legal and acrimonious battles over custody of children.

The factors which make it more or less difficult to cope with stress

There are many factors that can make it more or less difficult to cope with stress.

- Exhaustion, both mental and physical, which can affect a person's ability to cope and think logically.
- Worry and uncertainty about the future.
- A feeling of helplessness, feeling out of control or lacking hope that things will improve.
- Too many pressures to enable the parent to manage their time effectively.
- Feelings of guilt and/or shame that they are not coping or providing adequately for their child, for example if they do not have enough money to afford food for a balanced diet.
- Low self-esteem and self-confidence.
- Feelings of insecurity and lacking trust in others.
- Depression, which can last for a long time and is often not recognised or diagnosed.
- Fearful of their own safety, their child's safety, or both.
- Anger towards the other parent.
- Feelings of isolation.
- Seeing the child as yet another problem that has to be dealt with.

Some people cope with stress better than others, indeed some believe that a bit of stress can be healthy because it stops them becoming complacent. People deal with stress in different ways. Some find that doing physical exercise can help relieve the symptoms of stress, whereas others do creative activities such as painting, dance, drama, make music or sing.

Caring for children can be stressful at times and it is important that you are able to recognise the symptoms of stress and do something about them. Seeking help and/or support is not a sign of weakness but a professional way of dealing with certain situations in your work.

Link to assessment

E4 Discuss two sources of stress that parents may experience.

Hint

Read over the list of possible sources of stress on page 214.

Ask yourself why these situations may be stressful for some parents. Write about two sources of stress and say why these might affect the family and the well-being of the children.

Understanding why you should not be judgemental or stereotype families

Some parents will openly share their difficulties with you and may seek your advice. However, other parents may not be able to express how they feel or may not want to talk about it. You must take your cues from the parents and never force a situation.

Most parents will find that they have a bewildering mixture of feelings about their children, ranging from overwhelming love to sheer frustration and annoyance. Not everyone is a 'natural' parent and bonding with their child does not automatically happen. Every parent will raise their child in a different way and you must respect their wishes and views.

Supporting parents experiencing difficulties

It is very important that you do not blame or appear to blame parents who are experiencing difficulties, including negative feelings about their child. Being judgemental or having stereotypical attitudes and values is unprofessional.

Keys to good practice

- Make sure that you have good and effective communication skills and do not breach confidentiality.

- Make sure that the parents know that you trust and respect them.

- When a parent is feeling negative towards their child you can help by encouraging them to express their positive feelings, especially about their child's achievements and progress.

- Talk to the parent about what they like in their child. This will boost their self-esteem and confidence.

- The way that you talk to and interact with the children can give parents ideas on how to be a positive role model.

- When giving advice make sure that you are passing on correct and up-to-date information; this can include appropriate referral to experts or support agencies.

- Try to avoid giving direct advice, help parents to reach their own solutions.

- Encourage the parents to take 'ownership' of the problem and talk through the situation. In this way the parents may be able to come to their own decision, which will be more effective in the end.

- Remember that parents are central to their children's lives and usually know the most about that child. You should not appear to take away the significance of the parents' role. You are not a substitute parent, and it is good practice to ask parents for information about their child even when they are struggling. This shows that you respect their contribution and value their input.

Case Study

Vanessa is a registered childminder, minding Karl and his sister Kylie after school. One evening a very tearful mum turns up to collect the children with the news that her mother has terminal cancer and is not expected to live for more than six months.

How can Vanessa support the mother?

How can Vanessa help Karl and Kylie understand this situation?

Link to assessment

E8 Discuss ways to support a parent experiencing an identified stress.

Hint

You have already identified two potential sources of stress in **E4** (see page 215). Write about the ways that you can support and help a parent while still offering continuity of care to the child.

Supporting parents who want to access government guidance and funding for early years education

Early years education for children between three and five years is funded by central government in the form of the Foundation Stage (in England), Desirable Learning Outcomes (in Wales), Curricular Guidance for Pre-School Education (in Northern Ireland), and Curriculum for Excellence (in Scotland from 2007). Early years education for children under five can be followed in a variety of settings, such as nursery and reception classes, pre-school playgroups, daycare nurseries and accredited childminders.

For a variety of reasons parents may not wish to add another setting into the life of their child and may ask their childminder to deliver early years education. At the present time only accredited childminders who are part of an approved childminding network can offer early years education. Such people will have to plan, implement and assess activities that follow the appropriate curriculum for two and half hours each day for five sessions. They will also have their educational provision inspected by Ofsted in England, Estyn in Wales, Her Majesty's Inspectorate of Education in Scotland, and the Department of Education in Northern Ireland.

Information on early years education for under-fives can be found on the Parents pages on www.dfes.gov.uk. The related documents for England and Wales are available from QCA Publications and the Curriculum and Assessment Authority for Wales (ACCAC) respectively; details for both are given at the end of this book. Many early years partnerships hold information sessions for parents on aspects of early years education and have produced leaflets to support and guide parents.

Working Tax Credits or childcare vouchers issued by employers should not be used to pay for early years education. Both of these benefits are designed to help with the cost of childcare.

Confidentiality, data protection and the law

Confidentiality has already been discussed in Unit 1, but it is such an important issue that it needs to be revisited.

What is meant by confidentiality?

Home-based childcarers acquire a lot of information about the children and families that they work with. Some of it may be told directly by the parents or by other professionals such as teachers (with parental permission), and some of it may be picked up indirectly, perhaps from the children. The crucial characteristic of confidentiality is not sharing with other people or passing on personal information about the families with whom you are working.

Key Term

Confidentiality is about privacy and discretion, trust and respect.

Be careful that you do not breach confidentiality when talking to other childcare professionals

The importance of handling information about children and families in a confidential way

Children and their families have a legal right to privacy. The Data Protection Act 1998 is designed to prevent confidential and personal information being passed on without a person's consent and now includes not just information stored on computers but also on paper and screen, including photographs.

Whilst you may be very careful with written or digitally stored information, it is all too easy to breach confidentiality in general conversations with other home-based childcarers and practitioners. For example, when talking about your work, planned activities or behaviour difficulties at a toddler group you could inadvertently breach confidentiality and give away enough information for the child and their family to be identified by another person. Always think very carefully before you start to discuss professional issues with other people.

Why and how confidentiality must be maintained and the circumstances in which it can be breached

The information that you need to share with parents is confidential, as is the information that they share with you. This can include:

- contract details, such as fees, hours, addresses and contact details
- information about yourself, your qualifications, experience, training
- information about a new child at your setting, such as how often the child asks for the toilet, if they have special words with specific meanings
- what you will do in an emergency
- routine events, such as nappy changing, toileting, ways to meet parents' and children's needs
- medical issues
- education records
- contact details
- parent's employment details
- religious beliefs
- children's likes and dislikes
- how and when you exchange information daily.

It is important to remember that written information should not be removed from the setting or home, so medical cards, for example, should remain in the child's home if at all possible. Some registered childminders have cupboards or filing cabinets which can be locked, and also

Keys to good practice

- Never discuss one set of parents with another.
- Take care with casual conversations amongst your own friends and family.
- When preparing assignments and coursework make sure that you do not identify any child and their family. Do not refer to them by their real names, use initials or a pseudonym.
- Discuss with parents what to say when dealing with other professionals and get their agreement and permission to share information about the child.

Link to assessment

E6 Identify information that needs to be shared between the home-based childcarer and the parents.

Hint

You will need to name and briefly describe the different kinds of information that you will want from the parents *and* what information you need to share with parents.

- In what situations might you find yourself likely to pass on information when you should not – is this gossip?

- Are there people or circumstances that put pressure on you to share information in ways that you know you should not?

- What can you say to people when they are trying to get you to breach confidentiality?

- How do you respond if another childcare practitioner shares confidential information with you in an inappropriate way?

password-protect their computer files. This ensures that information can be kept confidential and is not accessible to other adults or children.

Most parents want the best for their children, including the support and help of other professionals so that the needs of their child can be met. This may mean that certain information will have to be shared. The only exception to this is a child protection issue, when sharing information may put the child at greater risk.

There are only two sets of circumstances in which confidentiality can be breached:

- if parents have given permission for you to do so

- if it essential to do so in the interests of a child.

There may be times when another professional wishes to discuss or share information about a child, such as a teacher if you collect children from school, or a health visitor if you have taken a child for a health check. If you have not got parental permission to discuss or share information with these professionals then you will need to explain that to do so would breach confidentiality and be unprofessional. Discuss these incidents with parents and reach agreement on what you should do.

Case Study

Confidentiality with permission

Mel is a nanny for Roisin who is having speech therapy. Roisin's parents both travel extensively and have given written permission to the speech therapist for Mel to attend appointments and consultations on their behalf and discuss Roisin's therapy.

Sadia is a registered childminder and has noticed bruises on the arms and legs of one of the children in her care. She is concerned that the child may be in need of protection and so contacted the Local Safeguarding Children Board (formerly the ACPC) to report her concern. Sadia did not tell the parents that she had done this.

Link to assessment

E7 Describe how you keep information confidential.

Hint

Write about how you make sure that any information concerning children and their families, whether spoken or written in any shape or form, is kept safe.

D Explain how and when the home-based childcarer should breach confidentiality.

Hint

This is a development of **E7**. You will need to write about when information should be shared with someone on a 'need-to-know' basis, whom you should inform and how you do this. You will also need to consider professional and legal responsibilities and the rights of the child.

Contracts and complaints

Contracts were discussed in Unit 1 (page 83) and it cannot be reinforced enough how essential it is that you negotiate a contract with parents *before* you start to care for their children.

The importance of monitoring and reviewing contracts at agreed intervals

Childcare is a dynamic profession, constantly changing, not necessarily because of government policies but as a result of the natural development of the children. You would not do an activity with a baby and continue to do it unchanged for years, no matter how much of a favourite it was; there would need to be some variation or progression. It is the same with your contract. Your situation will change as the children change and develop. For example, when you signed the contract with the parents you may not have had to pick their children up from school or nursery, and may now be doing this. In the same way, when you started caring for a baby he or she may not have been weaned, so you may now be feeding the baby in different ways. In both of these scenarios your responsibilities have changed and there are many factors that have also changed, such as safety in transporting children, possible allergies or dietary requirements. Some home-based childcarers review their contracts with parents once each year, others do it more frequently. Some childminders review all of their contracts every time a new child starts because the care circumstances change. Some nannies sign their contract at the beginning of their employment and do not look at it again until they leave. This is not good practice and nannies need to review their contracts regularly.

How often you review your contracts is really up to you but what is important is that they get reviewed.

Review contracts with parents regularly

Case Study

Karly was employed through a nanny agency to care for twins in their family home. She signed a contract when she started employment. Eighteen months later a new baby arrived and Karly's workload significantly increased, but she didn't review her contract. When she complained to her employers that she was not getting her agreed hours off work, they were not sympathetic. Karly had to go back to the agency to get another contract agreed, which took several weeks and damaged her working relationship with the parents as they thought that she was being unreasonable.

What mistakes did Karly make?

In what ways could she improve her working relationship?

Keys to good practice

- Set a date for a review of the contract when you first negotiate it with the parents.

- Set a review date no later than 12 months from the date that it was first signed; many people will set this date every six months.

- Make sure that you have agreed to everything in the contract and are completely familiar with its contents.

- Be prepared to review and reconsider aspects of the contract every time your situation changes, even if the agreed review date has not been reached.

Complaints policy, procedure and protecting yourself against complaints

Writing policies was discussed in Unit 3 on page 185, so it would perhaps be a good idea to review this section before reading further.

Dealing with complaints can be stressful; nobody likes to be told that they are not doing something right, even if they know that they have made a mistake. Most home-based childcarers pride themselves on following best practice at all times and it can be hard to deal with any complaints. However, it is realistic to recognise that there will be situations when parents will not agree with you, so you must be prepared for such occasions.

You may find yourself in a potential conflict with parents over:

- the breaking of agreements or contractual arrangements, for example not paying for childcare, always being late to collect the child

- breaches of confidentiality, such as overheard gossip or secondhand information

- different attitudes to childrearing, such as approaches to routines

- different attitudes to behaviour management, such as how to deal with unwanted behaviour – you might want to use 'time-out' as a last resort, but the parents may disagree and want you to negotiate and explain

- poor communication leading to misunderstanding.

You may decide that you want to formally write a policy which sets out how you will deal with complaints. You may want to include and consider:

- details of the complaint, including who made it, when it was made and who else was involved

- what you will do initially, whether you will talk it through with the parents immediately or agree another time to discuss it

- who you will involve and what their role will be. This might be another home-based childcarer, a childminding support worker, another nanny, or a union representative

- issues of confidentiality.

- Stay calm at all times, breathe deeply and keep your head up, try to maintain eye contact with the other person.

- Listen very carefully to what is being said, if necessary check that you have heard correctly, by asking the other person to either repeat what they have said, or ask open-ended questions.

- Accept any statements that are true.

- Ask for clarification of statements that you feel are untrue.

- Stick to the facts, do not involve emotions, feelings, personal opinions or suppositions.

- Repeat factual information that you have given verbally if necessary.

- Never get drawn into an argument, this is unproductive and unprofessional.

- Ask for suggestions as to how the complainant thinks you could improve.

- Take action as soon as you can.

- Provide the person who made the complaint with the information needed to follow up their complaint if they are not satisfied.

The role of the regulator and other bodies in dealing with complaints

Ofsted in England, CSIW in Wales, Education and Training Directorate in Northern Ireland and HMI in Scotland regulate home-based childcarers, particularly childminders. If a parent or another person contacts the regulator with a complaint against you, there is a legal responsibility for the regulator to investigate. They will make arrangements to interview both parties involved before they make a decision. You do have the right of appeal, provided that you have not committed a proven criminal offence. If it is proven that you have committed a criminal offence, such as put a child at risk or harm, the regulator will hand over details of the case to the police. The Criminal Prosecution Service will then make the final decision as to whether there will be further action.

Involving the police is the worst-case scenario; most complaints can be dealt with by the home-based childcarer and the parents without involving any other parties. Many people find that their local authority's Early Years Team can be very helpful in offering advice and support. NCMA also have a legal helpline for members and will offer support, advice and guidance.

Link to assessment

E5 Describe how to resolve two potential areas of conflict between a parent and the home-based childcarer.

Hint

Think about the issues that could lead to potential conflict, write about two possible areas for conflict and how you could resolve these issues. Think about the needs of the family, how you deal with confrontation and communicate in professional ways.

Communication with the child's primary carer

The importance of regular and effective communication between you and the parents

See also Unit 1, page 58.

The key to any successful relationship is communication. Communication can be defined as an exchange of ideas, contact between individuals, consultation and interaction.

The two broad types of communication are verbal and non-verbal communcation. Non-verbal communication includes:

- eye contact

- gestures such as pointing

- body language

- touch

- written language, including email and text messaging

- pictures

- symbols.

Verbal communication encompasses the spoken language, including telephone conversations and face-to-face contact, and factors such as tone of voice.

We use most of these forms of communication every day; for example, have you ever used a different tone of voice to manage a child's behaviour?

Communication in any form is a two-way process that requires a 'sender' and a 'receiver'. For example, you are having a conversation with a child:

Child (sender)
'Can you read this book with me please?'

You (receiver)
'Yes of course, let's sit down together on this cushion.'

Communication requires time and effort from both sides. Lack of communication can lead to misunderstandings and misinformation. There are skills that you can learn which will help you become a more effective communicator, not just with parents, but also with the children that you care for, and indeed all the other people that you come into contact with in both your professional and personal life. There are basically four main communication skills.

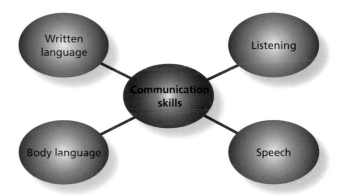

The four main communication skills

Listening

See also Unit 3, page 174.

Listening is a fundamental part of communication. It is not a passive activity, so it does not just happen. To be a good listener requires time, effort and concentration. Being a good listener does not come naturally to some people. They find that they are easily distracted, or that their feelings about a person can affect how well they listen.

There are several things that you can do to make sure that you are an effective listener. There are pitfalls that you can fall into if you are not aware. Researchers at the University of Leeds came up with a list of barriers to good listening, but also found all of the barriers could can be turned around into positive points of good practice!

Speech

You will be using some form of spoken communication every day with your family, the children that you care for and all the other people that you come into contact with. Speaking is possibly the most effective way of communicating with other people. Spoken words can help to build relationships. You can supplement your spoken words with facial expressions, gestures, body language and eye contact in ways that you can never do with telephone conversations, emails, faxes and written messages.

However, once said, words cannot be taken back. It is very easy to make a quick response to someone without really thinking about what you say. This can sometimes lead to misunderstanding and even distress. The old maxim 'engage the brain before the mouth' is good advice.

Another thing to be aware of is that spoken words are often not as exact as written words. It is common practice to have to write things down in order to make sure that everything is covered accurately and nothing is missed out, for example when making a speech or giving a talk. It is good practice to make written notes beforehand if you are going to speak to a parent or another professional about a specific or important issue. In this way you can be sure that you remember everything that you want to say, and that everything you say is accurate and factual.

Speaking on the telephone is commonplace and is a very important way of communicating with

Smiling when you're on the phone makes your voice tone warmer

people. If you are using the telephone for business it is good practice to remember the points in the box below.

Keys to good practice

- Try to speak more slowly than you would do if the person was standing in front of you.

- Try to speak as clearly as possible.

- Do not let your voice drop at the end of sentences. This will make it more difficult for the person on the other end to hear you clearly.

- If possible, try to use the telephone in a room or place where there is little background noise. Other noises will be distracting for both you and the listener.

- Smile – this will automatically give your voice a warmer tone.

Can you work out how these people are feeling from their body language?

Body language

Body language is also described as non-verbal communication. Your body is giving messages all the time you are talking and listening. Sometimes our bodies will be saying one thing and our mouths will be saying something else – this can be detrimental to communication. You should always try to maintain positive body language when dealing with parents, children and other professionals. In fact, it could be argued that you should always use positive body language!

Below is a chart of some of the most common forms of body language and their interpretations.

A word of warning – these are only possible interpretations and you should be careful not to read too much into another person's mannerisms. However, it is a good idea to be aware of some of the more common forms of negative body language so that you can avoid them, such as rubbing your nose when telling a parent how their child has behaved that day!

Body language	Possible interpretation
Erect brisk walk	Confidence
Standing with hands on hips	Readiness, or sometimes aggression
Sitting with legs crossed, foot kicking slightly	Boredom
Arms crossed on chest	Defensiveness
Walking with hands in pockets, shoulders hunched	Dejection
Hand to cheek	Evaluation, thinking
Touching or slightly rubbing nose	Rejection, doubt, or lying

Body language	Possible interpretation
Rubbing the eye	Disbelief or doubt
Hands clasped behind back	Anger, frustration, apprehension
Head resting in hand, eyes downcast	Boredom
Rubbing hands	Anticipation
Sitting with hands clasped behind head, legs crossed	Confidence, superiority
Open palm	Sincerity, openness, innocence
Pinching bridge of nose, eyes closed	Negative evaluation
Tapping or drumming fingers	Impatience
Steepling fingers	Authoritative
Patting or fiddling with hair	Lack of self-confidence, insecurity
Tilted head	Interest
Stroking chin	Trying to make a decision
Looking down, face turned away	Disbelief
Biting nails	Insecurity, nervousness
Pulling or tugging at ear	Indecision

Written language

There is an assumption that every professional is able to write effectively in every possible situation, such as keeping children's records, planning documents, and writing reports or messages for parents. However, this is not true. Many people have problems with writing, including feeling uncertain about things like spelling, grammar, the quality of their handwriting and a lack of confidence in what they write. There are many sources of help for adults who feel that they have problems with writing in any shape or form. Your college, local library and many other local amenity offices will be able to give details of the help that is available in your area.

Personal computers are a great help for people who have problems with the written word and worry about their handwriting. Computer programs have built-in spelling and grammar checks which can be very useful, but are not infallible. The printed word is still written, but because it comes from a printer rather than a person's own hand it will be easier to read.

Emails come under written forms of communication and can be very efficient. By using email you can send the same message to several people.

Case Study

Josie became aware that one of the children in her care had headlice. As a registered childminder she had to inform all of the parents of the children she cared for, so she sent one email directing parents to a website where they could get information on how to treat headlice. She also spoke directly to each parent when they collected their child.

Do you use email in this way?

Can you think of any benefits and disadvantages of contacting parents by email?

Communication difficulties and strategies for addressing them

Communication can be blocked or hindered if individual differences are not understood and respected. Communication with adults and children should reflect the individual needs of both parties. Communication difficulties can happen at a physical level, a sensory level and also at a cultural and social circumstances level, whereby the meaning of the communication may be misunderstood. It is important that you can adjust your style of communication to meet the needs of the person and the situation. This might mean that you may have to use more positive body language and gestures, pictures, photographs or a translator. You should never make assumptions or jump to conclusions, especially about what or how someone is communicating.

gestures, body language, pictures and symbols can often help to alleviate this difficulty.

Text messaging can be a very efficient way of communicating with people. We are all aware of the adverse publicity that the media has given text messaging due to the frequent lack of correct spelling or grammar within text messages. Text messaging can also be used to bully or be abusive. In spite of these issues it can be invaluable for communicating with a person who has a hearing impairment.

Using a different language

Different language can also include sign language, which may not be fully understood or can easily be misinterpreted. People using a strange language may not always be aware that sometimes their words can sound abrupt or unreceptive to the other person. This is where differences in communication styles can lead to misinterpretation. Do not raise your voice when trying to communicate with a person who does not speak the same language as you – shouting does not help and can appear aggressive. Speaking clearly, with lots of positive body language and gestures, can be beneficial. Also, give the other person thinking time to respond to you. Do not get impatient.

Communication difficulties

Find out!

Local authorities have translation services for people whose first language is not English, and also cover published information in Braille.

Find out if you can access this service to help you provide a more efficient service.

Using writing or print

Not everyone is able to understand or interpret the written word, but this does not necessarily mean that the person is not able to communicate. Using clearly spoken language with lots of positive

Using the telephone

Telephone communication is commonplace in today's world, but we sometimes forget that some people do not find it easy to use a telephone. People with hearing impairments can get a minicom service which allows them to read the words of the speaker. In such situations text messaging can be an acceptable alternative to making a phone call. It is also important to remember that telephone conversations do not have the added benefit of gestures, facial expressions and body language to supplement the spoken word. Without these there are more opportunities for either side to misinterpret what is being said. Some individuals need face-to-face conversations in order for them to fully understand what is being said.

Hearing and speech impairments

These impairments should not be regarded as communication difficulties as with respect and tolerance, communication can effectively take place. Be very careful not to stereotype, be judgemental or label an individual who has physical reasons for communication difficulties.

Find out!

Makaton and British Sign Language are just two different forms of communication. Many colleges and local authorities run training classes for people to learn alternative forms of communication.

Find out if there are classes near you that you could join to help you become a more effective communicator.

Poor communication

Poor communication can be caused by misinterpretation of what has been said or incorrect information being received. To avoid this you can write things down, if appropriate, or simply check with the other person that they have understood you.

Using sign language

Poor communication can also happen when people do not understand what each other is doing, or what their role is. Parents can misunderstand your role and perhaps think that you are trying to replace them in their child's life. This can be avoided by clearly explaining your role and responsibilities before you start to care for a child.

Poor communication can also happen when too much technical jargon is used, including abbreviations. This can be very daunting for the people involved who do not understand the terms being used.

Environmental factors

Problems like noise and poor light can create communication difficulties, as can speaking from too far away. Make sure that if you have important information to share, you are both in a reasonably quiet and well-lit place. This does not just apply for face-to-face contact but also for telephone conversations.

Time factors

Effective communication takes time, so you must make sure that you got have enough time to get across the message in whichever way you consider appropriate. Time pressures can lead to people not listening effectively and messages being misunderstood or only half received. It is good practice to try to make a specific, agreed time to talk to parents if you or they have something important to discuss.

The importance of maintaining the balance between the personal/ friendly and the business/ contractual aspects of the relationship

For the benefit of everyone, including the children, it is very important to be clear about any business or contractual aspects of home-based childcare which could be a potential source of misunderstanding. This is why negotiating and agreeing upon a written and signed contract is essential (see Unit 1, page 63, for an example contract).

Most home-based childcarers get on very well with parents and it is natural that you want to be on good terms. You are very high on the list of people that the parents trust. However, there is a big difference between being friendly and becoming friends. If you get too familiar it can sometimes be difficult to maintain the business side of the relationship.

You should give careful thought to socialising with parents. Sometimes this can be a difficult situation for a nanny, particularly if they are on

Case Study

Debbie had established a monthly newsletter which she gave out to parents of her childminding service, telling them about things that the children had been doing, what plans she had and also any training events that she had been on. During a conversation with one parent Debbie realised they did not know that she had recently achieved her NVQ Level 3, even though she had been giving regular updates in the newsletter over the last few months. Debbie knew that the parent had received the newsletter, but did not realise that they could not read it. Debbie now hands over the newsletter, points out the pictures to the parent and tells them briefly about her plans.

How else could Debbie ensure effective communication with this parent?

Should she still continue to give this parent the newsletter?

holiday with the family. You also need to give careful thought to situations where parents may try to persuade you to do them a favour, or change contractual arrangements so that they interfere with your personal life. It is possible that you may find yourself under pressure to offer more to the family than you wanted to.

Case Study

Aaron's parents have set up a direct debit to their nanny's bank account to pay her salary each month, which works well for Jude, the nanny. However, they have started to question the amount that they are paying and are asking for some money back, for example they do not want to pay for Bank Holidays, or times when Aaron goes to a friend after school and is not collected and cared for by Jude. The parents do not want to pay Jude for when they are away and she cares for Aaron overnight. Jude thought that she had sorted out salary details when they negotiated the contract, but now she feels that she is being taken advantage of.

What can Jude do?

It is vitally important that you review and renegotiate the contract every time that circumstances change. Some people think that this can become pedantic, but it will make sure that your relationship remains professional and businesslike, and makes the boundaries for both parties very clear.

Conflict resolution

There may be circumstances that you find yourself in where, no matter how good your communication skills are, there is conflict between you and one or both parents. It is important to remember that children will pick up on the atmosphere between you very quickly and may become distressed. However, do not ignore potential conflict situations, hoping that they will go away or that they will resolve themselves. They won't.

It is good practice to deal with the situation as quickly as possible, but at the same time do not act on impulse. Take time to think about the situation in an objective and unemotional way. Be prepared to find a solution that suits you both. This could mean that both you and the parents will have to be prepared to be flexible and make compromises. Do not expect to resolve a conflict situation in one meeting, it may take several, but it is important that you keep all lines of communication open.

If in the worse possible case, though this rarely happens, you and the parents cannot resolve your difficulties after all ways have been explored, then you will have to end your contract with the parents. To continue in a situation like this would not be beneficial to the children in the long term.

If you are involved in a conflict or even concerned about the possibility of one, it is always worth thinking about and reflecting upon how it has, or might have, occurred.

- Some conflicts are a result of mis-communication, someone taking a comment the wrong way, not hearing properly or thinking that the other person is either not interested or does not care.

- Sometimes emotional pressures can cause a conflict situation to occur, because one person might be under pressure that you are not aware of. This can affect their responses and reactions.

- Lack of confidence can be a potential cause of conflict. A person might be worried that they are not good enough, not clever enough or that the other person knows more than them. This can result in a person being unhelpful, possibly becoming aggressive and lashing out.

- Conflicts can happen when one person becomes angry and aggressive. They may demand that they are right and will want to come out on top of the situation. An assertive person does not become submissive in such situations, which would only make the situation worse. A submissive person is someone who expects to either be put down or be in the wrong. An assertive person does not get into win/lose situations but is able to handle a situation so that both sides achieve, a 'win/win' result and therefore resolve the conflict.

Keys to good practice

- Deal with the situation as quickly as you can.

- Keep calm, do not raise your voice; keep your body language, gestures, or facial expressions positive and non-threatening.

- Keep your emotions under control.

- Make sure that you communicate in a calm and non-threatening way.

- Acknowledge and show the other person that you are actively listening to their point of view.

- If you are unsure of what someone is saying, ask them to clarify it, using open-ended questions to get more information.

- Try to use 'I' statements, for example 'I can care for your child after school during term time'. This is clear and unambiguous, whereas saying 'If you want, I can care for your child after school' is not clear.

- If appropriate write the main points down.

- Watch the other person, observe them and see if there are any indications that they might be under pressure or stress.

- Try to increase your knowledge of different cultures and speech differences.

- Try to be assertive, not argumentative.

Link to assessment

A Evaluate the concept of working in partnership with parents.

Hint

Look in the study skills section on page 289 to find out what the term 'evaluate' means.

Write about:

- parents who may feel powerless, or the shift of power may not be equal

- the mismatch between the expectations of the parents and those of the home-based childcarer

- how partnership with parents impacts positively and negatively on children's needs and well-being

- relevant research on partnerships with parents.

Planning to meet the children's individual learning needs in the home-based setting

It is essential that you do everything you can to meet children's individual needs in all aspects of your work. This involves much more than just meeting basic physical and health needs, it also includes creating an environment where everyone is respected, having responsibilities, opportunities, choices and freedom. There will inevitably be times when some children's individual needs and wishes cannot be met because of what is necessary for the rest of the children that you are caring for. If this is the case it is important that you explain to the children why their freedom and needs might occasionally have to come second.

This unit is assessed by one assignment which can be presented in a variety of formats. It will be marked by your tutor and then externally moderated by CACHE.

This unit will teach you about:

- observation and assessment of children's development in a home-based setting
- preparing, implementing and evaluating plans for home-based groups of children of different ages and abilities
- meeting individual learning needs in the home-based setting.

Observation and assessment of children's development in a home-based setting

The planning cycle

Everybody makes plans at some point in their lives. They can be short-term plans, such as what you will wear that day, or longer-term plans, such as booking a holiday three months in advance and putting £50 aside each month to save up. Writing a shopping list is a form of planning, as is making a 'things to do today' list.

Planning is really about preparing, making certain arrangements and checking that those arrangements will work. For example, you plan to wear a certain top one day so:

- you need to check that it is clean, and
- if it is not, make arrangements to wash it.

But you may need to ask yourself the following questions.

- Have I got time to wash the top and get it dry?
- If not, should I plan to wear a different top?

You are now back to where you started, thinking about which top to wear, so you have in effect gone round in a circle. However, it is not a meaningless circle. You did the following:

You *planned* – which top to wear?

You *assessed* and *observed* – is it clean?

You *evaluated* – have I got time to wash and dry the top?

Do I need to choose a different top?

You *implemented* your plan – either by wearing the top or by choosing another one.

Which top shall I wear?

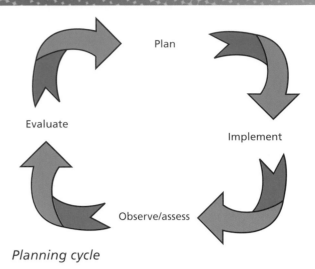
Key Terms

Plan – to prepare, set up and organise activities or experiences.

Implement – to put into practice, carry out.

Assess – to measure, consider, or weigh up.

Evaluate – to look at and consider the positive and negative aspects of something.

Observing children

Rationale for and methods of child observation and assessment

To observe means to watch, study, examine or scrutinise. These are things that you will do every day as part of your childcare practice. You will watch children to make sure that they are safe, and so that you can tell their parents what they have been doing. You will do this almost automatically. However, there are other reasons why you need to observe children. Many practitioners carry a small notebook and pen or pencil in their pocket and jot down interesting things that they notice about the children. This is a form of observing and often provides the information for more formal ways of observing children.

Key Term

Observation – watching, studying, examining or scrutinising the actions of others.

Formally observing someone is not always as easy as it sounds and takes practice. It can last for ten minutes or more in one period, or can be in the form of a series of short periods over a length of time, depending on what you want to observe.

You cannot possibly write down everything that a child does or says in ten minutes, and will inevitably get distracted. The way around this is to decide on something specific to write about, in other words decide on an *aim*. This makes you focus on one thing and get as much information as possible about it; for example, you might decide to focus on how well a child manages to build a tower with a construction set, or your aim might be to make a special note of how many times a young child shows aggressive behaviour towards other children. It is important that you keep your aim simple and focused, but do not forget to consider how other areas of development or aspects of behaviour may impact on your aim and subsequent evaluation.

Some of the reasons why you need to observe children

Case Study

Paramjeet's parents have asked their nanny to make a note of how many times he does not respond to her voice (this is an aim) during a normal working day. The parents are concerned that Paramjeet may have a hearing difficulty (this is the reason for the observation). The nanny kept a notebook and pencil in her pocket and made a note of the time, what they were doing and how Paramjeet responded.

Have you ever been in a similar situation?

What did you do?

Why do I need to observe children?

To learn more about children's needs

Making time to specifically observe one child will help you identify their particular strengths and weaknesses, or perhaps confirm what you may have

suspected for some time. Sometimes the evidence that you produce can be used to help get the child appropriate specialist help. If you know what the needs of the children are you will be able to provide specific activities for them and so meet their needs.

To provide information for parents and other professionals

The information that you pass on to parents must be accurate. Parents need to know how their child is progressing. If you keep records of observations that you have made you will show the parents that you are not only a professional childcare practitioner, but that you see their child as an individual that you really know and understand. Sometimes a child may already be receiving help and support from other professionals for a specific problem. These professionals may ask you to provide them with information about the child, which must be accurate and helpful.

To check to see if a child is developing and growing

Doctors and health visitors regularly check babies and children to see if there are any growth or developmental problems. Although these checks are regular, you spend a lot of time with the children in your care and are in a very good position to check the children more often than doctors or health visitors. You can make a game of measuring children to see how much they have grown, or check to see if a baby is progressing to the next developmental milestone in an informal way.

To help plan activities

The more information that you have about the children in your care, the better equipped you will be to provide them with appropriate things to do. You should not, for example, plan to make a collage of pictures cut from a catalogue if the child involved in the activity cannot use scissors. Let the child use scissors and practise cutting, but make your collage of both cut and torn out pictures.

To check that planned activities are appropriate for the children

Sometimes you may plan a particular activity that has a specific purpose, such as using scissors. It is very useful to observe the child while they are doing the cutting to see if what you have planned is effective in helping that child develop scissor control. The idea of checking the effectiveness of activities is often referred to as evaluation.

To help sort out a particular problem

Sometimes a parent may tell you about a concern they have about their child and ask for your

help in solving the problem. If you carry out observations on the child you will have more information that could either help reassure the parent that there is no reason for concern, or identify a problem. You will then have enough information to act upon and if necessary seek professional help.

Different forms of observation

There will be times when you want to record something that a child has done both quickly and

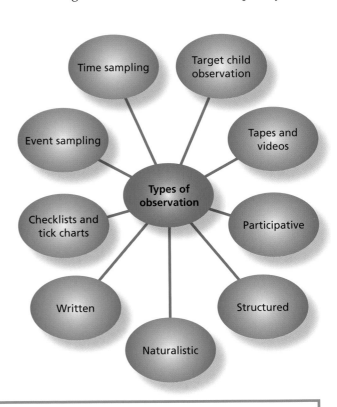

Link to assessment

E1 Include three observations that you have carried out on one child.

Hint

You do not have to include these observations in the main body of your assignment. You should put them in an appendix section and then they are not included in your word count. However, you must make constant reference to the observations throughout your assignment.

See also Link to assessment after the different formats for observations (page 241).

E2 Discuss why it is important for the home-based childcarer to observe children in their care.

Hint

Re-read the section above and think about the reasons for observing children. Try to think of some occasions when you have observed children and why the information you gathered was important. Think about what makes up the planning cycle and how observations can help you meet individual needs.

informally. On the other hand, there will be times when you will want to record something in a more formal, organised way. There are several different ways, or methods, that you can use to record information about children.

Written

Written observations are ways of recording information about a child's growth and development or behaviour over a short period of time. They provide a description of what happened at the time of the observation. Written records are usually written in the present tense, for example 'She sits and looks at the book, holding the book with her right hand and turning the pages with her left.'

Plus and minus points

Written observations require little preparation, just something to write on and with, and can be done quickly. However, this type of observation can only be used to record short periods of time and it is difficult to make a note of everything that is happening.

Below is an example of part of a written observation that a home-based childcarer could make; it does not have an evaluation or assessment section, and is descriptive only. Note that this is not the child's real name, it has been changed so as not to breach confidentiality.

Checklists and tick charts

There are many checklists and tick charts that are published to record different aspects of development, such as whether the child recognises all the letters of the alphabet or different colours. Amongst other things, health visitors and other medical professionals use these forms to record a child's height and weight at a given age. These charts are usually referred to as centile charts and can be a very useful way of comparing children's growth and development with other children of the same age and sex. You can produce your own checklists to record specific information about how a child is behaving or how they complete a task that you have given them.

Name: Ahmed Hameed

Date: 28 February 2006

Age: two years and four months

Time: 10.15am

Place: in the childminder's home, with two other children in the room.

Ahmed is sitting, with his legs folded underneath him, on the carpet of the playroom. Two other children are also sitting with him. There is a box of DUPLO® in front of Ahmed. He reaches into the box with his right hand and takes out two pieces. Ahmed looks at one of the other children and smiles at her. He then looks very closely at the DUPLO® in his hands and tries to put the two pieces together. When he has fixed them together he reaches into the box again and takes out two more bits. Concentrating, he tries to fix one piece to the other two, but as he pushes all the pieces separate. Ahmed sighs loudly and tries to put them together again. The girl sitting next to him says, 'let me do it'. Ahmed says, 'no, me do it' in a loud voice. He tries again to put all the pieces together, but can't do it. Ahmed stands up and throws the DUPLO® pieces across the room. I stopped writing at this point.

Concerns: Ahmed throwing the DUPLO® around.

What to do next: help Ahmed to join DUPLO® pieces and make sure he knows why he should not to throw toys

To be continued at a later date.

Plus and minus points

Checklists and tick charts are quick and simple to use and can be used again at a later date to see if there has been any change. You can also use checklists and tick charts for more than one child, if, for example, you are evaluating children's responses to a particular activity. The main disadvantage of checklists and tick charts is that their design limits the amount of information that you can record and also what you observe. Another problem is what to tick. Do you tick something off the first time a child does it, and then find that the next day they cannot do it? Or do you tick when they have done something consistently and well?

Event sampling

Event sampling is a formal way of observing and recording patterns of behaviour. This is generally used if there is something a child is doing that both you and the parents want to change, such as sucking a thumb. Using this method of recording, you make a note of something only when you observe it happening, so the actual observation can carry on over quite long period of time, such as several days. You make a note of what actually happened and for how long the child did the behaviour or action.

Below is an example of an event sample that has been partly completed, although it is not evaluated and there is no assessment section. This is not the child's real name, it has been changed so as not to breach confidentiality.

Plus and minus points

Over a period of time event samples build up a picture of a particular behaviour or action that you, the parents, or another professional want

---

Name: Susie

Date: 15 November 2005

Age: four years and two months

Time: 8.30am until 12.20pm

Aim: to make a note of when Susie sucks her thumb.

Event	Time	Situation	Comment
1	8.30am	Has just been dropped off by mum. Susie is a bit upset.	Susie finds saying goodbye to mum difficult. Sucked thumb for about 5 mins.
2	9.00am	Another child has just been dropped off by their mum.	Maybe this has reminded Susie of her mum? Again sucked thumb for about 5 mins.
3	10.15am	Listening to me read a story.	Susie was sitting very close to me, we were both relaxed and comfortable. She was listening to the story and asking questions. She sucked her thumb throughout the story, about 15 mins.
4	11.45am	Sitting at the table with other children, waiting for me to put lunch on the table.	Sucked thumb for about 3 mins.
5	12.20pm	Sitting at the table waiting for one child to finish his yoghurt.	Sucked thumb for about 3 mins.

information on. Event samples are quick and easy to use. However, you need to carefully prepare the form that you use and may have to ask other adults to help you record each event. Parental involvement is not included here as a minus point, but it is something for you to think about.

Time sampling

Time sampling is a different form of event sampling in that you make notes of what the child is doing at fixed times or intervals throughout the day, such as every fifteen minutes throughout a morning or for two minutes in every thirty minutes. As with all observations you will need to decide exactly what it is that you want to find out more about. You will need to prepare a sheet beforehand as with event sampling, but will not need the column headed 'event'.

Plus and minus points

Once you have prepared the recording sheet, the process of time sampling is quick and easy to do. You can record specific behaviour and things that a child does, as well as more general activities. However, you will need to keep an eye on the time throughout the period of the observations. In a busy day it is very easy to get involved in something and forget that it is time to make an observation. As with event sampling, you may have to involve the parents if the observation is to go beyond one day.

Target child observations

Although this type of observation is not really an appropriate method for childminders to use it is useful for you to know about. It is inappropriate because it requires an adult to focus on one child for a long period of time, something that you will not be able to do without neglecting your other charges. Target child observations are used in day nurseries, nursery classes and pre-school groups. This method of observation requires codes, because it would be impossible to write everything down. For example, TC means target child (the one you are focusing on), A means adult, C is another child, Sol means solitary play.

A target child observation focuses upon one child, usually for 10 minutes. A record is made of what the child plays with, who they talk to, what they say, how the adult interacts with them, and how the child interacts with other children and adults. After 10 minutes a pattern may emerge that gives you an idea of the child's social and language skills. You can also learn about their levels of concentration and which activities engage them most by carrying out target child observations.

Plus and minus points

Several specific activities can be observed at the same time, but whoever is doing the observation has to be able to understand and use the codes, and must concentrate very hard.

Tapes and videos

You will need the written permission of the parents to make any form of recording of their child. You may also need to consider the quality of the equipment that you are using, because some recording equipment used in the home also picks up all the background noises.

Plus and minus points

If the child is not aware of the equipment you can often get some very good spontaneous reactions and behaviour. However, some children will act up to the camera or tape recorder so you will not end up with a natural observation. If you are using a normal tape recorder you may find that all the background noises have been recorded as well, and it may be difficult for you to hear what you wanted.

Participative

Participative observations are those where you participate or get involved with the activity, such as cooking, playing with a construction set or reading a story. Note that if you are part of the activity it will be a lot more difficult for you to write notes, so you will have to rely on your memory to help you record what happened.

Plus and minus points

You can set up an activity and, because you are involved, you can have a certain amount of control over such things as how long it will last and the learning that will take place. On the other hand, if you have not got a very good memory, or will not have the chance to write down what happened immediately after the activity is over, this may not be a very successful method of observing for you.

Structured

Structured observations are so called because you set up a situation so that you can observe the child or children. You are likely to set up an activity to observe one specific skill, such as pencil control, recognising colours, or putting on a coat or jacket. It is important that you choose an activity the child enjoys, so that you will get a true picture of their abilities. You will need to decide how you are going to organise this observation, for example are you going to show the child what you want them to do, or are you going to ask them questions?

Plus and minus points

You can set up this observation at a time to suit you and the other children. You are more or less in control of what is going on. However, the child may become distracted and not complete what you wanted to observe. This does not mean that you have to abandon the observation, as you can carry on with it later.

Naturalistic

Naturalistic observations are the opposite of structured ones. You simply observe the children or child in the normal routine of the day. You make notes on what they are doing, who they are doing it with and what they are saying.

Plus and minus points

This observation takes place in a normal situation. You should therefore get children behaving and doing things spontaneously. The downside of this method is that you do not really have any control over the situation and it may be difficult to stick to your aim.

Longitudinal records

If you are regularly observing the children in your care and keeping records of their growth and development, you will build up a set of observations which will show progress and changes over a long period of time. Each set of records and observations for each child is part of a longitudinal record. These will enable you and the parents to identify important milestones in the child's development and learning.

In all of the examples of observations you will notice that the date and age of the child is clearly

given – you must include this information. You also need to keep your observations focused and will find it easier to do this if you identify an aim. The aim can be quite straightforward, for example to look at fine motor skills, or to look at vocabulary development. However, you must remember that all areas of development are interrelated and whilst an aim will help you focus, observing other aspects of a child's development at the same time may help you make valid assessments. For example, if you are observing a child with the aim of assessing social skills, these skills might be affected by physical development, such as hearing difficulties, which can make a child unwilling to join group activities.

Keys to good practice

When writing observations make sure that you:

- have the written permission of the child's parents before you carry out the observation

- include the date and time that the observation was carried out

- decide on your aim and make a note of it – this will help you to stay focused

- do not breach confidentiality by naming the child, instead use their initials or a pseudonym

- it may be acceptable to use the child's name or first initial, but you must make absolutely sure that this observation remains between you and the child's parents alone if they have asked you to carry out a specific observation of their child

- make a note of the child's age, either in years and months or months and weeks

- keep your observations factual, do not write anything down that you do not actually see or hear

- make sure that the actual observation record is kept confidential and shared only with the child's parents, or other professionals if appropriate (and with written parental permission).

Link to assessment

E1 Carry out three observations of one child to include in your assignment for this unit.

Hint

Try to do the observations using different formats/methods and try to focus on different aspects of development.

Make sure that you have parental permission before you begin.

Think carefully about the format that you use, look at the plus and minus points of each observation method before you begin.

You may have to do more than three observations as the format that you selected might not have been the most appropriate method for that specific aim.

E4 Describe the interest and learning needs of the child that you have observed.

Hint 1

Carefully read your observations and write about the evidence that you have gathered which shows:

- what the child enjoys doing
- if they can remain focused and on one task or activity for a period of time
- what their developmental needs are.

Hint 2

Think carefully about issues of confidentiality before you write about the interests and things that the child enjoys. You may decide to use other recorded information on top of your observations, such as the initial contact form, so that you can identify one learning/development need for each area of development.

Hint 3

You *must* identify one learning/development need for each of the following areas of development:

- social
- physical
- language
- cognitive
- emotional.

D Explain why it is important to include the child's interests when planning.

Hint

Look at the section on planning in this unit on page 243.

Write about:

- how children learn (see also Unit 2, page 141)
- theory of constructiuism (see also Unit 2, page 142)
- the social and emotional benefits to children.

Interpretation and evaluation of observations

You are very busy throughout your working day and do not want to do anything that takes you away from the main point of your work – looking after the children. Because you are so busy, it is possible that you give your attention to a particular child only when they need it. As a result you could miss something important. Not only do you need to be aware of things that the children can do, you should also be aware of things that they need help with, and what they can almost do on their own.

Some practitioners think that writing down observations adds to their workload and therefore takes them away from caring for the children. It is very important that you do not see observing children as an additional workload, but as a central and fundamental part of providing the best possible care for the children. The more accurate the information you have about the children is, the more able you are to provide appropriate activities for them and therefore improve the quality of the service you offer. You need to include times in your daily routine when you can watch and listen to the children, getting information about their progress and development. Using this information you can assess and evaluate the activities that you have provided, and think up new ones if appropriate. Doing observations has the added advantage of giving children time and space to play as they choose and guide their own activities, while still being supervised by you.

The information, or evidence, that you collect when you do an observation can be invaluable for several reasons.

1 It can show that you understand how children learn, grow and develop and that the activities you provide take this into consideration.

2 Observations will give you information that you can use to check if the activities provided are at the right level and if the children have learnt or progressed in any way. This is called *assessment*.

3 The information that you have, plus your own knowledge and experience, will help you to plan appropriate activities. The observations may have made you more aware of the particular needs of a child, which would make you able to plan a suitable activity to help that child.

4 As a professional childcarer you have a busy workload and you want to make sure that everything you do for the children is for their benefit. Sometimes, when you are working very closely with children, it can be difficult to decide if the activities you are providing are really meeting all the children's needs. In other words, you need to be able to reflect upon and evaluate what you are doing. One way that you can reflect on and evaluate the activities is to make observations of the children while they are playing. This will then provide you with evidence that you can look at in a quieter moment and decide if the activity really did what you intended it to do.

Key Term

Assessment – making an informed judgement about something or a measurement of it, for example the development of a specific skill.

Assessment of a child's needs must be objective and impartial if it is to be meaningful. You will need to think about the information that you have gathered in several ways.

- Did the method/format that you used provide the information that you needed?

- Have you sufficient evidence to make an assessment? One observation is rarely sufficient to provide enough information.

- Have you recorded everything that you saw or heard, or have you got gaps?

- Is your information accurate, and not based on speculation or guesswork?

- Can you draw a sound conclusion from your evidence or do you need to make more observations?

- Who do you need to share this information with and why?

Assessments can be either formative or summative.

- **Formative assessments** are ongoing, such as a daily diary recording eating and sleeping patterns over a period of time. They do not give an overall conclusion, but can provide an ultimate assessment of that child's development and needs.

- **Summative assessments** put together the findings of several observations, so they will have an overall or ultimate conclusion.

Essentially, when put together, a set of formative assessments will lead towards a summative assessment of a child's needs.

The reason for assessment is not to label a child at a particular age, but to help you best meet that child's needs and help them to progress and achieve. You should not compare one child with another, each child is an individual and will develop and progress at their own individual rate.

Using observation and assessment to inform planning

Any observation that you carry out will give essential and valuable information about that child's individual needs from the assessments that you have made. These assessments will allow you do make informed decisions about the activities and experiences that you provide and plan to provide.

You need to decide what you would like to accomplish with any child, what you and their family want them to be able to do, and goals to work towards. These could be new skills and new ways of behaving, in other words the results of the assessments. Then you will need to decide how you are going to achieve these goals – your strategies or plans. You will need to think about how much time you realistically have to give to each child in order to meet their needs and how you may have to change your routines.

After you have carried out an activity you will need to observe the child again to see if you can make different assessments as a result of your planning.

- Have you got evidence that the goals have been either partial achieved or fully achieved?
- If the answer is no then you will need to decide if the goals were unrealistic, did you choose

unsuitable activities, or did the activities not go as well as you had expected?

This is part of the evaluative process of planning and will provide information for you to continue the planning cycle.

Think about it

Read the written observation of Ahmed again on page 237. An assessment has been made that Ahmed needs to be encouraged to put the DUPLO® pieces together and also to learn that he should not throw toys.

What activities could you plan to meet Ahmed's needs?

The planning cycle is ongoing, it is constantly changing and developing as you make assessments of children's needs. It must be flexible so that you can adapt and change activities and experiences depending on the observation information that you have gathered.

Case Study

It was coming up to Bonfire Night and Sharon, a registered childminder, planned for the children, aged from two years and three months to five years and six months, to make firework pictures with glitter, different sparkly papers, glue sticks and wax crayons. Sharon supervised the activity, but was able to make written notes on how one of the children, aged two years and 10 months, used the materials. She observed that this child had difficulty using the glitter pens.

It would very easy to decide not to use glitter pens with this child again for a while, but Sharon felt that this was not meeting their needs.

Why do you think she felt like this?

How could Sharon use the information from this observation to inform her planning for future festive activities?

Monitoring and evaluation of the planning cycle

It is important that you reflect on what you are doing with the children in your care. This can sometimes be quite different from what you had originally planned, but if you are flexible in your approach you can take individual needs and interests into consideration. For example, you might have planned to collect natural materials to make a seasonal collage, but one child finds a woodlouse under a log and you all get involved in finding out more about mini beasts.

Key Term

Monitoring – checking or keeping an eye on something.

It is important that you evaluate and monitor your plans. You may need to think about:

- why some things were more successful than others

- what you could have done differently and why

- what resources you used and if they were suitable.

Think about it

Look again at the section about being a reflective practitioner in Unit 3 on page 165.

Try to relate this to the planning cycle and ways that you can reflect on your practice, and the activities and experiences that you provide for the children in your care.

Record-keeping and sharing information with families

The Children Act 1989 requires group providers of children's care to observe children and assess learning and development whilst reporting and recording it. However, the guidance in the Children Act acknowledges that maintaining detailed formal records is less feasible in home-based settings, but refers to the significance and importance of sharing information with parents and making notes rather than relying on memory.

You should keep notes about each child that you care for, regardless of how long or short the care time may be. Many home-based childcarers have a separate wallet for each child and start with the first time that they met the child and the parents. Records are not intended to grade or label a child but should aim to provide an overall picture of a child that is constantly updated, monitored and evaluated.

There is no prescribed or specified format in which records or observations should be kept.

Keys to good practice

All records that you keep should:

- be simple and straightforward

- be objective, factual and impartial

- be confidential

- be dated

- use language that is not ambiguous, vague or has generalisations

- avoid jargon, abbreviations and long words that could be misinterpreted or appear obscure

- be positive and focus on what the child is achieving, rather than on what they are not doing.

Do not worry about the quality of your spelling or handwriting. What is more important is that you and the parents can understand what has been recorded and then make use of it.

Parents should be shown what you record about their children's needs, development and progress. They should also be actively encouraged to

Parents should be shown what you record about their child's needs

contribute to the records, correct any incorrect information that you may have and support you in planning the next stage for their child. This will lead to a consistent approach between you and the parents, who are after all the first educators of their child and therefore experts on that child.

Make sure that you use these records/observations, otherwise there is no point in doing them. Do not put them away in a file or wallet and forget about them until you get an inspection date. Records are of use only if they are referred to, reviewed, and become part of your planning cycle.

NCMA produces straightforward records for home-based childcarers. It is important that you are aware of the many commercially produced record-keeping aids that have shortcomings, such as inappropriate or unnecessary information. Many of these commercially produced record-keeping systems are based on checklists and tickboxes, which can be very limiting and are not necessarily relevant to individual children. In addition, checklists and tickboxes might

Link to assessment

E7 Discuss the information the practitioner may record following the implementation of activities/experiences described in **E5**.

Hint

Look again at the good practice list of what information you need for an observation (page 242).

- Think about what information you may need for your future planning and feedback to parents, and other professionals if appropriate.

- Think about the development or attainment of the child, how you might adapt this activity, what recommendations you might make for helping the child to progress and/or develop more skills.

- What additional resources might you need?

inadvertently be seen as targets or goals for a child to achieve, rather then a list of reminders to check significant aspects of development.

Some checklists describe goals or targets that are specific to one ethnic group; for example, one goal on such a checklist could be to use a knife and fork. However, many children can skilfully use other types of eating implements such as chopsticks, but not knives and forks. This does not necessarily mean that their development is delayed.

Prepare, implement and evaluate plans for home-based groups of children of different ages and abilities

Some home-based childcarers think that if they are planning and supporting children's learning, they have to write lots of things down in a formal way and 'teach' all children in the same way that teachers would do in schools. This is not the case.

As professional childcare practitioners, childminders and nannies plan activities and support children's learning in many valuable ways. Experienced practitioners do this almost instinctively and do not always appreciate the full extent of their work in this area. They can and often do provide children with an excellent start to their formal years at school and also support all aspects of a child's growth and development in ways that could not be achieved in schools. This is one of the many benefits of parents choosing a home-based childcarer to care for their children.

Implementing your plans involves some form of teaching or educating. As a professional home-based childcarer you will be educating the children that you care for all the time, helping them to learn, to grow and to develop in every way. You will probably not set aside times of the day when you make a conscious decision to educate the children, but may include time to play with them in your daily routine. You do not have to provide worksheets and special educational

toys to teach the children, but will talk to them and play with them, helping them to do things that they couldn't do before, such as feeding themselves or fastening up their own coat.

Your teaching methods include all of the things that you do as part of your childcare service.

- Talking – all children learn through talking and communication.

- Providing a safe environment and safe equipment for the children to play with, because children learn through play and first-hand experiences.

- Offering a wide range of activities and experiences, as children learn through exploring the world around them.

- Playing with the children and guiding them.

- Joining in and supporting their play.

How various approaches categorise areas of children's development and learning in different ways

Birth to Three Matters Framework (England)

See also Unit 2, page 153.

The Birth to Three Matters Framework was published in 2002 to support all individuals caring for and working with children up to the age of three years. As you can see in Unit 2, page 153, it categorises children's development and learning into four aspects.

- A strong child.

- A skilful communicator.

- A competent learner.

- A healthy child.

Each aspect is further divided into four components, which provide broad descriptors of the type of development that may take place. The Birth to Three Matters Framework is not a curriculum, and as such it is not prescriptive or regulatory. It emphasises that all children are unique and that development is holistic. Ofsted will expect home-based childcarers to show understanding of the framework and show how it underpins their practice in practical ways.

Find out!

You can download the text of the Birth to Three Matters Framework from the Sure Start website at www.surestart.gov.uk

You can also get a copy of the Scottish framework from the following website: www.ltscotland.org.uk/earlyyears/files/birth2three.pdf

Birth to Three – Supporting Our Youngest Children (Scotland)

This approach looks above all at the role of the practitioner and is organised around three key features of practice which should be established:

- relationships
- responsive care
- respect.

The chart below shows the key considerations of this approach.

Both the Scottish and English frameworks support the use of observations and assessments in day-to-day practice to help practitioners plan and develop appropriate experiences and activities for the children in their care.

Early Learning Goals/Desirable Outcomes for Children's Learning

Much research has been done on early years education and appropriate learning experiences for children aged between three and five years. In 1990 the Rumbold Report was published and as a result the Desirable Learning Outcomes for Children's Learning on Entering Compulsory Education were published.

In 1998 all four-year-olds in England were able to receive free nursery education if their parents wanted it. So that all children were offered the

Key feature	Key considerations
Establishing effective relationships	• Providing opportunities for the child to establish warm and affectionate bonds with significant people. • Providing opportunities for the child to interact with others, both adults and children. • Maintain respectful and inclusive partnerships between all those involved with the child. • Developing environments that promote security and consistency. • Developing environments that promote trust and understanding.
Establishing responsive care	• Building up a knowledge of the individual child. • Building up an understanding of the needs and dispositions of each child. • Ensuring adults are interested, appreciative and affectionate. • Using flexible, relaxed and personalised approaches. • Working to enhance respect and sensitivity.
Establishing respect	• Valuing diversity in terms of each child's language, faith, family circumstances and ethnic background. • Respecting children's different experiences. • Being sensitive to and understanding of differences in order to ensure fairness, equality and opportunity.

same standard of education, all settings that received the nursery funding had to be inspected by Ofsted and agree to follow a curriculum, or set of goals. In England this curriculum was initially called the Desirable Learning Outcomes on Entering Compulsory Education. The funding for nursery education was later extended to three-year-olds. In 1999 the Qualifications and Curriculum Authority (QCA) published the Early Learning Goals for the Foundation Stage intended for children receiving funding in England. During the following year QCA published detailed guidance on how to implement the Early Learning Goals.

In 2000 the Qualifications, Curriculum and Assessment Authority for Wales (ACCAC), published the Desirable Outcomes for Children's Learning. The Welsh Assembly has a ten-year strategy called the 'Learning Country' which is to establish a framework for children's learning under which the Foundation Stage will be for children from five to seven years old.

In Northern Ireland the Northern Ireland Executive is moving towards providing one year of full-time pre-school education before the child is five years old.

Scotland intends to implement its Curriculum for Excellence in 2007, focusing on bringing together the curriculum guidelines for children between three to five years and five to fourteen years. It will emphasise the importance of focused and well-planned play.

At the present time the nursery education grant in England and Wales is made available through local Early Years Development and Childcare Partnerships (EYDCPs). The EYDCPs will allocate the funding to settings that show what they plan and provide for the children helps them to make progress towards achieving the Early Learning Goals.

What are the Early Learning Goals? (England)

By the time that most children reach their fifth birthday they are in a reception class. The period of time from the age of three to the end of the reception year is described as the Foundation Stage. The Early Learning Goals describe what most children should be able to do by the end of the Foundation Stage, when they are approaching their sixth birthday. The Early Learning Goals are divided into six areas.

1   Personal, social and emotional development.

2   Communication, language and literacy.

3   Mathematical development.

4   Knowledge and understanding of the world.

5   Physical development.

6   Creative development.

Each of these areas is divided into smaller goals called stepping stones. It is intended that a three-year-old would start on the first stepping stone in any area and progress along until they reached the last stepping stone at around the age of six. This is a planned approach to children's learning, with clear goals and stepping stones. The planning of play activities comes from the goals and stepping stones. As the child develops, grows and learns, the stepping stones and the goals change to match the development of the child.

Find out!

A copy of the curriculum guidance for the Foundation Stage is available from QCA Publications, telephone number 01787 884444.

What are the Desirable Learning Outcomes? (Wales)

The Desirable Learning Outcomes differ from the Early Learning Goals in that they cover the play and activities that most children are expected to be able to do before compulsory school age. The Early Learning Goals are what children are expected to have achieved after they have started compulsory school and have been in school at least one year.

Like the Early Learning Goals, the Desirable Learning Outcomes are also divided into six areas of learning.

1 Personal and social development.

2 Language and literacy.

3 Mathematical development.

4 Knowledge and understanding of the world.

5 Physical development.

6 Creative development.

Curricular Guidance for Pre-school Education (Northern Ireland)

Parents of children in Northern Ireland are also able to receive nursery funding if they wish their child to have pre-school or nursery education. The curriculum, or set of goals, is very similar to both the Early Learning Goals for the Foundation Stage and the Desirable Outcomes. There are plans to introduce a Foundation Stage for children aged from three to six years.

Curriculum for Three to Five Years (Scotland)

The current curriculum for three- to five-year-olds is based on five areas of learning.

1 Emotional, personal and social development.

2 Communication and language.

3 Knowledge and understanding of the world.

4 Expressive and aesthetic development.

5 Physical development and movement.

A childminder who meets specific requirements will be able to gain accreditation and offer early years education to the children that they care for. This means that they will be able to receive funding for three-year-olds and four-year-olds in their care, but must plan and implement activities that follow the Early Learning Goals or the Desirable Learning Outcomes for two and a half hours per day for five sessions each week. The EYDCPs will pay the nursery education grant only to accredited childminders who are members of the National Childminding Association approved 'Children Come First' networks.

Unless you intend to become an accredited childminder in a network, the play and activities that you provide for children between three and six years do not have to rigidly follow the Early Learning Goals or Desirable Learning Outcomes. You also won't have to show how you plan. You will not be inspected on the education you offer unless you are accredited. However, Ofsted (in England) or CSIW (in Wales) will still inspect your home to check that it provides a safe and caring environment and that you are providing suitable play for the children.

National Curriculum

Home-based childcarers are often employed to care for children before and after school and during school holidays. Quite often these will be children that you cared for before they started full-time schooling and you will know them well. So that you can support the development, growth and learning of school-aged children it is important that you have some understanding of what they will be doing in school.

Children between the ages of five and eleven years attending state schools all study the same nine subjects. These subjects, in England and Wales, are referred to as the National Curriculum. Scotland and Northern Ireland have their own, similar versions. The National Curriculum also covers subjects studied by children in state secondary schools, but they do not all study the nine subjects listed below.

• English.

• Mathematics.

• Science.

• Physical education.

• Technology.

• History.

• Geography.

• Art.

• Music.

Children in Wales also study Welsh. The National Curriculum is divided into four Key Stages.

- Key Stage 1 for children five to seven years.
- Key Stage 2 for children from seven to eleven years.
- Key Stage 3 for children from eleven to fourteen years.
- Key Stage 4 for children from fourteen to sixteen years.

The National Curriculum was first introduced into schools in 1988 to ensure that all schools would provide a consistent standard of education. Each subject is divided into attainment targets, or levels, so that children can be assessed against the targets. State schools must offer all nine subjects

Case Study

Val is a very experienced childminder, having looked after children for almost twenty years. At the moment she cares for a baby and two other children who are three and four. The four-year-old goes to the local nursery class each morning, which uses topics to plan the Early Learning Goals; their current topic is 'shapes'. Val wants to support what the nursery is doing and as the nursery staff always put a copy of its medium-term (topic) plan on the parents' notice board, Val can see what activities are planned. One afternoon she takes all three children out on a shape hunt to look for squares, triangles, circles and rectangles that are all around them.

Have you ever noticed that some road signs are circles, some are triangular and some are rectangular?

Various shapes of road signs

Prepare, implement and evaluate plans for home-based groups of children of different ages and abilities

(plus Welsh in Wales) to all the children. The only exception to this is for children who have a statement of special educational needs.

Like any other form of educational provision the National Curriculum is constantly being assessed and examined. The most recent changes have been to introduce the Literacy Hour in September 1998 and the Numeracy Hour in September 1999. Both were intended to help raise the standards in English and Maths, so that all children, by the time they left primary school at eleven, could read and have a good understanding of mathematics. From September 2005, Standard Assessment Tasks (SATs) became be more informal and now cater more for the individual needs of the child.

Find out!

There are several alternative curricula that offer appropriate experiences and activities for children.

Find out about:
HighScope
Maria Montessori
Rudolph Steiner

Promoting children's development through planned and unplanned experiences and play

Why do home-based childcarers need to plan?

In order to work effectively and efficiently you need to plan your day and your working week. How you do that will be a matter of individual choice, and you may not write down much of what you plan. However, if you are prepared to take a planned approach to your work with the children and make records of what you do, not only will you build up a collection of activities and things to do with children that you can refer to in the future, but you will also become more professional.

If you intend to claim nursery education funding in the future and become an accredited childminder who provides education for children, you will need to keep written plans. Standard 3 of the National Standards for under-eights day care and childminding, which took effect in September 2001 (within England), clearly says that the registered person (you the childminder) plans and provides activities and play opportunities which will develop a child holistically. In England the Ofsted inspectors can ask to see how you plan play and other activities for the children.

All childminders are registered in accordance with the Children Act 1989, which requires anyone who is providing group care to observe children, assess their learning and development, and report and record it. In order to meet with this requirement you must do some form of planning.

How to plan

It is very important to remember that there is no right or wrong way to plan. The way that you plan is up to you. Your methods of planning will be different to the way that your friends or other course members plan; this is because you are a unique person, and the children you care for are also unique.

Your plans have to meet the needs of the children you care for and your own needs, therefore they cannot be the same as anyone else's. You do not have to write down your plans in any particular way, or fill in any special sheets or forms. The important thing to remember is that your plans must work for you and your children. If they do not, then change them.

Before you start to write anything down, you need to decide what you and the parents of the child you are caring for want them to achieve. What are the goals, or new ways of behaving that you want the child to develop? Decide upon a time-frame in which you hope to achieve these goals. This will then help you see the difference between long-, medium- and short-term plans. Share your plans, in whatever form, written or in your head, with the parents and the children. They should be involved, if possible and if appropriate, in deciding what activities you plan to provide.

Some home-based childcarers like to plan to themes, topics or areas of development. This will very much depend on the age and number of children that you care for. Some practitioners find following a theme, for example, restricts them and does not allow for spontaneous activities and some forms of free play. Again, it is very much up to you what you want to do.

Case Study

Kate is studying for the Diploma in Home-based Childcare. She cares for Jessica who is 20 months old and intends to write a medium-term curriculum plan of learning experiences for Jessica for a two-week period. Kate decides to make a chart covering the ten days that Jessica is with her, with each day broken down into approximate time slots. In each time slot Kate intends to write in an activity that will cover one area of Jessica's growth and development. Kate intends to try to link the activities to aspects and components of the Birth to Three Matters Framework. By doing it this way Kate feels sure that she will be able to check if she has covered as many areas of learning and development as is possible in a two-week plan. She can also make sure that anything missing is covered later.

When talking to other course members Kate realises that some are writing spider plans, some are making lists, some are writing their plan like a diary, in fact, nobody seems to be doing the plan in the same way. Kate mentions this to the tutor and the group spend a few moments after the coffee break discussing the best way to produce plans. There is little or no agreement amongst the group. Kate is concerned, but the tutor points out that they are all caring for different children with different and individual needs, so their plans cannot be the same.

Think about how you plan to meet the individual needs of the children in your care.

Link to assessment

E3 Discuss the importance of planning for individual children's development and learning needs.

Hint

Refer to the three observations that you have previously made of one child in your care (from the assessment on page 236). Write about:

- how the children are more likely to make progress and achieve when your planning considers their individual needs
- how your planning links to an appropriate framework or curriculum
- how your planning is age and stage appropriate for the child
- how you consider the child's needs, abilities and interests (see also links to assessment **E4** page 241).

B Analyse the importance of planning for all children. This criterion is linked to **E3**.

Hint

Look at the study skills section on page 289 to make sure that you understand what is meant by the term 'analyse'.

Think about why you plan and write about:

- your professional responsibilities to consider the needs of children when planning
- the individual needs of the children
- their different learning styles
- long-term and short-term effects on children's development and learning
- the positive effects on the children, their families and yourself
- the rights of children
- links with an appropriate curriculum
- how planning informs your decisions about resources and equipment.

There will be many valuable learning experiences that are unplanned, such as watching raindrops run down the windows on a wet day and talking about the patterns they make, or for older children, how rain is formed and even perhaps the water cycle. Do not underestimate or forget about these experiences. You can reflect on them later and think about how you met children's individual needs.

Case Study

Jenna drives five-year-old Tom and eight-year-old Natasha to and from school along the same route each weekday. One day, on their way home, there is a diversion as a lorry has 'jack-knifed' at the roundabout.

When they get home Jenna and the children get out a map of the local area to look at the diversion route and see if there were any other ways that they could have gone. They decide that one day in the coming holidays they will walk one of the routes and take the map with them so that they do not get lost.

Think about some of the unplanned events that have happened when you have been caring for children.

How did or could you have used these as learning/development opportunities for the children?

Implementing frameworks for early education and learning

Your role is to support the children's learning, helping them to grow and develop. However, in order for you to do this, you will need to have an understanding of the curriculum or framework appropriate to the country in which you live, and the framework or curriculum that is appropriate to the age of the children with whom you are working.

The Birth to Three Matters Framework is designed to support those practitioners working with children up to three years. The Foundation Stage curriculum is appropriate for children from three to five years. The Foundation Stage is completed at the end of the year in which the child has had their fifth birthday. The National Curriculum is appropriate for children from five to sixteen years.

Whilst there are some differences between the curricula of England, Scotland, Wales and Northern Ireland, for children between three and five years, all support a play-based approach to children's learning.

Much training and awareness raising has been taking place in England, in particular to help all practitioners develop their understanding and confidence in implementing the Birth to Three Matters Framework. It must be remembered that the framework is designed to support practice and is not a curriculum.

Case Study

Rachel, a registered childminder, attended a Saturday training group on the Birth to Three Matters Framework, organised by her local early years team. Rachel had received her pack some months ago but didn't know how to use the materials. She said that attending the training helped her to become more familiar with each aspect and its components and she became aware that she was actually covering much of the framework already, but didn't realise it!

Have you attended training in the Birth to Three Matters Framework?

Match your current practice to the framework, and think about any changes that you may have to make.

There are plans in England to develop a curriculum/framework that will support practitioners working with children from birth to five years. It will be known as the Birth to Five Framework.

You will need to be aware of these plans as they will impact on your practice if you are working with children from birth to five years. More information will be posted on the DfES website as it is released: www.dfes.gov.uk

Early years refers to children and babies up to the age of five years.

Look again at Unit 1, page 40, on play. Play is very important to children and we should do everything that we can to support and extend it. Children's play changes as they develop and acquire more skills. Today play is accepted as an essential part of the early years curriculum, but children of all ages need to have opportunities to learn by experimenting and exploring.

There are five main types of play:

- creative
- imaginative
- social
- manipulative.
- physical

These are described in the table below.

In addition, play can be spontaneous or structured.

Unless you have been accredited and can access nursery education funding you will not be expected to implement the Foundation Stage curriculum, but many home-based childcarers use the curriculum for guidance to help them plan and stimulate their own ideas. It also can provide a useful link between the care environment and the nursery school, extending and developing the children's skills. You are not expected to implement the National Curriculum, but it is a good idea to have an understanding of this curriculum so that you can support school-aged children during homework tasks.

You will also need to have a good understanding of the benefits of play and how children learn through play before you can implement an early years framework or a curriculum.

Key Terms

Spontaneous play is when children play in their own way, and the adult needs to provide as much variety of equipment and resources as possible, with opportunities and time for exploration and experimenting.

Structured play happens when the play is planned by adults, such as a cutting activity with scissors to develop fine motor skills.

Type of play	Main features	Suggested activities	Links to framework/curriculum
Creative	Exploring Experimenting Sensory development No 'end product' needed	Sand both wet and dry and other tactile materials such as sawdust, pasta, jelly Water Painting and drawing	*Birth to Three Matters Framework:* A competent learner *Foundation Stage:* Knowledge and understanding of the world

Type of play	Main features	Suggested activities	Links to framework/ curriculum
Creative (*continued*)	Links to all areas of development	Malleable materials such as clay, play dough

Making constructions from recycled materials as well as commercially produced sets | Creative development
Physical development

National Curriculum:
Art
CDT |
| Social | *Four stages:*
0–2 years – solitary play (playing alone)

2–3 years – parallel play (play alongside others but not with them)

3 years onwards – associative play (children watch and copy the play of others)

3 years onwards – cooperative play, most children from three years onwards also begin to play together, deciding what to do and how to play | Treasure baskets and heuristic play, but all activities

Construction, malleable materials, outdoor play and all activities can be part of parallel play

Role-play

Games with simple rules | *Birth to Three Matters Framework:*
A strong child
A healthy child
A skilful communicator
A competent learner

Foundation Stage:
Personal, social and emotional development
Communication, language and literacy
Physical development

National Curriculum:
Physical education
Drama
CDT
English |
| Physical | Children use large muscles and exercise their whole body

Develop control of small muscles, coordination, balance and control

Expend surplus energy | All equipment should offer challenges for those who are ready, yet be appropriate for those who need to consolidate and practise their skills, and should take into account children with special needs

All equipment should be safe and hygienic, risk assessments should be carried out and regularly checked (see also Unit 1, page 9)

Physical play should be supervised at all times | *Birth to Three Matters Framework:*
A healthy child
A strong child

Foundation Stage:
Physical development

National Curriculum:
Physical education |

Type of play	Main features	Suggested activities	Links to framework/ curriculum
Imaginative	Children pretend that they are in different situations or may be other people. Can be instigated by the adult so that the child can explore familiar situations or fantasy worlds, such as a visit to the dentist, or under the sea Links to all areas of development	Role-play, indoors and outdoors Rich variety of materials, equipment and resources, e.g. large boxes that can be cars, boats, caves, dens, trains, pieces of material that can be made into cloaks, covers can be used to create dens, hide things	**Birth to Three Matters Framework:** A competent learner A skilful communicator A strong child **Foundation Stage:** Creative development Communication, language and literacy Personal, social and emotional development **National Curriculum:** Drama CDT Art English
Manipulative	Using hands, fine manipulative skills, coordination and control Concentration Sensory development	Finger play, rattles, baby gym Treasure basket Crayons and other drawing materials Beads and threading items such as pasta Puzzles, small-world toys, computer games (use of the mouse)	**Birth to Three Matters Framework:** A healthy child A competent learner **Foundation Stage:** Physical development Creative development **National Curriculum:** Physical education CDT Art

Keys to good practice

Before you can implement any curriculum or use a framework you will need to make sure that you have a range of suitable equipment and resources that:

- are safe (look for a recognised safety mark)

- are hygienic

- are age and stage appropriate

- provide opportunities for children to explore, experiment, develop and extend their skills

- are appropriate and accessible to all children.

Physical play

Link to assessment

A Evaluate the implications of using an inappropriate curriculum or framework for children.

Hint

Look in the study skills section on page 289 to make sure that you understand what is meant by the term 'evaluate'.

Think and write about the short- and long-term negative effects on the children, including:

• their learning and development in all areas

• the pressures that can be exerted by parents

• regulatory requirements, those of Ofsted for example

• the behaviour of the children.

Think about the positive benefits of using the right framework or curriculum when meeting children's individual needs.

Curriculum plans

Key Term

Curriculum – a set of activities, opportunities and experiences which help and support children's learning and development. Some can be planned and some unplanned.

The purpose of having a curriculum

A curriculum will help to ensure that you cover all aspects of a child's development and learning in a balanced manner. Sometimes it is easy to forget about one particular aspect or to spend more time on one than another. Being aware of a curriculum will help you to offer developmentally appropriate activities, and through your knowledge of each child you will be able to build on their interests in a meaningful way. Children who are interested will be motivated to explore, find out and learn more. Recognising their interests also shows the children that you are interested in them as individuals and concerned about their development.

Many of the activities, opportunities and experiences that you offer to children are play-based and can emerge from routine events involving you and the children.

Planned curriculum events are the ones that you have thought about and decided upon in advance. You will have thought about the age and stage of development of the children, your role, the time needed and what resources you may need. Unplanned curriculum events are spontaneous and arise from the unexpected. These can be valuable learning opportunities and you will need to quickly draw on both your knowledge of children's development in general and your specific knowledge of individual children.

Curriculum plans – long, medium and short term

Long-term plans

These are for goals and skills that you want to develop over a period of time.

- You might decide on a long-term plan of eight weeks to help a seven-year-old remember to bring their library book back from school on a Wednesday, and all of their sports kit back from school on a Friday.

- You might decide on a long-term plan of one month to help a three-year-old learn the colours red, blue, green and yellow.

Red
- Painting with red
- Water play with red food colouring
- Red play dough
- Look for red cars when walking
- Ask mum to dress him/her in something red

Blue
- Collage with pictures or bits of paper that have different shades of blue
- Blue play dough
- Make a collection of blue things from around the house
- Make sure I wear something blue
- Play with construction sets with blue pieces

Colours

Green
- Have snack or meal with everything green
- Make green with yellow and blue food colouring
- Make green jelly
- Read stories about green things

Yellow
- Build Duplo® model with only yellow pieces
- Make yellow cakes and decorate with yellow icing
- Look for yellow marks and signs on the road when out walking
- Make a yellow sunflower with hand prints

A plan for teaching colours

- You might decide to have a long-term plan of a whole year that covers all areas of growth and development for a two-year-old.

Medium-term plans

Each box in the spider plan on page 258 could become a medium-term plan that would last a week, with the goal of helping the child identify either red, blue, green, or yellow through a range of different activities.

Medium-term plans can focus on one particular aspect of learning, growth and development, such as one colour for a three-year-old, fine motor skills for a two-year-old and reading skills for an eight-year-old. It is at this point in the planning process that you decide what your role will be, whether or not the activity will be structured and led by you, or if the child will take the lead.

Short-term plans

Short-term plans can be either for one day or just one specific activity. You could have a short-term plan to do some cooking that is part of a medium-term plan to develop physical skills, which is in turn part of a long-term plan to make sure that the activities you provide for the children cover all areas of their growth and development.

Each box in the spider plan could be a separate short-term plan, with the aim or goal, for example, to help the child recognise blue by collecting only blue things from around the house.

Planning for individual children's learning, and in mixed-age groups

All children learn through:

- play
- first-hand experiences
- talking and communicating with each other, their parents and other sensitive and caring adults.

These three fundamental aspects of learning should be at the heart of all activities that you plan regardless of the age of the children. These aspects of learning can be identified through learning styles.

Learning styles

Learning in all shapes and forms should enable the child and young person to:

- explore their environment
- investigate and participate in new activities and experiences
- develop new skills and abilities
- discover how things work in the world around them.

Link to assessment

E5 Describe three activities/experiences that would meet the developmental needs of a child you have observed.

Hint

Look back at the development/learning needs of your observed child (page 242) and use the appropriate framework or curriculum guidance to support you.

It is good practice to include details of:

- the aim/purpose of the activity
- what resources you will need

- how you and the child will be involved in the activity/experience
- what health and safety issues you might have to consider.

E6 Identify the learning that may occur for the child during the activities you have described to meet criterion **E5** (above).

Hint

Write about the child's learning that may occur for each of the three activities.

How children achieve these things will depend on the learning style that they adopt.

If you are familiar with differing learning styles you will be more able to plan activities and experiences that meet the individual needs of the children in your care. Learning styles have close links with sensory development (what we see and hear). Children can use different learning styles in different situations, at different times of their development, or they may combine more than one learning style at a time (see table below).

Key Term

Learning style – the way in which we process information. Most people will have a preferred learning style.

Learning styles can be influenced by:

- who the child or young person is with during the activity / experience
- the number of children or adults around the child
- where the child is, the learning environment
- what resources are available to the child and if they can access and use them independently.

Case Study

Jo provided a treasure basket for a nine-month-old baby in her care. She recognised that this baby learnt in a tactile way and needed opportunities to touch, handle and feel a wide variety of objects.

She also provided a CD of a favourite story for the five-year-old that she cared for. This child preferred the auditory style of learning and would laugh out loud as he heard the different voices on the tape.

How could you provide for a kinaesthetic learner who is seven years old?

How could you provide for a visual learner who is ten years old?

Learning style	Features
Auditory (concerned with hearing)	**Talkers and listeners** Talkers have to hear information. Listeners have to retain and recall information. *Both*: Prefer the spoken word. Love different voices. Enjoy explanations. Enjoy communication with others. When reading often mentally hear what they are reading.
Kinaesthetic (concerned with spatial awareness in relation to senses)	Need to sense position and movement in relation to the situation in which they are in. Like and need to touch, examine and feel something in order to learn.
Tactile (concerned with tangible, concrete experiences)	Want and need to touch, handle and experiment in a sensory way. Can sometimes be perceived by others as being disruptive.
Visual (concerned with what is seen and perceived)	Enjoy pictures in books. Enjoy visual descriptions of things. Like to watch people speak as well as listening to them. Look for shapes and forms in pictures and words.

Planning for babies and toddlers

When you start to consider how to plan, or take a planned approach to children's learning, it is good practice to remember that babies and toddlers are learning through their senses and explorations. Therefore, if you are thinking about an overall framework for a long-term plan for children of this age, you should relate your plan to the aspects and components of the Birth to Three Matters Framework. Many babies are tactile learners initially.

A long-term plan should include opportunities for:

• sensory, intellectual and creative development

• physical skills and well-being

• language and communications

• social and emotional development.

The goal would be to provide activities that will stimulate and promote all areas of growth and development, supported and underpinned by the Birth to Three Matters Framework and sensitive and caring adults.

A medium-term plan for babies and toddlers could perhaps focus on physical skills, such as coordination. The goal could be to develop coordination skills. The component of a 'Strong and healthy child' should provide plenty of stimuli for activities and experiences.

A short-term plan could include play and activities such as:

• playing with a baby gym for a small baby

• doing a large puzzle with few pieces with a toddler

• feeding themselves with finger foods.

You could do a written observation of a baby playing under a baby gym for about ten minutes, with the aim of observing hand–eye coordination, or an event sampling to see how many times the baby's hand manages to pat or connect with the objects on the baby gym.

You could use the information from your observation to decide or assess if the baby needs to have more opportunities to play with the baby gym, possibly because they did not often manage to connect with the objects. Alternatively, you could decide if the baby needs to be introduced to a different play activity to develop their skills, such as a toy that when touched or patted makes a noise.

Whatever you decide as a result of your observation, you will need to provide or implement another play opportunity, and the planning cycle will go around again. You could carry all this information around in your head, write it down, or even type it up onto your personal computer.

Planning for three- to five-year-olds

Many of the activities that are suggested in the QCA guidance for the Foundation Stage (England) are things that you will be doing in your home all of the time, such as:

• cooking

• dressing-up

• looking at books

• counting

• talking about what the children did at the weekend with their parents

• putting aprons on before painting

• singing rhymes.

Each one of these suggested activities covers one or more of the areas of learning. Cooking, for example, involves:

• personal, social and emotional development, as the children share and take turns

• mathematics, as they count, weigh and measure the ingredients

• knowledge and understanding of the world, as they see the ingredients change while they are being mixed together and cooked

• physical development, as the children handle the cooking utensils and, possibly, put on their own aprons

• creative development, as they make something and perhaps decorate the tops of cakes, or pizzas

• communication, language and literacy – have you ever cooked in silence with children!

Some home-based childcarers find it helpful to use learning goals from the Foundation Stage for planning purposes, even though they are not required to do so (unless accredited childminders delivering Nursery Education). Their long-term plan might include considering overall development within each area of learning as a medium-term plan.

Children of this age can be tactile, visual, kinaesthetic and auditory learners, depending on the activity or experience.

Planning for school-aged children

You will probably be caring for school-aged children before and after school, along with some school holidays. You will not be expected to deliver the National Curriculum, but will need to offer support to the children. Your role is not to provide activities that are best suited to the classroom, but to support their learning. You can do this in a variety of ways.

• Develop your own understanding of the National Curriculum so you can support homework activities.

• Develop and establish good lines of communication with the child's teachers. It is helpful if you ask the child's parents to write a letter to the school explaining your role and responsibilities; this should avoid misunderstandings and potential breaches of confidentiality.

• Help the children to gain independence in personal hygiene, self-help skills, road safety and stranger danger. All of these can be developed through planned and unplanned activities while the child is in your care.

• Plan activities to help older children deal with peer group pressures and, in the worst case scenario, bullying. This can be done through role-play, discussions, and activities that meet individual needs.

• Provide a quiet place for homework and plan activities for younger children that do not disturb or interrupt homework.

School holidays should be fun for everyone. Your routines may have to change during school holidays, and you could have more children to

Planning play for mixed-age groups can be challenging

Prepare, implement and evaluate plans for home-based groups of children of different ages and abilities

care for, or sometimes fewer. Many practitioners find that caring for school-aged children during the holidays can be demanding. You can cope with this by planning ahead, and knowing when the holidays are enables you to be well-prepared.

It can be quite a challenge to provide activities for mixed-age groups of children and to be realistic about coping – just how many children can you cope with and still enjoy your work? You could take advantage of the local facilities in your area, such as a swimming pool and sport centres, and talk to the parents about their school-aged children enrolling on play schemes.

Case Study

During the school holidays Debbie cares for four children in one family, aged one, two and a half, seven, and ten years old. During these times her routines have to be more flexible, but at the same time accommodating the sleep and rest needs of the two younger children. In the mornings Debbie plans activities that involve all the children, such as trips to local attractions, and in the afternoon, while the two youngest are asleep, she tries to plan activities that are more suitable for the older children. These involve art, crafts such as model making, cooking, den making.

Can you think of any other activities that Debbie could do to meet the needs of all the children and those of the specific age group?

When planning for mixed-age groups you need to consider:

- differing learning styles – children can display a range of learning styles within any one activity or experience

- the interests and needs of the children

- the children's health and safety

- the stage of development, remembering that children develop at different rates

- any special needs of the children

- the wishes of the parents

- ways to encourage diversity and equality of opportunity for all. This does not mean that all children have to engage in the same activities, but that you treat them fairly, taking their individual needs into consideration.

Link to assessment

E8 Describe how the home-based childcarer may adapt activities/experiences described in the previous link to assessment (page 259) for children at a different age or stage of development.

Hint

All children develop at different rates even though they all pass through the same stages, so think about each specific activity/experience and write about how and why you could adjust it to meet the needs of a younger/older child or one who is more or less able.

C Explain how to meet the learning needs of mixed-age groups in a home-based childcare setting.

Hint

Write about the ways in which you can recognise, manage and organise the differing learning styles and needs:

- through observations

- by linking to an appropriate framework or curriculum

- meeting needs and abilities of different ages of children

- meeting stages of development.

Care and learning needs of older children and young people

Seven to nine years

Children between seven and nine years do not develop as rapidly as they did in the early years.

Although they continue to grow in height and weight the main area of development is the way that they think and reason. Most children are developing increasing competency in reading, writing and numeracy. They are more in control physically and coordinated in their actions, so they can 'fine-tune' their skills. Children of this age begin to play in more organised ways, following rules and making them up to suit their play. They usually enjoy hands-on activities in which they have to work things out for themselves and solve problems. Children are usually cooperative and respond well to adult recognition and praise of their efforts and behaviour. Children in this age group establish same-sex friendships and there are quite noticeable differences in the activities that interest girls and boys.

Children need adults who can support their play and learning, knowing when to intervene and when to stand back. They need adults who will praise their efforts and behaviour and will listen to them and respect their views. They need opportunities to become more independent, such as sleepovers with friends.

Young people can be concerned about their appearance

Nine to eleven years

Children between nine and eleven years can be at a changing point in their lives, especially girls, who may be approaching puberty. At this age they have often developed firm and stable friendships and need time to be with their peers. They respond well to responsibilty and opportunities to be independent but still need adults to offer safety and security. Children still want and need adult approval – adults and parents are important people in their lives and they will respond positively to praise and recognition.

Eleven to thirteen years

Young people between eleven and thirteen years will be experiencing great physical changes that may impact on their emotional and social development. This is often a time of change at school, when many young people have to cope with different routines and new relationships, whilst at the same time have a growing need for independence. They may want to get to and from school by themselves, using public or school transport, or walking or cycling.

Prepare, implement and evaluate plans for home-based groups of children of different ages and abilities

Children in this age group may develop anxieties about school work, relationships with their friends or their appearance, and can become rebellious of boundaries that they regard as imposed by adults. Young people need opportunities to enjoy being a child without pressures, such as to enjoy watching cartoons.

Adults need to be very sensitive to the changing and developing needs of children. By giving clear boundaries that have been explained and negotiated beforehand young people should be able to see the reasoning behind them and are more likely to adhere to them.

Children in this age group are developing rapidly and need opportunities for exercise and rest as well as a balanced diet. These things cannot be imposed but sensitive adults can explain and inform in non-threatening ways.

Thirteen to sixteen years

Young people between thirteen and sixteen years are young adults facing decisions about their future. This is a common time for young people to rebel and they may drop out of school, avoid participating in sport, turn truant or become disruptive. Being with their friends and peers is more important than being with family members; however, those who have not got a group of friends can become depressed, over-anxious and feel that they are missing out. Young people of this age will have developed and probably established their own style of clothes, choice of music and friends, all of which can be potential areas of conflict with adults. Whilst this can be a difficult time for some young people it can also be a most enjoyable and fun time as they become more independent and social.

Adults should try to be non-judgemental and listen to young people's views and opinions. They can help young people find out about career opportunities, further training and education, drugs, sexuality and alcohol.

Young people, like children, will display a range of all learning styles appropriate to the experience and the situations that they are in. They will have a preferred learning style which may show itself in how they respond to different teachers at school. For example, a tactile learner may be more successful at Design Technology, whereas an auditory learner may enjoy Drama.

The importance of helping children to have high expectations and aspirations

As was mentioned in Unit 2, self-image and self-esteem are not only important factors of a young person's emotional development, but are highly significant in all areas of development. Children who are positive and confident feel good about themselves and will be willing to be adventurous in all areas of their learning and development.

For children, part of having high self-esteem and a high self-image is knowing that the important people in their lives believe in them and have confidence in their abilities. This shows children that we have high, but realistic expectations of them.

By the time children are about six years old they begin to compare themselves, their skills and learning to others. This helps them to learn about themselves and understand not only their personal limitations but also what they can achieve. Children who have high expectations of themselves are confident and feel good about themselves.

As children get older they start to think about what they would like to be – their 'ideal self'. This can be influenced by other children and adults in their lives, but also by individuals that they see through the media. Children with low self-esteem who are lacking in confidence do not have high aspirations for themselves and believe that they cannot achieve their ideal self. Adults who care for and work with children must make sure that they help children of all ages to feel good about themselves, which should lead them to develop a positive self-image.

Whilst it is important that you encourage children to have high expectations of their own abilities and potential, it is also very important that you do not inadvertently put pressure on them. Your expectations and those of the child's parents must be realistic and achievable. If they are not, they can have a very damaging effect on a child.

The importance of valuing and celebrating differences amongst people and helping children to learn about cultures different from their own

Every individual is a unique being and should be respected as such. A child's home background has a significant influence on that child, who they are and who they will become. Children will naturally want to share aspects of their home life with you, especially if you are caring for them outside of their own home. They will want to tell you about things that they have done with parents or other family members, meals that they have shared and places that they have been.

It is possible that children may not feel accepted and respected by others because they dress in a different way, eat different food or speak more than one language. Rather than being proud of their culture, children can lack confidence and hide cultural differences from their peers; home-based childcarers and practitoners should do everything that that they can to combat this.

Children become aware of differences at an early age and will therefore learn about possible prejudice, stereotypical views and discrimination. To help them grow up without prejudice, respecting all cultures equally and not seeing one as better or superior to another, you must show as much respect for other people's culture as you do for your own.

You should find out as much as you can about the child's home life and their culture if it is different from your own. One way that you can do this is to look at cultural differences in food. Food is a common feature in all cultures, used to celebrate significant events as well as being part of everyday life. Every culture has different ways of eating food and an accepted etiquette that goes along with eating. Children who are aware of more than one culture will learn to adapt their own eating habits by watching other adults and children. This will enable them to become more tolerant and understand more about the differences between cultures.

Think about it

Should you celebrate a festival from a culture that is not your own or that of a child that you care for? The festival might have significant meaning for other people and you might be criticised for copying aspects of the celebration without any understanding. It shows more respect to ask the child's family about the festival and ways that you can contribute to the celebrations.

There is a danger that in our attempts to encourage children to learn more about different cultures we become tokenistic, for example putting a length of sari material in your dressing-up box does not teach children about people who wear saris or their culture or religion, because the children are quite likely to use the material to make a den, a 'super-hero' cloak, wings or something completely different. In the same way, having a black doll or a wok in your toy box does not teach about cultural differences. You should not introduce children to information and images that glamorise a culture or stereotype a group of people, for example by finding out a little bit about a culture and then assuming that all people from that culture behave or live in the same way.

Keys to good practice

- We need to talk to children about how families have different traditions.

- We need to provide positive images of people in different cultural groupings.

- We should try to get written materials in various languages.

- Culture is not just about festivals and holidays, it is about what and how we eat, how we dress, how we bring up children, how we wash and care for ourselves, and how we decorate and furnish our homes.

- Show respect for all cultures.

Assessing and evaluating children's learning in the home-based setting

How can evaluations be meaningful? How can realistic conclusions and assessments be made that will help children progress? Considering the ideas, theories and views of others through researching a topic will in part answer the above questions. This will help you to develop an understanding of how children behave in certain situations and why they react to certain stimuli, and should help you to make appropriate recommendations that meet the individual needs of the child.

When you start to consider theories it is important to remember that apparently contrasting ones do not necessarily mean that one is right and the other is wrong. You should evaluate these theories and views together with your own professional judgement about the needs of the child. However, contrasting theories and views can make it confusing when trying to decide which theory or view to focus on. It is important that you do not try to look for a theoretical viewpoint that will conveniently fit the evidence that you have gathered in your observations. Ask yourself:

• What was I trying to find out?

• Why?

Adults who live and work with babies and young children will acquire an abundance of anecdotal evidence. However, such evidence can be unreliable and subjective. For instance, many parents believe that their children can do things that they are not actually capable of, not necessarily because they want their child to be better, faster or cleverer than others, but because they are emotionally involved with their child, and emotions can cloud judgements. Also, some parents may not want to admit that there might be a cause for concern with their child – they may feel guilty and blame themselves.

Case Study

A nanny has made a written observation of twin boys aged two years and nine months while they are playing with their toy garage and cars. Her aim was to look at their language development because the parents were concerned that the boys might have a language delay. The written observation showed that the boys did not talk very much during their play, and spent much of their time watching their sister on the computer.

This observation could be assessed and evaluated in several different ways.

• The nanny could decide that the boys had not yet reached Piaget's stage of pre-operational development as they did not use the toys as symbols in their play (this is a feature of Piaget's cognitive development theory). In addition they did not use language to develop their play.

• On the other hand, if the nanny had become involved in the boys' play she might have been able to develop and extend it. This relates to Vygotsky's theory about the importance of adults extending and developing children's learning.

• The nanny may have suggested that the boys played together at this time and perhaps they did not choose the toys, which could have affected their interest and motivation in the activity.

What is relevant to this observation in order to make a meaningful evaluation and assessment?

Jan and her partner both work full-time and have placed their seven-month-old baby with Anita, a registered childminder.

Anita has become aware that the baby does not respond to sounds, especially those out of his line of vision, such as the telephone, but he is beginning to babble. Anita discussed her concerns with Jan, but she insists that there is no problem at home and suggests that Anita's house is too noisy for her baby to distinguish sounds. Anita is not convinced and during quiet times does a series of observations which show that the baby will only respond when he has full eye contact or when he can see the object or person that is making a noise. Anita shows Jan her observations and explains how she reached her assessment and evaluation. She suggests

that Jan do similar observations at home. Jan does this and has to admit that Anita could be right to raise these concerns. She makes an appointment with the GP, which shows that the baby has limited hearing in one ear.

Anita had knowledge of child development and developmental milestones. She also knew about the theory which suggests that language and communication skills can be learnt through reinforcement (B. F. Skinner), and if the baby did not respond then reinforcement could not take place. This knowledge of children's development and some theoretical perspectives improved, supported and developed Anita's professional practice.

Research the work of B. F. Skinner on reinforcement theory.

Meeting individual learning needs in the home-based setting

Throughout the earlier units the importance of meeting individual needs has been emphasised many times, but why is it so important in a home-based setting? In order to be an effective childcare practitioner it is essential that you learn the skills and techniques of identifying the individual needs of every child that you care for.

All children have a range of needs which have to be met in a variety of ways. These needs are shown in the spider chart below.

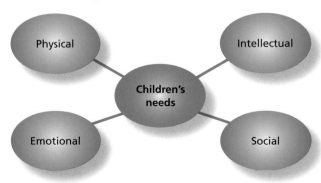

Children's needs

Physical needs

- Warmth.
- Shelter.
- Food.
- Exercise.
- Sleep and rest.

Intellectual needs

- Intellectual stimulation.
- Challenge and interest.
- Opportunities to learn.
- Access to new information.
- Positive responses to new discoveries and explorations.

Social needs

- Contact with others.
- Friendship.
- Sharing.
- Belonging to a group.

Emotional needs

- Security.
- Affection.
- Close relationships with others.
- Unconditional love.

You must make sure that you consider and think about the full range of a child's needs while you are caring for them, and do not just concentrate on one or two aspects. However, do not think that everything that you do as a home-based childcarer must consider every need all the time, something that is simply not possible to do. Over a period of time you should ensure that you have planned opportunities in which these needs can be met. Some needs, such as physical ones, you will meet every day, whereas others, such as social needs, may be met only once or twice each week, for example when you and the children attend a toddler group.

The importance of identifying the child's individual needs through observation and assessment

Understanding how children develop and grow is an essential skill. One of the basic means of developing this understanding is through observation. Watching children in a focused manner will help you to identify their individual needs, allowing you to plan and provide activities and experiences that will interest, stimulate and be enjoyable for those children. We know that children develop at different rates, but pass through the same sequences, or stages. A child can be more advanced in one area of their development than another, for example a child with well-developed intellectual skills may not be able to interact very well with their peers. In such a situation it is possible that you may not be fully aware of this child's social needs, but careful and sensitive observation should help you to develop your understanding and therefore meet these needs.

Children of the same age chronologically can be very different, for example twins can be quite different in their behaviour and abilities even though they are the same age. In the same way, one nine-month-old baby may be crawling whilst another at the same age may not be making any attempt to get mobile. Careful, focused observation will avoid you making generalisations about development and will make you a more effective practitioner, reinforcing the fact that you cannot respond to all children in the same way because all children are different.

Legislation and funding for special educational needs in home-based childcare

There have been significant changes in legislation over recent years to ensure that children with a disability and/or special education needs are supported and included in ways that meet their individual needs.

The Disability Discrimination Act 1995

This Act defines a disabled person very broadly as 'someone who has a physical or mental impairment which has a substantial and long-term adverse effect on their ability to carry out normal day-to-day activities'. This includes children who have:

- physical impairments
- intellectual or mental impairments
- a learning disability
- sensory impairment
- diabetes
- severe dyslexia
- epilepsy
- HIV/AIDS
- incontinence
- progressive conditions such as muscular dystrophy
- severe disfigurements.

This Act has statutory powers in England, Scotland, Wales and Northern Ireland.

The Education Act 1996

This piece of legislation is for England only and defines a child as having 'special educational needs' if they have a learning difficulty which requires special educational provision to be made for them. This is provided for under the statementing process, which is explained later in this unit.

The Special Educational Needs and Disability Act 2001

This act supports the Code of Practice 2002 (page 271) and supports children in their right to be included in mainstream education facilities and associated services, which will include extended schools, after- and before-school clubs, holiday play schemes and wrap-around care. This affects home-based childcarers who may be involved in wrap-around care and extended schools.

Funding for special educational needs

Since April 2003 all local authorities had to have a direct payments scheme whereby money is given to the disabled person, or their parents and carers in the case of a child under sixteen years, in order that the individual may purchase the services needed from a private or voluntary agency. In the case of home-based childcarers this could mean that if you are caring for a child with special educational needs the parents could use the direct payments scheme to pay you to care for their child during the school holidays.

Once a child has a statement they will attract extra funding to provide for the service to support their needs. However, this does not always mean that a child will have a full-time support worker as the school has the final decision on how the money will be allocated and may decide to spend it on resources, equipment and other aids to support the child.

The role of the practitioner in working with children who have special educational needs

In England the Education Act 1996 describes a child with special needs as an individual who has a learning difficulty which means that special provision in the education setting will have to be made. This is provided for under the special educational needs framework, which can include a statement of the child's needs. In Scotland children are covered by the Disability Strategies and Pupils' Educational Records Act 2002. It is possible that a child with a disability as described by the Disability Discrimination Act 1995, may also have a learning difficulty and therefore a special education need (see Unit 2, page 103).

Despite this legislation some parents find that before- and after-school care and holiday care for a child with special education needs can be difficult.

In many parts of the country registered childminders belonging to a network have been

Case Study

Melissa, aged nine years, has multiple sensory impairments, and she attends a special school which does not yet provide extended hours. Her parents both work and they struggled to find suitably experienced people to care for Melissa while they are at work. The local Children's Information Service was able to give them the details of registered childminders with vacancies who were suitably experienced, qualified, and who might be willing to care for Melissa.

Why do you think Melissa's parents experienced problems finding suitable care for her?

What would a home-based childcarer need to consider before agreeing to care for Melissa?

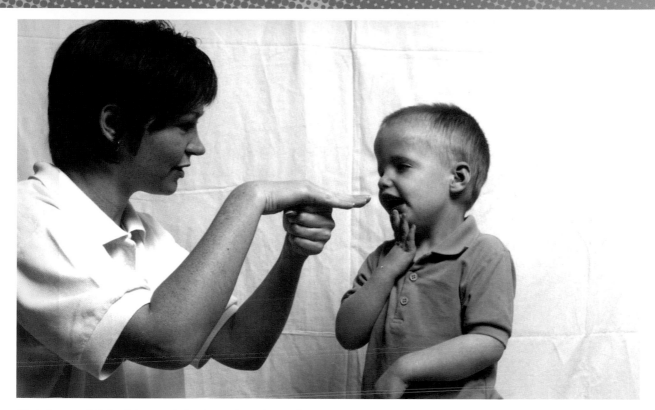

Helping a child with special educational needs

able to offer respite care for children with special educational needs or in need of protection. Such practitioners have their registration details amended by Ofsted in order for them to offer this service.

The Code of Practice 2002

The Code of Practice 2002 is supported by the Special Education Needs and Disability Act 2001. The Code states that children have special education needs if they have learning difficulties that require extra educational provision. Children can have a wide range of special educational needs, some of which can affect them all their school lives and some of which can be of a temporary nature. It is thought that around 20% of school-aged children will have a special educational need at some point in their life, and about 2% have a need that is significant. It is this 2% of children that are assessed by their local authority, which issues a statement setting out how their needs should be met (DfES 2002). This process is usually referred to as 'statementing' and

is clearly set out in the Code of Practice.

The main aspects of the code are:

- children with special educational needs have more rights to be educated in a mainstream school

- local education authorities are required to give advice and information to parents

- settings have a duty to let parents know when they are making special educational provision for their child

- schools and nurseries have the right to request a statutory assessment of a child.

The Code of Practice also encourages the early identification of children who may have special educational needs. Pre-schools, nurseries and childminding networks are asked to draw up special needs policies and to have someone to coordinate special educational needs. This person is usually referred to as the SENCO, or Special Educational Needs Coordinator.

Statementing: the graduated approach and supporting a child's primary carer through the process of statementing

The principal idea behind the statementing process is to ensure that children with special educational needs are given support. The Code of Practice uses the term 'a graduated response' within the framework of identifying, assessing and providing for young children.

Since statementing began there have been concerns expressed that too many children were gaining statements which were not required because they were already receiving support in other ways. The statementing process can be very lengthy and time-consuming, and some local authorities felt that too much time and money was being spent preparing reports and administration when the money would have been better spent on actually providing the required support. Recent changes to school funding includes a budget to support children with special educational needs, which means that fewer statements should be needed.

The graduated approach of the Code of Practice is basically separated into three stages.

1   Early Years Action (for children under statutory school age) or School Action. As you are already keeping records of the children in your care, you could be the first person to identify that a child has an additional need. You will already have good lines of communication with the parents, so together, and using the Code of Practice as your guide, you should devise an individual education plan for the child. This is usually referred to as an ILP, or individual learning plan, and there is no set format of ILPs for children under school age. This may seem like an additional workload for you, but given that you are regularly observing and recording information about the children, it is just formalising something you are doing already.

2   Early Years Action Plus or School Action Plus is the next stage, when other professional and outside agencies, such as educational psychologists and speech and language therapists, can be called upon to provide specialised help and support for the child.

3   Producing a statement of special educational needs (statutory assessment). This describes in detail the child's needs and all the special help and resources that he or she needs. It is produced by the local education authority (LEA) after they have made a detailed assessment of the child. The LEA could seek the home-based childcarer's views on the child's progress and may want to see copies of records, observations, assessments and the child's ILP.

It is worth noting that children under the age of two very rarely have a statement, but they might be supported by other professionals, such as portage workers, if they have a medical condition. However, parents have the right to ask for a child under two years to be assessed and given a statement if appropriate.

Supporting a child's primary carer through the statementing process

Many parents find that the statementing process can be time-consuming and difficult. It is important that you are as supportive as possible during this time. Make sure that you provide plenty of opportunities for parents to talk to you in order to discuss their worries and concerns. You will need to make sure that you have good communication skills (see Unit 1, page 58, and Unit 4, page 222) It is also important to remember that all the discussions you have with parents are confidential.

One way to support parents is to be aware of the timescales involved in the statementing process.

Timescales involved in the statementing process

If the local education authority makes a statutory assessment of a child's educational needs then the resulting statement, where appropriate, will be sent to the child's school and parents. However, this process can take several weeks to be completed and many parents can find this a frustrating time. In reality, a local education authority has six weeks to make a decision if it will carry out a statutory assessment of a child once the request has been received.

If the local education authority decides to assess, they have 10 weeks to seek advice from parents and a range of other professionals. After receiving all of the advice, the local education authority has two weeks to decide whether or not to make a statement. If the decision is made to issue a statement, they then have eight weeks to make the final statement.

If parents or a setting make a request for a statutory assessment of a child's special educational needs and are refused, they can appeal against this decision and have 29 days to lodge their appeal. The appeal is heard at a Special Educational Needs Tribunal.

Following a statutory assessment of a child who already has a statement, the local education authority must decide whether or not to amend the existing statement, cease to maintain the statement or maintain the statement without any changes. The local education authority has two weeks to make this decision following completion of a re-assessment, but this re-assessment can take several weeks. Parents have the right to meet with the local education authority to discuss the re-assessment and must ask for a meeting within 15 days of receiving the local education authority's decision.

In addition to being aware of the timescales, it may be helpful to remind parents who are going through the statementing process to ask themselves specific questions when reading the documents received from the local education authority.

The Children Act 2004 and *Every Child Matters* have far-reaching requirements. One of these is a new standardised approach to assessing children's and young people's needs; this is referred to as the Common Assessment Framework (CAF). It is designed to help practitioners communicate and work together more effectively. In addition, a process has been established through which agencies can share information to better meet the needs of children and young people with whom they are working. This is referred to as Information Sharing and Assessment (ISA). Many parents will find these new terms confusing; one way in which you could support parents is to explain these terms and how they may affect their child.

See also Unit 3, page 190.

Find out!

In the DfES document *Every Child Matters: Change for Children,* a real-life case study is given, on page 19, of early intervention and how the information sharing and assessment coordinator and a common assessment were able to form a team around a child to support both their needs and the needs of the family.

This document can be downloaded from www.everychildmatters.gov.uk or www. teachernet.gov.uk/publications

Parents may also be under stress during the statementing process, so you will need to use tact, sensitivity, professional understanding and knowledge in order to give appropriate support. Remember that you should be working in partnership with the parents at all times, with the best interests of the child or children always put first.

The role of the SENCO in supporting home-based practitioners

The role of the SENCO has now been recognised as an increasing influence in special education needs developments at both national and local levels. Due to an increase in inclusive practices the overall perception of special educational needs has changed within the community, especially in education.

Childminding networks will have an individual who has a SENCO role. Their role is to:

• support home-based childcarers in recognising and responding to the needs of children with special educational needs

• help network members to develop their own special educational needs policy

• help network members to put their policies into practice by supporting their planning

• liaise with and provide a link for parents, network members and other professionals who may be involved in the statementing process

• help network members develop an ILP (or IPP) to support the child's needs

• support network members to collect, record and update all relevant background information to support the statementing process and the child's needs

• help network members access appropriate resources to support the child and their family.

Sources of support and information for home-based practitioners and parents

There are many sources of support and information that you can use, if appropriate to the child and their parents.

Sources of support and information

• The health visitor of the child.

• Your network coordinator if you are a registered childminder.

• The SENCO.

• NCMA.

• Your Early Years Workforce team.

- Your local children's centre.

- The local library.

- The Internet.

- National organisations that are concerned with one specific condition or disability, such as the national autistic society (further details of these organisations can be found at the end of this book).

Sources of support and information for children

- You.

- Their health visitor.

- Books from the library.

- The Internet.

- Their school counsellor, teacher, welfare assistant and/or SENCO.

- The children's centre in the local area.

- National organisations that are concerned with one specific condition or disability.

Sources of support and information for parents

- You.

- Their health visitor.

- Their GP and/or medical professional concerned with their child.

- Their child's school counsellor, teacher, welfare assistant and/or SENCO.

- The children's centre in the local area.

- Books from the library.

- The Internet.

- National organisations that are concerned with one specific condition or disability.

- An information sharing and assessment coordinator.

Working with parents and others in meeting children's individual learning needs

As stated several times throughout this book, parents are the first educators of their children and should know their child very well. You must respect this knowledge and work in collaboration with parents for the overall well-being of the child.

It is also important to identify a child or young person's individual and preferred learning style if you are to effectively meet their needs. For example, you will not meet the learning needs of a tactile learner if you provide them only with books to read or CDs to listen to. You need to have a varied approach to meeting children's needs that considers and accommodates their learning styles as well as their age and stage of development and learning.

Case Study

Gareth, aged twelve, has a preferred visual learning style, and is achieving well at school, especially in the more academic subjects. He attends the after-school club three times each week and willingly gets involved in craft and hands-on activities. He has asked one of the adults at the club if he can use the Internet to find a picture of a model that he could copy.

Why do you think Gareth wanted a picture?

How could you support his learning and achievement?

Most families and children with special needs will gain support from agencies and professionals. Before 1994, many parents felt that there was little communication between the different agencies and professionals that were dealing with their children, leading to much frustration at times.

The Code of Practice 1994 improved the support for families and focused on creating multi-disciplinary teams. Today great care is taken to involve both parents and children in any decision-making processes.

Parents generally act as advocates for their children, or the children are able to speak for themselves if the issues are explained to them.

Key Term

Advocate – a supporter, someone who speaks on behalf of another with the needs of that individual in mind.

The Children Act 2004 and *Every Child Matters* took the multi-disciplinary approach further with the establishment of the Common Assessment Framework (CAF), which aims to provide a user-friendly assessment of all the child's individual, family and community needs. This assessment can be built up over time, and with parental consent, shared between practitioners. It is envisaged that all local authorities and their local partners will be able to implement the CAF by 2008.

The establishment of children's centres across the country will mean that multi-agency teams can be based in one location. This will make it much easier for parents and home-based childcarers to access information and support.

The stresses and strains of caring for children with special needs can be alleviated by respite and holiday care. Several childminding networks across the country have established links with other professionals, which has led to the development of a register of childminders who are able to offer respite care. This service offers parents opportunities to have time with their other children if appropriate. This service also helps parents address other issues that may affect the care of their children, such as drug or alcohol abuse.

Assessment guidance and study skills

Each assessment will require a significant amount of work, including personal research and reading. You will need to take this into consideration when planning your time and commitment to the course. Planning study time for yourself should be done in the same way that you carefully plan routines, activities and experiences for the children that you care for. You will also need to think about where you can work. Some people like to work in a quiet place without distractions, whereas others can work equally well where there are other people, perhaps even with music or a television on in the background. It is a matter of personal preference and you must choose to work in the surrounding that most suits your individual needs.

This unit will help you by:

- explaining the assessment procedures, including grade boundaries, and completing CACHE documentation
- giving hints and suggestions for answering multiple-choice questions
- giving hints and suggestions for presenting your assignments
- giving definitions and explanations of some of the most frequently used terms
- giving hints and suggestions for working towards the higher grades
- helping those undertaking personal research, referencing and compiling a bibliography.

Introduction

All of the units for the Diploma in Home-based Childcare have some form of assessment. In order to achieve the full award you must successfully complete all five assessments to E grade or above, apart from Unit 1, which is only marked as Pass or Refer.

Unit 1 is assessed by 25 multiple-choice questions that are externally marked by CACHE. You can achieve only a Pass grade for Unit 1. Units 2, 3, 4 and 5 are assessed by an assignment set by CACHE and marked by your tutor. These assessments are graded from E to A, and marks are awarded according to grade boundaries that will be explained later on in this unit. The overall grade for the award is determined by the total number of points gained; again, this will be explained later on in this unit.

Further information can be found in your candidate handbook for the award, the documents entitled *Finding the Level* and *Assignment Guidance*, both of which can be downloaded from the CACHE website: www.cache.org.uk

Explanation of the assessment procedures

Sometimes assessment procedures can seem quite complicated, but they are fairly straightforward once you are aware of and understand the processes involved.

External assessment by multiple-choice questions paper

The multiple-choice questions paper assesses your knowledge and understanding of Unit 1. You will not be able to see the paper in advance so it is important that you:

- are confident about everything that you have learnt in Unit 1

- understand how to answer multiple-choice questions (this will be looked at in greater detail later in this section).

Key Terms

Multiple-choice questions

There will be two types of multiple-choice question:

- Each question has several possible answers from which you must choose one.

- Each question has several options from which you have to choose one option as the correct answer.

External assessment – your work is marked by a moderator or a computer, not your tutor. This ensures that everyone's work is marked in the same way and to the same standard.

The multiple-choice questions paper is written and marked by CACHE. It is available monthly so you will have plenty of time to prepare yourself. The paper consists of 25 multiple-choice questions. You can achieve only a Pass or a Refer for this unit. Results will be sent to your centre within 14 days. For example, if you take the multiple-choice questions paper on 14 November 2006 the results will be sent to your centre by 28 November 2006.

A different set of questions will be issued by CACHE each month and a date will be set when that paper can be answered. You will only be able to be submit a paper if your centre has previously let CACHE know the date for which you have been entered. For example, if your centre has informed CACHE that you will be answering the paper in November you will not be able to sit the paper in October. However, if you do not get the required number of correct answers you can be re-entered for papers set after November.

If you are referred it means that you did not answer enough questions correctly to achieve a pass, but do not get too upset, your centre can re-enter you to take the paper again until you achieve a pass. However, you will not answer the same questions in subsequent papers, since each paper is different. You will be able to take the paper again on the published dates during your three-year registration period.

As with all CACHE assessments your centre can request a re-mark if both they and you do not think that the result is a true reflection of your abilities. However, you should remember that each paper is optically marked by a computer and the result is unlikely to change.

CACHE is planning to introduce electronic assessment (e-assessment) for multiple-choice questions at some centres and to assess on demand. More information on both these initiatives will be posted on the CACHE website.

Special arrangements

If you need to have special arrangements made in order for you to complete the multiple-choice questions paper, you must discuss this with your tutor, for example the need for extra time or a reader because of a recognised condition such as dyslexia. Different conditions and requirements apply to different circumstances – your centre has all of the CACHE regulations and will apply to CACHE on your behalf.

Assessment of Units 2–5

Each unit has a separate assessment that is set by CACHE and can be found in Section 4 of your CACHE candidate handbook. In order to successfully be awarded with the unit assessment you have to attempt all of the E grade criteria. You do not have to attempt the higher grades if you do not want to, but why stop at E?

Handing-in dates

Your centre and tutor will set the handing-in date for each assignment. These are very important dates and failure to comply with them can have a significant knock-on effect on the assessment process, and also when you and the rest of your group get the results of the assessment. Each centre has its own policy for dealing with any extenuating circumstances that may affect the handing-in date.

It is very important that you speak to your tutor as soon as possible if you realise that you may not be able to hand in your work on the set date.

Presenting your work

Your assignment should be submitted on A4 paper, where appropriate to the format. It can be typed, handwritten in ink or word-processed. If you submit handwritten assignments your work must be legible. Handwritten work in pencil is not permitted.

On each sheet of paper you should put your:

- name
- CACHE personal identification number (PIN)
- centre name
- centre number.

Note that if you are using a computer to produce your assignment this information can be put into a 'header' or 'footer' using the View menu (in Microsoft Word) and will automatically be printed at the top or bottom of each page.

It is also a good idea to number each page clearly, just in case pages become detached during the assessment process. Using a numbering system such as 1/10, 2/10 etc. clearly shows the marker how many pages you have submitted and they will be quickly be able to identify if any have gone missing.

Using the grading criteria

The assessment for Units 2–5 has grading criteria. These are printed in your CACHE candidate handbook with each assessment task. The criteria describe the information that you will need to provide for each grade.

The grading criteria can be used as a checklist to make sure that you have completed all of the assesment tasks. Your tutor, or whoever marks your work, will use the grading criteria to award marks. If you have not provided evidence of a grading criteria you will not be given any marks for it.

In general terms, the more correct information you provide, the more likely you are to achieve higher marks, providing of course that the information is appropriate to the criterion and within the word limit.

At the end of marking your work, the marker will total up the number of points awarded and allocate the grade accordingly. You need:

80–100 points for an A grade
70–79 points for a B grade
60–69 points for a C grade
50–59 points for a D grade
40–49 points for an E grade

If it is below 39 points your work will be referred.

Keys to good practice

- Use the grading criteria to help you structure each assignment.

- Look for the links between the grades where appropriate, which will save you repeating yourself. The Links to assessment sections in each unit shows the links between the grades.

- Use the grade boundaries on pages 25 and 26 of the CACHE candidate handbook to identify where you can gain more points.

- Talk to your tutor, making sure that you understand exactly what is required of you to complete the assignment task.

Overall grade for the award

The overall grade for the Diploma in Home-based Childcare is established by the number of points gained within the ranges shown below.

A = 19–21
B = 15–18
C = 11–14
D − 8–10
E = 5–7

These totals are taken by adding up the number of points awarded for Units 2–5 as shown in the following table.

Unit	Grade A	Grade B	Grade C	Grade D	Grade E
2	5	4	3	2	1
3	5	4	3	2	1
4	5	4	3	2	1
5	5	4	3	2	1

Supposing you had achieved:

- A grade for Unit 2
- B grade for Unit 3
- A grade for Unit 4
- C grade for Unit 5.

You would have 5 + 4 + 5 + 3, a total of 17 points. This would mean an overall grade of B for the full award.

No points are awarded for Unit 1 as you can only pass this unit.

Completing CACHE documentation

As mentioned earlier, on each page of your assignment you should put your:

- name
- CACHE personal identification number (PIN)
- centre name
- centre number.

The front sheet of your assignment should be signed and dated before it is handed over. You are effectively signing it to say that the work is all your own. You should also write your PIN, centre name and number on the front sheet, indicating the number of words that you have used. Your tutor can use this front sheet to give you written feedback after marking your work. Sometimes the internal moderator may sign this sheet to indicate that your work has been moderated.

It may be that your work will have to be posted to either the external or internal moderators so you need to think about what you use in order keep all of the assignment documents together. Try to avoid using bulky files, often a thin plastic wallet is sufficient.

Hints and suggestions for answering multiple-choice questions

Multiple-choice questions are all usually of a similar format. There is more often than not a statement or a question followed by four possible answers, for example:

What does the home-based childcarer need to check before outdoor play? This is the **question**, following it are four **statements**:

1 That the weather is warm.
2 That the gate is locked.
3 That the surface is smooth.
4 That the equipment is safe.

In this case there are four possible **answers**:

a. 1, 2 & 3 only correct.
b. 1 & 3 only correct.
c. 2 & 4 only correct.
d. 4 only correct.

If you think that a. is the right answer you are saying the home-based childcarer needs to check that the weather is warm, the gate is locked and the surface is smooth before outdoor play.

If you think that b. is the right answer you are saying the home-based childcarer needs to check that the weather is warm and the surface is smooth before outdoor play.

If you think that c. is the right answer you are saying the home-based childcarer needs to check that the gate is locked and that the equipment is safe before outdoor play.

If you think that d. is the right answer you are saying the home-based childcarer needs only to check that the equipment is safe before outdoor play.

When you have made a decision you will find on the answer paper that there are four numbered boxes next to the question number, for example:

1. a. ☐
    b. ☐
    c. ☐
    d. ☐

You must make a clear mark in pencil through **ONE** letter only. Remember that this part of the assessment is marked by a machine, so if you make a mark in more than one box your answer will not be legible and will therefore be recorded as incorrect. If you change your mind or make a mistake you must completely erase your original mark and put your mark in a new box. There is no point writing a comment on the answer paper, such as 'Dear marker, I intended box c to be my answer for question 1, not box b, but my rubber isn't very good.'

The optical reader is a machine, not a human and cannot respond to your messages!

This will be different with e-assessment and you should refer to the CACHE website at www.cache.org.uk for any information on this type of assessment.

The benefit of answering multiple-choice questions on a computer is that any mistakes or changes can be done very easily with a click of the mouse.

So what do you think is the correct answer? What should you do, or what do you do as part of your normal practice before outdoor play? Let us hope that most home-based childcarers would answer c!

Sometimes multiple-choice questions may not have four possible statements and four possible answers set out as above, for example:

Question/statement
Confidentiality is **most** important because it means that the home-based carer can:

a. Protect children and their families
b. Keep information about children inside the work setting
c. Be sure that children are not compared with each other
d. Avoid some children having all the attention.

In this question there is only one correct answer – a.

At the end of each section in Unit 1 you will find examples of multiple-choice questions, with the answers. These are designed to test your knowledge of the topics covered in that unit and to help you prepare for the actual multiple-choice questions paper. In addition here are some more multiple-choice questions for you to try.

1 A child falls and hits the back of their head. What should the childcarer do first?

   1   Give them a drink of water and wash their face.
   2   Let the child rest and keep them warm.
   3   Phone the parents and describe the child's accident.
   4   Observe the child and check if they feel sick or tired.

a. 1 and 3.
b. 2.
c. 2 and 4.
d. 4.

The answer is d.

2 The wheel on a toy car has come off. What do you do?

   1   Stick it back on with superglue and give it back to the children.
   2   Remove the toy from the children's reach and repair it later.
   3   Throw it away.
   4   Put the wheel on a high shelf and let the children play with it as it is.

a. 1.
b. 2.
c. 3.
d. 4.

The answer is c.

3 A simple board game for three-year-old children can encourage:

   1   The development of all the senses.
   2   Self-awareness.
   3   Fine manipulative skills.
   4   Turn-taking.

a. 1 and 2
b. 1 and 3
c. 2 and 3
d. 3 and 4.

The answer is d.

Keys to good practice

- Make sure that you are confident about your knowledge of Unit 1 before you decide to take the multiple-choice paper.

- A pass does a lot more for your self-esteem and self-confidence than a referral!

- Read each question or statement carefully before you make your decision.

- Read each of the possible answers carefully, taking all combinations of possible answers into account.

- Make one mark only on the answer paper.

- If you make a mistake or change your mind make sure that your original mark is clearly erased or removed.

- Use the examples above and those at the end of each section of Unit 1 as discussion points with your course group members.

- Talk to your tutor if you are not sure whether you are ready to answer the paper.

- Have confidence in your own professional abilities – you can do it!

Hints and suggestions for presenting your assignments

Units 2–5 are each assessed by an internally marked assignment which can be presented in a variety of formats or layouts. These are:

- a report

- a reflective account

- an audiotape and transcript

- a guidance handbook

- a set of case studies

- an essay

- a diary

- an information booklet

- or any other format or combination of formats which allows you to present the information required in the assessment task.

There are quite distinct differences between each format and you will have a personal preference, depending upon the assignment task. It is good practice, however, to discuss the most appropriate format with your tutor.

All assessments for the Diploma in Home-based Childcare are at Level 3 and so should have references and a bibliography. This is one of the E grade criteria. References and compiling a bibliography will be discussed later on in this unit (see page 292).

You will also need to make sure that you show good understanding of anti-bias/anti-discriminatory practices, where appropriate, regardless of format. This is one of the E grade criteria. Anti-bias/anti-discriminatory practice appropriate to this award will be discussed later in this unit (see page 288)

Whatever format you choose you must make sure that you maintain confidentiality at all times. Always use false names or initials when referring to children or other adults. You should not identify specific places by name, such as drop-in centres, network offices, leisure centres and so on. These can be referred to by initial letters or simply not named at all, for example:

'One way in which children's overall physical development can be stimulated is through involvement in activities at the local sports complex, such as swimming or martial arts classes.'

Presenting a report

A report is:

- a written account

- a set of statements

- a detailed piece of information.

It can cover more than one topic in its content, for example you could complete a report on safety, and include not only safety aspects inside and outside of the home, but also good hygiene practices, choosing appropriate equipment and ways of keeping children safe.

Reports often have headings to indicate sections and can contain bullet points and lists of relevant information.

For example, the assignment task may ask you to identify three factors that can affect children's behaviour. In a report this information could be presented in the following way:

Three factors that can affect behaviour

There are many factors that can affect children's behaviour depending on their individual needs.

Three significant factors could be:

- *the state of health of the child*

- *changes in the child's family circumstances such as the breakdown of a relationship*

- *peer pressure.*

Bullet points can be used effectively to present information using fewer words, than in sentences. Bullet points also have the added benefit of helping

Keys to good practice

- Discuss your assignment task with your tutor before you begin in order to decide upon the most appropriate format to use.

- Maintain confidentiality throughout your work regardless of the format you choose.

- Make sure that your work is referenced to develop or clarify a specific point.

- Make sure that you have a bibliography at the end of your work.

- You will need to show a good understanding of anti-bias/anti-discriminatory practice throughout your work.

you to set out your work in a clear way because you need to start a new line for each bullet point.

For example, in Unit 3 criteria E7 states, *'Identify one strength and one area for development in your practice.'*

A possible response could be:

One strength in my practice is:

• positive relationships with parents.

One area for development is:

• updating my policies.

Reports can also include diagrams, graphs, tables and charts to present factual information where it is required and appropriate. For example, you could be asked to identify the main constituents of a healthy and balanced diet. You could present this information in a chart or a table as shown below.

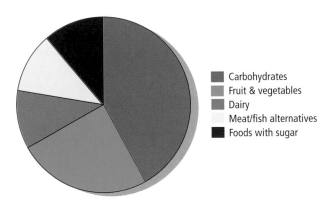

Carbohydrates
Fruit & vegetables
Dairy
Meat/fish alternatives
Foods with sugar

Information can also be presented in tables, which can be very clear and also use fewer words because the headings do not need to be repeated. For example, in Unit 4 criteria E2 states, *'Describe TWO different family structures.'*

A possible response could be:

Family structure	Main features
Step-families	• Children live with one birth parent. • May have step-siblings.
Extended families	• Grandparents may live with the family or nearby.

If you consider the overall structure and format of this book, it could be described as a report format.

Presenting a reflective account

An account is an explanation or a description of something. To be reflective means to consider something in detail. Therefore a reflective account is more than just an explanation of something, it needs to consider other factors that might influence or impact upon the topic that you are writing about.

It does not necessarily have to be evaluative, as an evaluative account should consider the positives and negatives, or strengths and weaknesses of a topic. A reflective account takes why something happened, or the reasons for something, into consideration.

For example, the assessment task could refer to professional development and training for home-based childcarers, a reflective account could include:

'On reflection the local authority offers many opportunities for childcare practitioners to attend professional development activities. However, as most of these events are scheduled during normal working hours, some home-based childcarers are unable to attend. It is not always possible for home-based childcarers to find alternative carers for their children and this issue prevents the professional development and attendance of childminders and nannies at these events.'

Presenting an audiotape and transcript

If appropriate you can record your assessment on to audiotape. You might want, for example, to present some information relating to an observation of children's language development. You may decide that the most effective way to do this is to actually record some children talking. However, note that you must also produce a written transcript in English of exactly what is on the tape.

It is also acceptable to present an assessment on tape with a transcript if you feel that other formats would not give a true reflection of your abilities, if perhaps you had difficulties with the written word or if English was not your first language.

A point to remember is that some home audio-recording equipment can produce tapes that have a lot of background noise, or distortion. If you think that using an audiotape is a good format for you, then it is a good idea to try to use the best possible recording equipment that you have access to.

Presenting a guidance handbook

A handbook is usually presented as a series of pages fastened together and gives factual information on a specific subject, such as your CACHE candidate handbook for this award. This handbook gives you specific information about the course, the syllabus, the assessment tasks and CACHE regulations.

Guidance is about making sure that the right direction is followed, for example a step-by-step approach to achieving the award. So if you were going to present your assessment as a guidance handbook you would produce a comprehensive, detailed and perhaps step-by-step approach to the subject, for example a detailed routine for healthy and safe practices when changing a nappy could be presented as a part of a guidance handbook.

A guidance handbook can also contain, if appropriate, diagrams, charts, tables and illustrations to make the information clearer.

Presenting a set of case studies

Case studies are detailed examinations or observations of a specific topic, for example a set of written observations on the same child or group of children carried out over a period of time, all with the same aim.

Case studies can also be in the form of the responses to a set of questions or activities. Childcare practitioners, for example, could

devise a set of activities for a child to complete and produce a case study about that child which records how they responded to the activities, their behaviour, language and so on.

The information from case studies can be assessed and evaluated as a whole, or individually in order to highlight specific issues. However, judgements made will usually be based on a complete set of case studies. For example, you may have concerns about the behaviour of a child. After talking to the parents you decide to carry out a set of case studies over two weeks, and so set yourself an aim. Some days you may have a lot of information in your study, other times not so much. At the end of the two-week period you and the parents can look at the case studies and decide upon a plan of action.

Presenting an essay

An essay is a piece of written work which does not usually contain any sub-headings. It also does not normally have bullet point lists, diagrams, charts or tables. Just like other formats, an essay should contain references to clarify and develop points made.

A good essay has a clear structure to it, for example an introduction, a development section, and a conclusion. Each new idea or topic is introduced by starting a new paragraph within the text. Quite often the writer of an essay will use the introduction to introduce the aim and also to indicate the structure of the piece of work. This makes it easier for the reader to follow the writer's ideas.

Presenting a diary

A diary records events that occur in the daily lives of individuals. These events can be recorded systematically at the end of each day, week, or spontaneously as and when they occur. Diaries can give a fascinating insight and commentary to social events of the time.

Sometimes pregnant women will keep a diary of their baby's development and carry it on into the first year or even longer. These diaries record significant events, such as the first scan, the first time she felt the baby kick, the baby's first smile, first tooth, first words and so on.

Diaries can include written pieces, pictures, charts, diagrams and sometimes real objects, such as a pressed flower or anything of meaning to the person writing the diary.

Diaries are not usually short-term pieces of work, they are often compiled over a series of months or years. However, as this registered childminder said, 'I kept a diary of the time that I was in hospital after I broke my leg. I recorded what I did, or didn't eat, which patients cheered me up, which drove me mad, generally insignificant silly things, but it made very entertaining reading afterwards!'

You could present information in a diary format if, for example, you were trying to explain how your routines supported children's well-being.

Presenting an information booklet

A booklet is literally a little book and should be a series of pages fastened together. It can include written text, pictures, diagrams, charts, tables and any other appropriate ways of presenting factual information.

Information could be described as facts that individuals need to know or will find useful and important. If you inform someone then you tell them something, bring them up to date or enlighten them. So an information booklet should be planned to increase another person's knowledge about a specific subject.

Registered childminders who put together a welcome pack probably have an information booklet about themselves, their experience, qualifications, special areas of interest and their practice. Nannies could also have a similar booklet that they give to prospective employers to provide a full and comprehensive picture of their skills and abilities.

Presenting a combination of the above formats or any other appropriate format

As you read through the assessment tasks for each unit you may decide that to keep to one format

through the assignment would not present the information as well as you may like and could even be restrictive.

For example, you may have decided to present your assignment for Unit 3 as a report. However, as you work through your report you might decide that the D grade criterion can be more effectively met in a short guidance handbook.

Remember that the above example is only a suggestion, and designed to help you identify how you can incorporate different formats into your work.

You can present your work in any appropriate format provided that the marker can understand your intentions and that you can demonstrate that you have met all of the criteria in sufficient detail to gain an E grade or above.

Anti-bias/anti-discriminatory practice at Level 3

Key Terms

Anti-bias – without prejudice, impartial.

Anti-discriminatory – fair, not bigoted, not judgemental.

Anti-bias/anti-discriminatory practice is all about understanding that everyone is different, unique and individual. There are enormous differences in people's ways of life within different cultures. This understanding should be an integral part of your assignment and not just a few additional sentences at the end of the work.

Anti-bias/anti-discriminatory practice is free from stereotypical assumptions and conjecture. For example, it would be wrong to write '*Girls who play football are often regarded as tomboys.*' All children have different interests and abilities.

Anti-bias/anti-discriminatory practice should be evident in all of your policies. It is also an important part of behaviour management, recognising children's rights and child protection. A true understanding of anti-bias/anti-discriminatory practice will be evident in the activities and experiences that you plan and provide for the children in your care. It is also shown in how you respond to and work with parents, and ways in which you maintain confidentiality.

Definitions and explanations of some of the frequently used terms

CACHE has produced a document called *Finding the Level* which can be downloaded free of charge from their website at www.cache.org.uk

This document clearly sets out the definitions of commonly used terms, with an example of how they may occur in an assessment task and an example from a candidate's work. This document is generic across all CACHE awards.

However, the following table shows some of the frequently used terms in the assessment tasks of the Level 3 Diploma in Home-based Childcare.

Keys to good practice

- Make sure that your understanding is shown throughout your work, and not just at the end of the assessment.
- Keep up to date with current legislation and changes in government policies.
- Be prepared to challenge prejudice, stereotypical attitudes and unfair practices.
- Be a positive role model at all times.

Word	Definition	Example
Analyse	• Break down into parts. • Investigate. • Reason. • Writing about the subject from more than one point of view.	*Analyse the importance of planning for all children.* Think about why you should consider children's needs, such as the positive effects, different learning styles, needs and abilities of different age groups.
Describe	• Give clear details. • Present understandable information.	*Describe how to market a home-based childcare service.* Think about the information that you will need to provide, such as the aims and values, how you market and advertise, working hours, special features.
Discuss	• Talk about, in a written format. • Argue a point. • Consider. • Debate.	*Discuss two sources of stress that some parents may experience.* Name two sources of stress and write about how each source could affect a family (you could possibly present this as a two-column table or a chart).
Evaluate	• Assess. • Judge. • Appraise. • Weigh up.	*Evaluate the implications of using an inappropriate curriculum framework for children.* Think about long-term and short-term

support worker and other like-minded people, can provide specific information and a different interpretation or view on something. Remember that you must maintain confidentiality at all times.

Referencing

Key Term

Reference – to quote from the work of someone else to support your own views or comments.

When you put a reference in your work you must acknowledge the fact that you did not write it. You do this by putting the author's name and the date of the work in brackets followed by the quote using quotation marks.

For example:

Sheila Riddall-Leech (2006, p81) states that 'a key person helps a baby and young child to cope throughout the day'.

Full details of the book that any quotes are taken from need to appear in the bibliography, so that readers can source the book in order to follow up on the information.

References should be related to and linked in some way to the topic that you are covering at that point in the text. It should not just appear out of the blue because you think it happens to meet the grading criteria, or makes your assignment look good!

If you change the words of another person, technically it is not a reference. For example:

The role of a key person can be to support children throughout their time with the childcarer.

Although the statement above says basically the same thing as the earlier reference example, it uses different words, so it is not a quote.

Key Term

Plagiarism – copying the work of another and claiming it as your own.

If you do not reference work that is not your own, this is plagiarism. By referencing and producing a bibliography you can show where you found your information.

Plagiarism can include copying another person's assignment and passing it off as your own, or two or more people working together on an assignment and then producing exactly the same piece of work individually. There is no harm in working together, indeed it can be very supportive, but you must produce an individual piece of work.

If your study centre can prove that your work is not your own, you may be subject to the centre's disciplinary procedures and your assignment will not be marked. You will be asked to submit another piece of work.

Developing a bibliography

Key Term

Bibliography – a logical list of sources of personal research.

Your bibliography should list all the sources of information that you have used to help produce your assignment. It goes at the very end of your assignment.

There is no set way of compiling this list, but it should be logical and consistent, so if you start by writing the name of the author of a book, for example, you should follow the same style throughout your list. However it is usual for the lists to be in alphabetical order – whichever style you choose!

It is a good idea to list all the books that you have used together, all the other publications together and all the websites together.

The information that you should include in your bibliography for books and professional journals is:

• the author's surname and forename or initials

• the date the book or article was written

• the title of the book, article or publication

• who published it.

This information can usually be found on the inside page at the front of a book, called the imprint page.

For example:

Riddall-Leech, S. (2005) *How to Observe Children*, Heinemann

Turnbull, M (2005) *Why Chatter Matters, Who Minds*, NCMA

The information that you should include in your bibliography for websites is:

• the full web address

• the date you accessed it

• the surname and forename or initials of the person who wrote the page (if available)

• the title of the website page.

For example:

www.cache.org.uk 05.12.05, Information for Centres, Finding the Level

Answers to multiple-choice questions in Unit 1

Answers to questions on pages 30–31
1 c.
2 d.
3 a.
4 b.
5 c.

Answers to questions on pages 39–40
1 b.
2 c.
3 c.

Answers to questions on pages 49–50
1 c.
2 c.
3 b.
4 d.

Answers to questions on page 59
1 b.
2 d.
3 a.

Answers to questions on page 66
1 b.
2 a.
3 d.
4 a.

Answers to questions on page 70
1 c.
2 b.
3 d.
4 d.

Answers to questions on pages 79–80
1 a.
2 a.
3 d.
4 c.

Answers to questions on page 93
1 c.
2 a.
3 b and c.
4 d.

Table of common dietary habits

Food	Buddhist	Hindu	Jewish	Mormon	Muslim	Rastafarian	Roman Catholic	Seventh Day Adventist	Sikh
Alcohol	✗	✗	✓	✗	✗	✗	✓	✗	✓
Animal fats	✗	Some	Kosher only	✓	Some Halal	Some	✓	✗	Some
Beef	✗	✗	Kosher only	✓	Halal	Some	✓	Some	✗
Cheese	✓	Some	Not with meat	✓	Some	✓	✓	Most	Some
Chicken	✗	Some	Kosher	✓	Halal	Some	✓	Some	Some
Eggs	Some	Some	No blood spots	✓	✓	✓	✓	Most	✓
Fish	Some	With fins and scales	With scales, fins and backbone	✓	Halal	✓	✓	Some	Some
Fruit	✓	✓	✓	✓	✓	✓	✓	✓	✓
Lamb/mutton	✗	Some	Kosher	✓	Halal	Some	✓	Some	✓
Milk/yoghurt	✓	Not with rennet	Not with meat	✓	Not with rennet	✓	✓	Most	✓
Nuts	✓	✓	✓	✓	✓	✓	✓	✓	✓
Pork	✗	Rarely	✗	✓	✗	✗	✓	✗	Rarely
Pulses	✓	✓	✓	✓	✓	✓	✓	✓	✓
Shellfish	✗	Some	✗	✓	Halal	✗	✓	✗	Some
Tea/coffee/cocoa	✓ but no milk	✓	✓	✗	✓	✓	✓	✗	✓
Vegetables	✓	✓	✓	✓	✓	✓	✓	✓	✓

✓ will eat or drink
✗ do not eat or drink

Fasting is often a matter of individual choice; however, the following times are observed:
Jews will fast at Yom Kippur, Muslims will fast at Ramadan, Mormons fast for 24 hours once a month.
Some Roman Catholics prefer not to eat meat on Fridays.

The Food Commission
94 White Lion Street
London N1 9PF
Tel: 020 7837 2250
Website: www.foodcomm.org.uk

**The Foundation for the Study of Infant Deaths
(FSID)**
Artillery House
11–19 Artillery Row
London SW1P 1RT
Tel: 020 7222 8001
Website: www.sids.org.uk/fsid

Health Development Agency (UK)
Holborn Gate
330 High Holborn
London WC1V 7BA
Tel: 020 7430 0850
Website: www.hda.nhs.uk

Health Information Wales
Ffynnon–las
Ty Glas Avenue
Llsnishen
Cardiff CF4 5DZ
Tel: 0800 665544

Hyperactive Children's Support Group (HACSG)
71 Whyke Lane
Chichester
West Sussex PO19 7PD
Tel: 01243 539966
Website: www.hacsg.org.uk

Kidscape
2 Grosvenor Gardens
London SW1W 0DH
Tel: 020 7730 3300
Website: www.kidscape.org.uk

Macmillan Cancer Relief
89 Albert Embankment
London SE1 7UQ
Tel: 020 7840 7840
Website: www.macmillan.org.uk

MIND (National Association for Mental Health)
15–19 Broadway
London E15 4BQ
Tel: 020 8519 2122
Website: www.mind.org.uk

MIND (Cymru)
3rd Floor, Quebec House
Castelbridge
5–19 Cowbridge Road East
Cardiff CF11 9AB
Tel: 029 2039 5123
Website: www.mind.org.uk

The Multiple Births Foundation
Hammersmith House, Level 4
Queen Charlotte's and Chelsea Hospital
Du Cane Road
London W12 0HS
Tel: 020 8383 3519
Website: www.multiplebirths.org.uk

Muscular Dystrophy Campaign
7–11 Prescott Place
London SW4 6BS
Tel: 020 7720 8055
Website: www.muscular–dystrophy.org.uk

National AIDS Helpline
1st Floor, Cavern Court
8 Matthew House
Liverpool L2 6RE
Helpline: 0800 567123
Website: www.aidshelpline.org.uk

National Childbirth Trust
Alexandra House
Oldham Terrace
Acton
London W3 6NH
Enquiries: 0870 444 8707
Breastfeeding line: 0870 444 8708
Website: www.nctpregnancyandbabycare.com or
    www.national-childbirth-trust.co.uk

National Childminding Association (NCMA)
Royal Court
81 Tweedy Road
Bromley BR1 1TG
Tel: 0845 880 0044
Website: www.ncma.org.uk

National Children's Bureau (NCB)
8 Wakely Street
London EC1V 7QE
Tel: 020 7843 6000
Website: www.ncb.org.uk

National Council for One Parent Families
255 Kentish Town Road
London NW5 2LX
Tel: 020 7428 5400
Website: www.oneparentfamilies.org.uk

National Drugs Helpline
Helpline: 0800 776600
Website: www.talktofrank.com

National Eczema Society (NES)
Hill House
Highgate Hill
London N19 5NA
Helpline: 0870 241 3604
Website: www.eczema.org.uk

National Extension College
Michael Young Centre
Purbeck Road
Cambridge CB2 2HN
Tel: 01223 400 200
Website: www.nec.ac.uk

National Lottery Funding
Tel: 0845 275 0000
Website: www.lotterygoodcauses.org.uk

National Meningitis Trust
Fern House
Bath Road
Stroud GL5 3TJ
Tel: 01453 768000
Website: www.meningitis–trust.org.uk

NSPCC
Weston House
42 Curtain Road
London EC2A 3NH
Helpline: 0808 800 5000
Website: www.nspcc.org.uk

National Association of Toy and Leisure Libraries
68 Churchway
London NW1 1LT
Tel: 020 7255 4600
Website: www.natll.org.uk

Northern Ireland Childminding Association (NICMA)
16/18 Mill Street
Newtownards
Co. Down BT23 4LU
Tel: 028 9181 1015
Website: www.nicma.org

Parentline Plus
Unit 520 Highgate Studios
53–79 Highgate Road
Kentish Town
London NW5 1TL
Tel: 020 7284 5500
Website: www.parentlineplus.org.uk

Parents Advice Centre
Floor 4, Franklin House
12 Brunswick Street
Belfast BT2 7GE
Helpline: 0808 8010 722
Website: www.pachelp.org

Parents Anonymous
6–9 Manor Gardens
London N7 6LA
Tel: 020 7263 8918

Qualifications and Curriculum Authority (QCA)
83 Piccadilly
London W1J 8QA
Tel: 020 7509 5555
Website: www.qca.org.uk

Relate
Herbert Gray College
Little Church Street
Rugby CV21 3AP
Tel: 01788 573 241
Website: www.relate.org.uk

Royal National Institute of the Blind (RNIB)
105 Judd Street
London WC1H 9NE
Tel: 020 7388 1266
Website: www.rnib.org.uk

**Royal Society for the Prevention of Accidents
(RoSPA)**
RoSPA House
Edgbaston Park
353 Bristol Road
Edgbaston
Birmingham B5 7ST
Tel: 0121 248 2000
Website: www.rospa.co.uk

The Samaritans
The Upper Mill
Kingston Road
Ewell
Surrey KT17 2AF
Helpline: 08457 909090
Website: www.samaritans.org.uk

Save The Children
1 St John's Lane
London EC1M 4AR
Tel: 020 7012 6400
Website: www.savethechildren.org.uk

SCOPE
6 Market Road
London N7 9PW
Helpline: 0808 800 3333
Website: www.scope.org.uk

Scottish Childminding Association
Suite 3
7 Melville Terrace
Stirling FK8 2ND
Tel: 01786 445377
Website: www.childminding.org

SENSE
11–13 Clifton Terrace
Finsbury Park
London N4 3SR
Tel: 020 7272 7774
Website: www.sense.org.uk

Sickle Cell Society
54 Station Road
Harlesden
London NW10 4UA
Tel: 020 8961 7795
Website: www.sicklecellsociety.org

St John's Ambulance
Edwina Mountbatten House
63 York Street
London W1H 1PS
Tel: 020 7258 3456
Website: www.sja.org.uk

Stillbirth and Neonatal Death Society (SANDS)
28 Portland Place
London W1B 1LY
Tel: 020 7436 7940
Helpline: 020 7436 5881
Website: www.uk-sands.org.uk

Terrence Higgins Trust (THT)
52–54 Gray's Inn Road
London WC1X 8JU
Tel: 020 7831 0330
Website: www.tht.org.uk

Twins and Multiple Birth Association (TAMBA)
2 The Willows
Gardner Road
Guildford GU1 4PG
Tel: 0870 770 3305
Website: www.tamba.org.uk

Vegetarian Society
Parkdale
Dunham Road
Altrincham
Cheshire WA14 4QG
Tel: 0161 925 2000
Website: www.vegsoc.org.uk

World Health Organization (WHO)
Avenue Appia 20
1211 Geneva 27
Switzerland
Tel: (+00 41 22) 791 21 11
Website: www.who.int

Further reading and information

Abbot L. & Moylett H. (1997) *Working with the Under Threes: Training and Professional Development*, Open University Press

Baldwin N. (2000) *Protecting Children: Protecting Their Rights*, Whiting & Birch Ltd

Bee H. (1998) *The Growing Child*, Longman

Bruce T. (1997) *Early Childhood Education*, Hodder and Stoughton

DfES (2004) *Every Child Matters: Change for Children*, DfES

DfES/QCA (2000) *Curriculum Guidance for the Foundation Stage*, DfES

DfES/Sure Start (2002) *Birth to Three Matters Framework*, DfES

Fawcett M. (1996) *Learning through Child Observation*, Jessica Kingsley Publishers

Lansdowne R. & Walker M. (1996) *Your Child's Development from Birth to Adolescence*, Frances Lincoln

Lord Laming (2003) *Victoria Climbié Inquiry – Report of an Inquiry by Lord Laming*, HMSO

Meggit C. (2006) *Child Development – An Illustrated Guide*, 2nd edition, Heinemann

Moyles J. (1989) *Just Playing the Role and Status of Play in Early Childhood Education*, Open University Press

Oates J. (ed.) (1995) *The Foundations of Child Development*, Blackwell

Pascal C. & Bertram T. (ed.) (2001) *Effective Early Learning*, Paul Chapman Publications

Pugh G. (2001) *A Policy for Early Childhood Services?* in Pugh, G. (ed.) *Contemporary Issues in Early Years*, Paul Chapman Publishing

Riddall-Leech S. (2003) *Managing Children's Behaviour*, Heinemann

Riddall-Leech S. (2005) *How to Observe Children*, Heinemann

Rodd J. (1998) *Leadership in Early Childhood: The Pathway to Professionalism*, Open University Press

Shah M. (2001) *Working with Parents*, Heinemann

Sheridan M. D. (1997) *From Birth to Three*, Routledge

Tassoni, P. and Hucker K (2005) *Planning Play in the Early Years*, Heinemann

Websites

BBC Children in Need
www.bbc.co.uk/cin

Department for Education and Skills (DfES)
www.dfes.gov.uk

Department for Environment, Food and Rural Affairs (DEFRA)
www.defra.gov.uk

Families Need Families
www.fnf.org.uk

Health and Safety Executive
www.hse.gov.uk

HemiHelp
www.hemihelp.org.uk

International Child Abuse Network
www.yesican.org

National Association of Citizens' Advice Bureaux
www.nacab.org.uk

Rights4me
www.rights4me.org.uk

Royal Society for the Prevention of Cruelty to Animals (RSPCA)
www.rspca.org.uk

Glossary

Abuse – when a child is suffering or may suffer considerable harm from physical abuse, emotional abuse, sexual abuse, neglect or bullying.

Advocate – a supporter, someone who speaks on behalf of another with the needs of that individual in mind.

Agency – an organisation or group of individuals with a specific purpose.

Allergy – sensitivity and/or an intolerant reaction to a particular food or substance.

Annual Performance Assessment (APA) – a yearly assessment of a council's specific contributions to improving outcomes for children and young people, carried out by the Commission for Social Care Inspection (CSCI) and the Office for Standards in Education (Ofsted).

Anti-discriminatory – fair, not bigoted or judgemental.

Anti-discriminatory practice – taking positive steps to counter and challenge discrimination.

Assertiveness – mental attitude of negotiation and solving problems rather than giving into emotional urges.

Assess – to measure, consider, or weigh up.

Assessment – making an informed judgement about something or a measurement of it, for example the development of a specific skill.

Attachment – unique emotional bond between a child and an adult.

Balance – a skill that requires coordination, but not necessarily from the eyes or ears. The ability to balance is developed by the body as the movements use information received from the central nervous system.

Balanced diet – one that includes a wide range and variety of foods.

Behaviour – way in which an individual acts or responds to a certain situation.

Bias – not a balanced comment or judgement, unfair or showing favouritism.

Bibliography – a logical list of sources of personal research.

Birth to Three Matters Framework – a framework to support those people working with and caring for babies and young children under three years old.

Challenging – responding and facing up to another individual in ways that are assertive, but not confrontational.

Child protection – defending the basic right of a child to be protected from abuse.

Children and Young People's Plan – single multi-agency plan covering the activities required to improve outcomes for children and young people.

Children's Trusts – a high-level partnership arrangement of agencies involved in children and young people's services.

Common Assessment Framework (CAF) – a new, standardised approach to assessing children's and young people's needs, designed to help practitioners communicate and work together more effectively.

Communication – an exchange of ideas, contact between individuals, consultation and interaction.

Conductive education – very intensive medical treatment that focuses upon a step-by-step approach, encouraging the child to gradually develop movement. Small movements are repeated frequently, sometimes to the point of exhaustion. The idea behind conductive education is that if the brain is forced to do something that it can't currently do, it will try to find a way to connect mind and muscle.

Confidentiality – privacy and discretion, keeping something secret.

Conflict – a clash, difference of opinion or argument.

Continuing professional development – the ongoing training and updating of skills and knowledge relating to your profession.

Contract – a written agreement which sets out the terms and conditions relating to the specific care of a child.

Coordination skills – of hand, eye and foot, and the ability to combine more than one skill or movement at the same time. An example of this aspect of development is when a child uses their eyes to guide their feet when going upstairs.

Criticism – disapproval of another's actions, speech, behaviours.

CSIW – Children's Services Inpectorate in Wales, the Welsh Assembly department for inspecting childcare and schools in Wales.

Curriculum – a set of activities, opportunities and experiences which help and support children's learning and development. Some can be planned and some unplanned.

Development – ways in which children grow and acquire skills and competences. Areas of development are sometimes categorised as physical, intellectual (or cognitive), language, social and emotional. All of these areas are interrelated and interdependent.

Developmental milestones (or norms) – quantitative measurements that provide typical values and variations in height, weight, and skill acquisition. These can also be referred to as norms.

Difficulty – a term that is often given to a situation or condition, such as emotional difficulty, that may can be overcome or treated. However, some learning difficulties cannot be overcome.

Disability – a physical or mental condition that limits a person's movements, senses, or activities, for example limited mobility due to cerebral palsy.

Disclosure – occurs when a fact, especially a secret, is revealed. For instance, if a child has told an adult or another child what has been happening to them.

Early Learning Goals – goals for five-year-olds at the end of the Foundation Stage.

Emergency – a crisis or situation that requires immediate action.

Empowerment – to give strength, confidence or power to someone.

Environment – the surrounding, setting or situation in which people live, in this case the one in which you work and care for children.

Equipment – all toys, utensils, furniture, fittings and materials that may be used with or by children.

Evaluate – to look at and consider the positive and negative aspects of something.

Evaluation – an informed assessment or judgement based on specific information.

External assessment – your work is marked by a moderator or a computer, not your tutor. This ensures that everyone's work is marked in the same way and to the same standard.

Family – a unit that provides a home and care for children.

Fine manipulative skills – small movements that are needed to write or draw.

Fine motor skills – small movements of the whole hand.

Fitness – levels of agility, suppleness, muscle tone.

Foundation Stage Curriculum – a set of activities and experiences divided into six areas of learning for children between three and five years.

Gross motor skills – movements involving all of an arm or leg, such as in throwing a ball.

Health – the physical condition of an individual.

Heuristic play – is a form of play that encourages babies and young children to explore everyday natural objects through their senses. Heuristic play is usually attributed to Elinor Goldschmied.

Holistic – the belief that the whole being is more than the sum of its parts.

Holistic development – focuses upon the development of the whole child, not just one aspect of the child's development.

Holistic treatment – focuses upon the whole person rather than just the symptoms of an illness or disability.

Impairment – a condition that negatively affects the ability to hear, see, walk or coordinate actions.

Implement – to put into practice, carry out.

Inclusion – the process of recognising, understanding and overcoming obstructions or barriers to participation.

Independence – allowing a child to have self-autonomy, freedom, self-reliance and therefore undertaking an activity or having an experience without intervention.

Individual learning plan (ILP) – sometimes referred to as an individual education plan (IEP) or an individual play plan (IPP), and usually drawn up by the SENCO, or parents and other professionals who may be working with the child.

Individuality – unique and different aspects of a person that make them different from everyone else.

Infection – a disease, illness, virus or bug.

Information Sharing and Assessment (ISA) – the process through which agencies can appropriately share information to better meet the needs of children and young people with whom they are working.

Inter-agency – a group of professionals from more than one profession working together, for example health care workers, medical staff, speech therapists.

Joint Area Review (JAR) – a review or inspection of all services for children and young people in a local authority area, to evaluate the way local services, taken together, contribute to the well-being of children and young people.

Key person – a named member of staff who has responsibility for a small group of children. The key person will try to welcome the child each time they arrive at the setting, talk to the parents, complete observations and assessments and provide continuity of care as far as is possible.

Key Stage – age divisions of the National Curriculum.

Learning style – the way in which we process information. Most people will have a preferred learning style.

Literacy – how we use words, either in writing or reading.

Local Area Agreements (LAA) – agreements made between central and local government in an area, aimed at achieving local solutions that meet local needs, whilst also contributing to national priorities.

Local Safeguarding Children Board (LSCB) – has replaced the Area Child Protection Committee (ACPC) and is a statutory body responsible for overseeing the safeguarding of children and young people in a local area.

Locomotive skills – controlled movements that children use to run, jump and walk.

Managing – the organisation, supervision, administration and running of your business/childcare service.

Marketing – advertising, promoting and selling your business/childcare service.

Medicine/prescribed drug – a remedy, tablet, pill, lotion or liquid that can help alleviate a medical or health problem.

Milestones – clearly defined stages within a sequence of development. Sometimes referred to as norms.

Monitoring – checking or keeping an eye on something.

Multi-Agency Teams (MATs) – co-located teams of practitioners from different agencies, working together to support children and young people in the area, but managed by their parent organisation.

National Curriculum – a set of learning activities and experiences for children between five and sixteen years of age.

National Service Framework (NSF) – national standards for children's health and social care.

Observation – watching, studying, examining or scrutinising the actions of others.

Ofsted – the Office for Standards in Education (England). The governmental department responsible for the inspection of childcare, schools and local education authorities.

Oracy – what is said and how it is said.

Physical development – how children get control of their bodies.

Plagiarism – copying the work of another and claiming it as your own.

Plan – to prepare, set up and organise activities or experiences.

Policy – what you have decided to do in certain situations.

Portage – when skills that children need are broken down into small steps, each one of which is mastered before progressing on to the next step. Portage workers come to the child's home, using play and everyday activities to help children learn each step.

Prejudice – narrow-mindedness, bigotry, unfairness, discrimination.

QCA – the Qualifications and Assessment Authority.

Reflective practice – thinking about and critically analysing your practice, actions and work with the intention of changing and improving what you do.

Risk assessment – a possible danger or threat to safety. Assessment means to measure, evaluate or make a judgement. Risk assessment is therefore a case of weighing up possible dangers or threats to safety and taking appropriate action.

Routine – a custom, scheduled event or activity that is usually planned with regularity.

Self-image – how a person sees themselves in relation to others, including physical and mental qualities. Self-image is related to self-esteem in that a person with a low self-image will also suffer from low self-esteem.

SENCO – Special Educational Needs Coordinator, the person responsible for coordinating special educational needs provision within a setting or network.

Spontaneous play – when children play in their own way, and the adult needs to provide as much variety of equipment and resources as possible, with opportunities and time for exploration and experimenting.

Statement – a legal document that outlines a child's special educational needs and the local authority's duty towards the child.

Stepping Stones – progressive stages of achievement within each area of learning in the Foundation Stage.

Stereotype – to label, put into artificial categories, to typecast.

Strength – the condition of the muscles.

Structured play – when the play is planned by adults, such as a cutting activity to develop fine motor skills with scissors.

Supervision – control, management or command of a situation or other individuals.

Sure Start – a government programme attempting to provide young children and their families with better life opportunities.

SWOT analysis – a critical consideration of an individual's strengths, weaknesses, opportunities and threats to practice.

Vigour – energy levels and vitality.

Well-being – often associated with happiness but in this case a positive state of overall good health.

Wrap-around care – care for children before and after school, and during school holidays, but not necessarily provided by the same person or organisation. For example, a registered childminder may provide care before school and during some of the school holidays, whereas an after-school club could provide care after school. Similarly, a holiday play scheme could provide care during part of the school holidays.